EXAM CRAM™ 2

The CISSP Cram Sheet

PHYSICAL SECURITY

1. Facility controls include

    Lighting—For lighting used to discourage crime, the NIST standard states that the area should be illuminated at 2 feet wide by 8 feet high.

    Fencing—A height of 8 feet with three strands of barb wire will stop a determined intruder.

    Perimeter controls include gates, guards, CCTV, turnstiles, mantraps, and alarms.

2. Locks can be either:

    Cipher locks—Programmable

    Preset locks—Used on doors

    Device locks—Used to prevent the theft of equipment

3. Facility management requires review of the facility:

    Proper construction and design should give attention to walls, doors, ceilings, windows, flooring, HVAC, and fire detection and suppression.

    The load of the building should be reviewed to ensure that it can support what is planned to be installed in it.

    HVAC should have positive pressurization to keep contaminants and smoke out of the facility.

4. The following are common power anomalies:

    Blackout—Prolonged loss of power

    Brownout—Power degradation that is low and less than normal

    Sag—Momentary low voltage

    Fault—Momentary loss of power

    Spike—Momentary high voltage

    Surge—Prolonged high voltage

    Noise—Interference superimposed onto the power line

    Transient—Noise disturbances of a short duration

    Inrush—Initial surge of power at startup

5. Hardware-protection mechanisms and expected life controls include

    SLAs—Ensure that vendors will provide the necessary maintenance.

    MTBF—Used to calculate the expected lifetime the device.

    MTTR—Used to estimate the amount of time between repairs.

6. Fire-suppression methods include

    Class A—Paper or wood, suppressed with water or soda acid.

Class B—Gasoline or oil fires, suppressed by using CO_2, soda acid, or halon.

Class C—Electronic or computer fires should be suppressed by using CO_2 or halon.

Class D—Fires caused by combustible metals, suppressed by applying dry powder or using special techniques.

7. Halon, an effective fire suppressant, has been found to be an ozone-depleting substance.

    Halon 1211—This type is found in portable extinguishers and is stored as a liquid.

    Halon 1301—This version is used in fixed flooding systems and is stored as a gaseous agent.

8. Halon fire-suppression systems can be left in place, but there are strict regulations on reporting discharges. EPA-approved replacements include FM-200, CEA-410, NAF-S-III, FE-13, argon, water, and aragonite.

9. Water sprinklers are an effective means of extinguishing Class A fires. Four variations are available:

    Dry pipe—Maintains no standing water. It reduces the risk of accidental flooding and gives some time to cover or turn off electrical equipment.

    Wet pipe—Widely used and ready for activation. This system is charged and full of water.

    Preaction—A combination system. Pipes are initially dry and do not fill with water until a predetermined temperature is reached.

    Deluge—Involves a large volume of water covering a large area quickly, similar to a dry-pipe system.

SECURITY-MANAGEMENT PRACTICES

10. Three goals of risk management are to identify risks, quantify the impact of potential threats, and find an economic balance between the impact of the risk and the cost of the countermeasure.

    · · · · · · · · · · · · · · · · · · a natural or man-made event that ········ organization.

    ········ ·ersight, or ········ sceptible to

    D1446002

    ···· with risk: ···· numbers or ·······termeasures

    and the amount of damage that can occur. Pure quantitative risk analysis is not possible.

56. Penetration testing is the process of evaluating the organization's security measures. These tests can be performed in a number of ways, including internal, external, whitebox testing, and blackbox testing.

57. Clipping levels are the thresholds implemented for certain types of errors or mistakes that are allowed without alarm.

BUSINESS CONTINUITY PLANNING

58. The Business Continuity Planning (BCP) process as defined by ISC2 has the following five steps:
    1. Project management and initiation
    2. Business impact analysis (BIA)
    3. Recovery strategy
    4. Plan design and development
    5. Testing, maintenance, awareness, and training

59. The BIA is the second step of the BCP process. Its role is to describe what impact a disaster would have on business operations.

60. BCP testing includes

    Checklist—Copies of the plan are sent to different department managers and business unit managers for review.

    Tabletop—Members of the emergency management team and business unit managers meet in conference to discuss the plan.

    Walkthrough—Actual simulation of the real thing takes place.

    Functional—Operations of the new and old site can be run in parallel.

    Full interruption—A complete a test of the BCP plan is performed.

61. Data center backup methods include

    Cold site—An empty room with only rudimentary electrical, power, and computing capability

    Warm site—Partially configured

    Hot site—Ready to go and an expensive option

LAW, INVESTIGATIONS, AND ETHICS

62. The ISC2 code of ethics states that CISSPs will

    Protect society, the commonwealth, and the infrastructure

    Act honorably, honestly, justly, responsibly, and legally

    Provide diligent and competent service to principles

    Advance and protect the profession

63. RFC 1087 states that the following activities are unethical:

    Seeking to gain unauthorized access to the resources of the Internet

    Disrupting the intended use of the Internet

    Wasting resources (people, capacity, computer) through such actions

    Destroying the integrity of computer-based information

    Compromising the privacy of users

64. The Computer Ethics Institute lists the Ten Commandments of Computer Ethics, which should also be reviewed before the exam.

CRYPTOGRAPHY

65. Two types of encryption algorithms exist: two-way and one-way functions. Two-way functions are used to operate on plain text to encrypt it with the intention of later operating on that cipher text in some way to decipher or decrypt it.

66. Two-way functions include symmetric and asymmetric algorithms.

67. Symmetric cryptography works by providing both parties the same key for encryption and decryption. It provides confidentiality and is hard to break. Its weakness is that the keys are subject to exposure and must be transmitted through a channel other than the message.

68. Data Encryption Standard (DES) is a block encryption algorithm that is based on IBM's 128-bit algorithm; 56 bits make up the key and 8 bits are used for parity. DES can be implemented in one of four modes:

    Electronic Code Book (ECB)—Native encryption mode that is used for small amounts of data. ECB is the weakest form of DES.

    Cipher Block Chaining (CBC)—Works by taking each data from the previous and applying it to the next.

    Cipher Feedback Mode (CFB)—Emulates a stream cipher and can be used when the encryption of individual characters is required.

    Output Feedback Mode (OFB)—Also emulates a stream cipher and generates random binary bits that are combined with the plain text to create cipher text.

69. Asymmetric algorithms use two different keys. The advantage is that key distribution is easier. Asymmetric algorithms are not as fast as symmetric systems.

70. Asymmetric algorithms include Diffie-Hellman, El Gamal, and Elliptic Curve Cryptosystem algorithms.

71. Common hashing algorithms include MD2, MD4, MD5, HAVAL, and SHA-1.

72. A public key infrastructure (PKI) allows individuals using the Internet to obtain and share cryptographic keys from a trusted authority. The PKI consists of four basic components and is governed by the X.509 standards:

    Certificate Authority (CA)—Used to verify and issue digital certificates. The certificate includes the public key and information about it.

    Registration Authority (RA)—Verifies authenticity for the CA.

    Repository—Accepts certificates and distributes them to authorized parties.

    Archive—Responsible for the long-term storage of archived information distributed from the CA.

Qualitative analysis—Looks at different scenarios of risk possibilities and ranks the seriousness of the threats and the sensitivity of the assets.

13. Formulas used for quantitative analysis include

EF (exposure factor) = Percentage of an asset loss caused by an identified threat

SLE (single loss expectancy) = Asset value × Exposure factor

ARO (annualized rate of occurrence) = Estimated frequency a threat will occur within a year

ALE (annualized loss expectancy) = Single loss expectancy × Annualized rate of occurrence

14. Other types of qualitative assessment techniques include

The Delphi Technique—A group assessment process that allows individuals to contribute anonymous opinions.

Facilitated Risk Assessment Process (FRAP)—Obtains results by asking questions. It is designed to be completed in a matter of hours.

15. Risk is dealt with in the following ways (these can be combined):

Risk reduction—Implements a countermeasure to alter or reduce the risk

Risk transference—Purchases insurance to transfer a portion or all of the potential cost of a loss to a third party

Risk acceptance—Deals with risk by accepting the potential cost and loss

Risk rejection—Pretends risk doesn't exist and ignores the risk

16. Security policies can be regulatory, advisory, or informative.

17. Security must flow from the top of the organization.

18. Types of security documents include

Policies—General statements produced by senior management

Standards—Tactical documents that are more specific than policies

Guidelines—Point to a statement in a policy or procedure by which to determine a course of action

Procedures—The lowest level in the policy that provide step-by-step instructions to achieve a certain task

ACCESS-CONTROL SYSTEMS AND METHODOLOGY

19. Identification (the process of claiming to be a certain person), authentication (the process of determining the legitimacy of a user or process), and authorization (granting access to a subject or an object after the object has been properly identified and authenticated) are access-control methods.

20. Authentication is typically verified through the use of a password, tokens, or biometrics.

21. Biometric systems include

FRR—The False Rejection Rate or Type I Error is the percentage of valid users who are falsely rejected.

FAR—The False Acceptance Rate or Type II Error is the percentage of invalid users who are falsely accepted.

CER—The Crossover Error Rate is the point at which the False Rejection Rate equals the False Acceptance Rate.

22. One-time passwords are used only once and are valid for only a short period of time; they are usually provided by a token device.

23. Single sign-on allows a user to enter credentials one time to access all resources.

24. Kerberos and SESAME are two examples of single sign-on systems.

25. Centralized access control such as RADIUS, TACACS, and DIAMETER can be used to maintain user IDs, rights, and permissions in one central location.

26. Attacks on access control can come in the form of DoS attacks.

Ping of death—Employs an oversize IP packet

Smurf—Sends a message to the broadcast address of a subnet or network so that every node on the network produces one or more response packets

Syn flood—Sends TCP connection requests faster than a machine can process them

Trinoo—A DDoS tool that can launch UDP flood attacks from various channels on a network

27. Data access controls are established to control how subjects can access data. Common types include the following:

The DAC model is so titled because the user controls who has access to the system he maintains.

The MAC model uses the system rather than the user to who has access. The MAC model is typically used by organizations that handle highly sensitive data.

RBAC models place users into groups to maintain access. These are used extensively by banks and other organizations.

SECURITY MODELS AND ARCHITECTURES

28. The Trusted Computing Base (TCB) is the total combination of protection mechanisms, including hardware, software, and firmware within a computer system that maintain security.

29. The reference monitor is an access-control concept referring to an abstract machine that mediates all accesses to objects by subjects.

30. The security kernel implements the reference monitor concept. The reference monitor concept has the following properties:

Provides isolation

Is invoked for every access attempt

Is impossible to circumvent and be foolproof

Is complete, verified, and tested

31. Resource isolation is the process of segmentation so that memory is separated physically, not just logically.

32. Rings of protection are used to isolate processes. The closer to the center, the more protected the resource. Lower numbers have higher levels of privileges.

33. Security models define the structure by which data structures and systems are designed to enforce security policy. Common security models include

    Bell-LaPadula—Enforces confidentiality and uses three rules: the simple security rule, the * property, and the strong star rule.

    Biba—Integrity model that has two basic rules: "no write up" and "no read down."

    Clark-Wilson—Integrity model with three goals: maintaining consistency, preventing unauthorized access, and preventing improper modification. Makes use of an access triple through a restricted interface.

    Noninterference—Prevents a subject or process from one sensitivity level from affecting subjects or process at other sensitivity levels.

34. **State machine**—Systems that operate in this mode are in a secure state upon bootup, during operation, and for each operation performed.

TELECOMMUNICATIONS AND NETWORK SECURITY

35. The goal of security is to protect confidentiality, integrity, and availability.

36. ARP poisoning sends fake ARP packets to change ARP cache tables and redirect traffic.

37. DNS spoofing is much like ARP poisoning, except the attack attempts to poison the DNS cache. Victims can be redirected to wrong Internet sites.

38. Sniffing is a passive attack that requires the attacker to gain some type of access to the network. Any clear-text information is at risk. FTP, Telnet, SMTP, and SNMP can be targets.

39. POTS is a voice-grade analog telephone service used for voice calls and for connecting to the Internet and other locations via modem.

40. ISDN is a communication protocol that operates similar to POTS, except all digital signaling is used. ISDN uses separate frequencies that are called "channels." It is configured as follows:

    ISDN BRI—Two 64Kbps B channels and one 16Kbps D channel

    ISDN PRI—Twenty-three 64Kbps B channels (US) and one 16Kbps D channel

41. The seven layers of the Open Systems Interconnect models are: application, presentation, session, transport, network, data link, and physical.

42. TCP/IP is the foundation of the Internet as we know it today. TCP/IP is similar to the OSI model but consists of only four layers. TCP/IP includes

    TCP—A reliable, slow, and connection-oriented protocol that ensures that packets are delivered to the destination computer

    UDP—A fast, best-effort, non-connection-oriented protocol

43. Routing protocols can be divided into two broad categories.
    Distance-vector protocols: RIP
    Link-state protocols: OSPF

44. TCP/IP data can be addressed as a unicast to one particular system; a multicast, which targets a group; or a broadcast, which goes to all systems.

45. Data can be transmitted into two fundamental methods, including analog or digital, which converts the signals to a binary value.

46. Information can move in two ways:

    Asynchronous communication—Two devices are not synchronized in any way.

    Synchronous communication—Two devices are synchronized and usually controlled by a clocking mechanism.

47. Baseband transmission means the cable is used for the transmission of data.

48. Broadband transmission means the cable is divided into channels so that different types of data can be transmitted at a time.

49. Firewalls are used as a choke point and to control traffic into and out of a network.

50. Common firewall terms include

    Demilitarized zone (DMZ)—A network segment that is located between the protected and the unprotected networks.

    Bastion host—A device that has been hardened and is to be deployed in the DMZ.

    Packet filtering—Considered a first level of defense. Access is based on rules.

    Stateful packet filtering—Method of control that keeps a state table to keep track of activity and control access.

    Proxy—Stands between the trusted and untrusted network.

51. Honeypots are computers that are used to attempt to lure attackers away from the real network assets.

APPLICATION AND SYSTEMS-DEVELOPMENT SECURITY

52. Polyinstantiation allows different records to exist in the same table at various security levels.

53. Database models can be relational, using attributes (columns) and tuples (rows); hierarchical, combining records and fields in a logical tree structure; or distributed, storing information in more than one database.

54. The system life cycle includes the following stages: project initiation, functional design and planning, system design, functional review, software development, product installation, operation and maintenance, and disposal and replacement.

OPERATIONS SECURITY

55. Operational security can be enhanced by implementing good employee controls, such as new hire orientation, separation of duties, job rotation, least privilege, and mandatory vacations.

EXAM CRAM™ 2

CISSP

Michael Gregg

CERTIFICATION

800 East 96th Street, Indianapolis, Indiana 46240 USA

CISSP Exam Cram 2

International Standard Book Number: 0-789-73446-X

Library of Congress Catalog Card Number: 2005925369

Printed in the United States of America

First Printing: September 2005

08 07 06 05   4 3 2 1

Trademarks

Warning and Disclaimer

Bulk Sales

Que Publishing offers excellent discounts on this book when ordered in quantity for bulk purchases or special sales. For more information, please contact

> U.S. Corporate and Government Sales
>
> 1-800-382-3419
>
> corpsales@pearsontechgroup.com

For sales outside the U.S., please contact

> International Sales
>
> international@pearsoned.com

Publisher
Paul Boger

Executive Editor
Jeff Riley

Acquisitions Editor
Steve Rowe

Development Editor
Ginny Bess

Managing Editor
Charlotte Clapp

Project Editor
Seth Kerney

Copy Editor
Krista Hansing

Indexer
Tim Wright

Proofreader
Kathy Bidwell

Technical Editor
Clement DuPuis

Publishing Coordinator
Cindy Teeters

Multimedia Developer
Dan Scherf

Interior Designer
Anne Jones

Cover Designer
Anne Jones

Que
CERTIFICATION

Que Certification • 800 East 96th Street • Indianapolis, Indiana 46240

A Note from Series Editor Ed Tittel

You know better than to trust your certification preparation to just anybody. That's why you, and more than 2 million others, have purchased an Exam Cram book. As Series Editor for the new and improved Exam Cram 2 Series, I have worked with the staff at Que Certification to ensure you won't be disappointed. That's why we've taken the world's best-selling certification product—a two-time finalist for "Best Study Guide" in CertCities' reader polls—and made it even better.

As a two-time finalist for the "Favorite Study Guide Author" award as selected by CertCities readers, I know the value of good books. You'll be impressed with Que Certification's stringent review process, which ensures the books are high quality, relevant, and technically accurate.

Exam Cram 2 books also feature a preview edition of MeasureUp's powerful, full-featured test engine, which is trusted by certification students throughout the world.

As a 20-year-plus veteran of the computing industry and the original creator and editor of the Exam Cram Series, I've brought my IT experience to bear on these books. During my tenure at Novell from 1989 to 1994, I worked with and around its excellent education and certification department. At Novell, I witnessed the growth and development of the first really big, successful IT certification program—one that was to shape the industry forever afterward. This experience helped push my writing and teaching activities heavily in the certification direction. Since then, I've worked on nearly 100 certification related books, and I write about certification topics for numerous Web sites and for *Certification* magazine.

In 1996, while studying for various MCP exams, I became frustrated with the huge, unwieldy study guides that were the only preparation tools available. As an experienced IT professional and former instructor, I wanted "nothing but the facts" necessary to prepare for the exams. From this impetus, Exam Cram emerged: short, focused books that explain exam topics, detail exam skills and activities, and get IT professionals ready to take and pass their exams.

In 1997 when Exam Cram debuted, it quickly became the best-selling computer book series since "...*For Dummies*," and the best-selling certification book series ever. By maintaining an intense focus on subject matter, tracking errata and updates quickly, and following the certification market closely, Exam Cram established the dominant position in cert prep books.

You will not be disappointed in your decision to purchase this book. If you are, please contact me at etittel@jump.net. All suggestions, ideas, input, or constructive criticism are welcome!

Ed Tittel

Dedication

*I would like to dedicate this book to my parents, W. P. and Betty Gregg.
They both sacrificed to help me achieve my dreams.*

ಸ

About the Author

Michael Gregg is the president of Superior Solutions, Inc., a Houston-based security assessment and training firm. He has more than 20 years of experience in the IT field. He holds two Associate's degrees, a Bachelor's degree, and a Master's degree. Some of the certifications he maintains include the following: CISSP, MCSE, CCNA, CTT+, A+, N+, Security+, CIW Security Analyst, CEH, NSA IAM, SCNP, DCNP, CCE, and TICSA.

Michael has consulted and taught for many Fortune 500 companies. Although consulting consumes the bulk of his time, he enjoys teaching. Michael has a proven reputation as both a dynamic and influential speaker. Teaching and contributing to the written body of IT security knowledge is how Michael believes he can give something back to the community that has given him so much.

Michael is a member of the American College of Forensic Examiners and of the Texas Association for Educational Technology. When not working, he enjoys traveling and restoring muscle cars.

Acknowledgments

I would like to offer a big "thank you" to Christine, Curly, Betty, Gen, and all my family. A special thanks to the people of Que who helped make this project a reality, including Jeff Riley and Steve Rowe.

We Want to Hear from You!

As the reader of this book, *you* are our most important critic and commentator. We value your opinion and want to know what we're doing right, what we could do better, what areas you'd like to see us publish in, and any other words of wisdom you're willing to pass our way.

As an executive editor for Que Publishing, I welcome your comments. You can email or write me directly to let me know what you did or didn't like about this book—as well as what we can do to make our books better.

Please note that I cannot help you with technical problems related to the topic of this book. We do have a User Services group, however, where I will forward specific technical questions related to the book.

When you write, please be sure to include this book's title and author as well as your name, email address, and phone number. I will carefully review your comments and share them with the author and editors who worked on the book.

Email: feedback@quepublishing.com

Mail: Jeff Riley
       Executive Editor
       Que Publishing
       800 East 96th Street
       Indianapolis, IN 46240 USA

For more information about this book or another Que Certification title, visit our website at www.examcram2.com. Type the ISBN (excluding hyphens) or the title of a book in the Search field to find the page you're looking for.

Contents at a Glance

Table of Contents

Chapter 5
System Architecture and Models

Introduction

Welcome to *CISSP Exam Cram 2*! This book covers the CISSP certification exam. Whether this is your first or your fifteenth *Exam Cram 2*, you'll find information here and in Chapter 1 that will ensure your success as you pursue knowledge, experience, and certification. This introduction explains the ISC2 certification programs in general and talks about how the *Exam Cram 2* series can help you prepare for the CISSP exam.

This book is one of the *Exam Cram 2* series of books and will help by getting you on you way to becoming an ISC2 Certified Information Systems Security Professional (CISSP).

This introduction discusses the basics of the CISSP exam. Included are sections covering preparation, how to take an exam, a description of this book's contents, how this book is organized, and, finally, author contact information.

Each chapter in this book contains practice questions. There are also two full-length practice exams at the end of the book. Practice exams in this book should provide an accurate assessment of the level of expertise you need to obtain to pass the test. *Answers and explanations are included for all test questions*. It is best to obtain a level of understanding equivalent to a consistent pass rate of at least 95% or more on the practice questions and exams in this book before you attempt the real exam.

Let's begin by looking at preparation for the exam.

How to Prepare for the Exam

Preparing for the CISSP exam requires that you obtain and study materials designed to provide comprehensive information about security. The following list of materials will help you study and prepare:

➤ The ISC2 website, at www.isc2.org

➤ The study guide available at the ISC2 website

➤ The CISSP open study guide website, at www.cccure.org

Many people form study groups to help them study for and master the material needed to pass the CISSP exam.

Practice Tests

You don't need to know much about practice tests, other than that they are a worthwhile expense for three reasons. First, they help you diagnose areas of weakness. Second, they are useful for getting used to the format of questions. Third, they help you to decide when you are ready to take the exam. This book contains questions at the end of each chapter and includes two full-length practice tests. However, if you still want more, a related Exam Cram 2 *CISSP Practice Questions Exam* book has more than 500 additional questions. The questions are in paper form so that you can practice in an environment similar to the real exam; they are also available electronically as a practice test CD in the back of the book. Many other companies provide CISSP certification practice tests as well.

Taking a Certification Exam

When you have prepared for the exam, you must register with ISC2 to take the exam. The CISSP exam is given throughout the year at various locations. You can find the latest schedule at https://www.isc2.org/cgi-bin/exam_schedule.cgi?displaycategory=1182. Many people decide to travel to the exam location; others wait until it is given at a location closer to them. ISC2 has implemented regional pricing: As an example, early registration is $499 in the U.S., compared to standard registration of $599. Check the ISC2 website at https://www.isc2.org/download/regional_pricing.pdf to get specific details.

You can register for an exam done online, by mail, or by fax. The online form is available at https://www.isc2.org/cgi-bin/content.cgi?category=542. After you register, you will receive a confirmation notice.

Arriving at the Exam Location

As with any examination, arrive at the testing center early. Be prepared! You will need to bring the confirmation letter and identification such as a driver's license, green card, or passport. Any photo ID will suffice. Two forms of ID are usually required. The testing center staff requires proof that you are who you say you are and that someone else is not taking the test for you.

You'll be spending a lot of time in the exam room. The total test time is 6 hours, so eat a good breakfast and take a snack and bottle of water with you to the testing area.

In the Exam Room

You will not be allowed to take study materials or anything else into the examination room with you that could raise the suspicion that you're cheating.

After the Exam

Examination results are not available after the exam. You must wait up to 4–6 weeks to get your results by email or snail mail.

Retaking a Test

You must wait at least 90 days to retake a failed examination. If you fail, you should use that time to brush up on your areas of weakness. Additionally, invest in some practice tests if you have not already done so. There is much to be said for "getting used to" a testing format.

Tracking Your CISSP Status

When you pass the exam, you still need to attest to the CISSP code of ethics and have an existing CISSP complete a endorsement form for you.

When you receive notice of your passing grade, a blank endorsement form will be sent with it. The endorsement form must be completed by someone who can attest to your professional experience and who is an active CISSP in good standing. If you don't know anyone who is CISSP certified, ISC2 allows endorsements from other professionals who are certified, licensed, or commissioned, and an officer of the corporation where you are employed. You can review complete information on the endorsement form at the ISC2 website.

About This Book

The ideal reader for an *Exam Cram 2* book is someone seeking certification. However, it should be noted that an *Exam Cram 2* book is a very easily readable, rapid presentation of facts. Therefore, an *Exam Cram 2* book is also extremely useful as a quick reference manual.

Most people seeking certification use multiple sources of information. Check out the links at the end of each chapter to get more information about subjects you're weak in. Practice tests can help indicate when you are ready. Various security books from retailers also describe the topics in this book in much greater detail. Don't forget that many have described the CISSP exam as being a "mile wide."

This book includes other helpful elements in addition to the actual logical, step-by-step learning progression of the chapters themselves. *Exam Cram 2* books use elements such as exam alerts, tips, notes, and practice questions to make information easier to read and absorb.

 Reading this book from start to finish is not necessary; this book is set up so you can quickly jump back and forth to find sections you need to study.

Use the Cram Sheet to remember last-minute facts immediately before the exam. Use the practice questions to test your knowledge. You can always brush up on specific topics in detail by referring to the table of contents and the index. Even after you achieve certification, you can use this book as a rapid-access reference manual.

The Chapter Elements

Each *Exam Cram 2* book has chapters that follow a predefined structure. This structure makes *Exam Cram 2* books easy to read and provides a familiar format for all *Exam Cram 2* books. These elements typically are used:

➤ Opening hotlists

➤ Chapter topics

➤ Exam Alerts

➤ Notes

➤ Tips

➤ Sidebars

➤ Cautions

➤ Exam-preparation practice questions and answers

➤ A "Need to Know More?" section at the end of each chapter

Bulleted lists, numbered lists, tables, and graphics are also used, where appropriate. A picture can paint a thousand words sometimes, and tables can help to associate different elements with each other visually.

Now let's take a look at each of the elements in detail.

➤ **Opening hotlists**—The start of every chapter contains a list of terms you should understand. A second hotlist identifies all the techniques and skills covered in the chapter.

➤ **Chapter topics**—Each chapter contains details of all subject matter listed in the table of contents for that particular chapter. The objective of an *Exam Cram 2* book is to cover all the important facts without giving too much detail; it is an exam cram. When examples are required, they are included.

➤ **Exam Alerts**—Exam Alerts address exam-specific, exam-related information. An Exam Alert addresses content that is particularly important, tricky, or likely to appear on the exam. Exam Alerts look like this:

Make sure you remember the different ways in which DES can be implemented and that ECB is considered the weakest form of DES.

➤ **Notes**—Notes typically contain useful information that is not directly related to the current topic under consideration. To avoid breaking up the flow of the text, they are set off from the regular text.

This is a note. You have already seen several notes.

➤ **Tips**—Tips often provide shortcuts or better ways to do things.

A clipping level is the point at which you set a control to distinguish between activity that should be investigated and activity that should not be investigated.

➤ **Sidebars**—Sidebars are longer and run beside the text. They often describe real-world examples or situations.

How Caller ID Can Be Hacked

Sure, we all trust Caller ID, but some Voice over IP (VoIP) providers allow users to inject their own Call Party Number (CPN) into the call. Because VoIP is currently outside FCC regulation, these hacks are now possible.

➤ **Cautions**—Cautions apply directly to the use of the technology being discussed in the Exam Cram. For example, a Caution might point out that the CER is one of the most important items to examine when examining biometric devices.

The Crossover Error Rate (CER) is the point at which Type 1 errors and Type 2 errors intersect. The lower the CER is, the more accurate the device is.

➤ **Exam-preparation practice questions**—At the end of every chapter is a list of 10–15 exam practice questions similar to those in the actual exam. Each chapter contains a list of questions relevant to that chapter, including answers and explanations. Test your skills as you read.

➤ **"Need to Know More?" section**—This section at the end of each chapter describes other relevant sources of information. With respect to this chapter, the best place to look for CISSP certification information is at the ISC2 website, www.ISC2.org.

Other Book Elements

Most of this *Exam Cram 2* book on CISSP follows the consistent chapter structure already described. However, there are various, important elements that are not part of the standard chapter format. These elements apply to the entire book as a whole.

➤ **Practice exams**—In addition to exam-preparation questions at the end of each chapter, two full practice exams are included at the end of the book.

➤ **Answers and explanations for practice exams**—These follow each practice exam, providing answers and explanations to the questions in the exams.

➤ **Glossary**—The glossary contains a listing of important terms used in this book with explanations.

➤ **Cram Sheet**—The Cram Sheet is a quick-reference, tear-out cardboard sheet of important facts useful for last-minute preparation. Cram sheets often include a simple summary of facts that are most difficult to remember.

➤ **CD**—The CD contains the *PrepLogic Practice Exams, Preview Edition* exam-simulation software. The preview edition exhibits most of the full functionality of the Premium Edition, but it contains only one exam's worth of questions. To get the complete set of practice questions and full exam functionality, visit www.preplogic.com.

Chapter Contents

The following list provides an overview of the chapters.

➤ **Chapter 1: "The CISSP Certification Exam"**—This chapter introduces exam strategies and considerations.

➤ **Chapter 2: "Physical Security"**—This chapter details physical security and the threats and countermeasures available for protecting an organization's resources.

➤ **Chapter 3: "Security-Management Practices"**—This chapter discusses the organization's information assets and means of protection, including policies, procedures, guidelines, and assorted controls.

➤ **Chapter 4: "Access-Control Systems and Methodology"**—This chapter covers the basics of access control. Items such as identification, authentication, and authorization are discussed, as are biometric access-control systems.

➤ **Chapter 5: "System Architecture and Models"**—This chapter discusses the ways to design, monitor, implement, and lock down computer systems.

➤ **Chapter 6: "Telecommunications and Network Security"**—One of the longest chapters, this chapter discusses telecommunication technology. Items such as TCP/IP, the OSI model, routing protocols, and networking equipment are discussed.

➤ **Chapter 7: "Applications and Systems-Development Security"**—This chapter discusses databases, malicious code, knowledge-based systems, and application issues.

➤ **Chapter 8: "Operations Security"**—This chapter covers security concepts, operation controls, auditing, and resource protection.

➤ **Chapter 9: "Business-Continuity Planning"**—This chapter covers all the aspects of the BCP and DRP process. Its goal is to help the reader understand what is needed to prevent, minimize, and recover from disasters.

➤ **Chapter 10: "Law, Investigations, and Ethics"**—This chapter covers all things legal, from international law and incident response to forensics. It also covers the ethical standards that CISSP candidates must understand and abide by.

➤ **Chapter 11: "Cryptography"**—This chapter discusses the methods, means, and systems used to encrypt and protect data. Symmetric, asymmetric, and hashing algorithms are introduced, along with PKI and cryptographic methods of attack.

➤ **Chapter 12: "Practice Exam 1"**—This is a full-length practice exam.

➤ **Chapter 13: "Answers to Practice Exam 1"**—This element contains the answers and explanations for the first practice exam.

➤ **Chapter 14: "Practice Exam 2"**—This is a second full-length practice exam.

➤ **Chapter 15: "Answers to Practice Exam 2"**—This element contains the answers and explanations for the second practice exam.

Contacting the Author

Hopefully, this book provides you with the tools you need to pass the CISSP exam. Feedback is appreciated. The author can be contacted at info@thesolutionfirm.com.

Thank you for selecting my book; I hope you like it. Good luck!

Self-Assessment

This Self-Assessment section enables you to evaluate your readiness to take the CISSP certification exam. It should also help you understand what's required to obtain the CISSP certification. Are you ready?

CISSPs in the Real World

Security continues to be on everyone's mind. The CISSP certification has again topped the list as one of the most sought-after security certifications. Increasing numbers of people are studying for and obtaining their CISSP certifications. Congratulations on making the decision to follow in their footsteps. If you are willing to tackle the process seriously and do what it takes to obtain the necessary experience and knowledge, you can pass the exam on the first try.

 You can also assess your CISSP skill set by using the MeasureUp Certification Mode.

The Ideal CISSP Candidate

The ideal CISSP candidate is likely to have a 4-year college education and have at least 5–7 years experience in one or more of the 10 CISSP domains. The most applicable degree is in computer science or perhaps a related field. A degree is not a prerequisite for taking the test. However, the 4 years of experience is a prerequisite. Don't be lulled into thinking that this is an easy test. Some words of caution might be in order:

➤ The CISSP exam requires the candidate to absorb a substantial amount of material. The test is 6 hours long and consists of 225 graded questions. Unlike Microsoft exams and most other IT vendor exams, it is not a computer-generated test.

➤ The pass mark is set high, at 700 points. The individual questions are weighted, which means that harder questions are worth more than easier ones.

➤ Most of the individuals attempting the exam are familiar with one to three of the domains. This means that studying for the exam can be overwhelming because there is so much material to cover. This book can help by guiding you to the areas in which you are weak or strong.

➤ To be eligible for the CISSP exam, students are required to have 4 years of experience, or 3 years of experience and a college degree.

Put Yourself to the Test

In this section, you answer some simple questions. The objective is for you to understand exactly how much work and effort you must invest to pass the CISSP certification exam. The simple answer to this question is this: The experience and education you have will dictate how difficult it will be for you to pass. Be honest in your answers, or you will end up wasting $500 or more on an exam you were not ready to take. From the beginning, two things should be clear:

➤ Any educational background in computer science will be helpful, as will other IT certifications you have achieved.

➤ Hands-on actual experience is not only essential, but also required to obtain this certification.

Your Educational Background

➤ Do you have a computer science degree?

You'll have a good base knowledge needed for 3 or more of the 10 domains, assuming that you finished your degree and your schooling and have some fairly sophisticated computer skills. Subject areas such as application development, networking, and database design are a great help.

➤ Did you attend some type of technical school or computer cram course?

This question applies to low-level or short-term computer courses. Many of these courses are extremely basic or focused in one particular area. Although the CISSP exam is not platform specific, training classes that focused on networking, security, hacking, or database design will help you pass the exam.

➤ Have you developed any security policies, performed security audits, performed penetration tests, or developed response plans?

If yes, you will probably be able to handle about half of the CISSP exam domains.

➤ Do you have a photographic memory?

If yes, you might have a vague chance of passing simply by reading this book, taking some practice exams, and using the Internet to brush up on the subjects you are weak in. However, the goal here is to gain a real understanding of the material. As a CISSP, you might be asked to lead, plan, organize, or control your organization's security operations; if that happens, you'll need a real understanding of how the various technologies and techniques work. Don't cheat yourself or gamble with your career.

Again, the education and requirements given here are by no means absolute. Still, an education can give you a very good grounding in any endeavor—the higher the level of education, the better.

Testing Your Exam Readiness

Whether you attend a training class, form a study group, or study on your own, preparing for the CISSP exam is essential. The exam will cost you about $500, depending on where you are located, so you'll want to do everything you can to make sure you pass on the first try. Reading, studying, and taking practice exams are the best ways to increase your readiness. Practice exams help in a number of ways:

➤ Practice exams highlight weak spots for further study.

➤ Practice exams give you a general perspective on the question format. Practicing the questions the way they are asked can help enormously on the actual testing day.

➤ Two full-length practice exams are provided with this book. *Exam Cram 2* also publishes a second book, *CISSP Practice Questions Exam*, with more than 500 practice CISSP test questions; it is an excellent supplement to this book.

After the Exam

After you have passed the exam, you will need to gain continuing education credits each year to maintain your certification. Your certification will come up for renewal every three years, so you'll need to obtain 120 continuing education credits (CPE) or retake the exam. Retaking the exam is probably not a likely choice. These are some ways to gain CPEs to keep your certification current:

➤ Write a book.

➤ Read a book. (Only one per year can be used for credit.) This will give you a couple of credits, but not enough to keep your certification current.

➤ Do volunteer work that is approved by ISC2. When you are certified, you can log on to the ISC2 website for more information. A variety of volunteer work is available, including proctoring the CISSP exam.

➤ Attend a training class. Just about any type of technology training class is accepted, as long as it is tied to one of the domains.

➤ Teach a training class.

➤ Attend a college-level security class.

As you can see, the goal here is to help you stay current. As technology changes, we all must continue to learn to keep up the pace.

Now that we have covered some of the ways in which to assess you exam readiness, let's move on to Chapter 1, "The CISSP Certification Exam," where you will learn more about how the exam is structured and some effective test-taking strategies.

The CISSP Certification Exam

Terms you'll need to understand:
✓ Common body of knowledge (CBK)
✓ Exam strategy

Techniques you'll need to master:
✓ Assessing exam requirements
✓ Determining whether you're ready for the exam
✓ Using practice questions
✓ Using your time wisely

Introduction

Welcome to the *CISSP Exam Cram 2*! The aim of this chapter is to help you become prepared for the CISSP exam and understand what to expect when you enter the testing area. For most people, exam taking is not something that they eagerly anticipate. The best way to reduce this anxiety is to be fully prepared before you attempt to pass the exam. Taking those extra steps will help you feel more relaxed and confident when you enter the testing area.

Before beginning your studies, take a few minutes to make sure you fully understand the CISSP exam process. This is something that you don't want to wait until the day of the test to figure out. Reviewing these details now will help you concentrate on the exam so that you aren't worried about how much time you have to answer each question. Finally, mastering a few basic exam-taking skills should help you recognize—and perhaps even overcome—some of the tricks or unusual verbiage you're bound to find on the exam.

In addition to reviewing the exam environment, this chapter describes some proven exam-taking strategies that you can use to your advantage.

Assessing Exam Readiness

Before you rush out and sign up for the CISSP exam, check out the ISC2.org website and review the CISSP Certification requirements. To be eligible to become a CISSP, you must qualify for and meet two separate requirements:

➤ **Examination**—This portion of the process requires that you submit the examination fee, assert that you possess a minimum of 4 years of professional experience in the information security field or 3 years plus a college degree (this is subject to audit and verification), review and sign the Candidate Agreement stating that you will legally commit to adhere to the CISSP Code of Ethics, and answer four questions regarding criminal history and background.

➤ **Certification**—This second step of the process requires that the candidate pass the exam with a score of 700 points or greater, submit a completed and executed Endorsement Form, and, in some cases, pass a verification audit regarding professional experience.

When you are confident that you meet these requirements, you can continue with your studies. To be fully prepared for the exam, I recommend that you read the entire text, review the practice questions, and review the additional resources identified in each chapter. After you read the book and test yourself with the questions and practice exams, you will have a good idea of whether you are ready to take the real exam.

Be aware that the *CISSP exam is difficult and challenging*; therefore, this book shouldn't be your only vehicle for CISSP study. Because of the breadth and depth of knowledge needed to successfully pass the CISSP exam, be sure to use plenty of study materials and use this book to help you gauge your strengths and weaknesses. The ISC² website is a good place to find additional study material, and so are the "Need to Know More?" sections at the end of the chapters in this book. The study guide pages on the ISC² website include 70 publications that are helpful when preparing for the exam.

Taking the Exam

When you arrive at the location of the exam, you need to sign in. You will be asked to show your exam confirmation and photo identification. You cannot take the exam without a photo ID and your exam confirmation number. After you've signed in, find a seat, get comfortable, and wait for the exam to begin.

The exam is completely closed book. In fact, you will not be permitted to take any study materials into the testing area; you will be given scratch paper to use that must be returned at the completion of the exam. The exam room usually contains a number of tables where the candidates will sit. Because the test has a 6-hour time limit, ISC² tries to make the candidates as comfortable as possible and allows you to bring bottled water and a snack. ISC² allows you to make comments regarding the training environment at the completion of the exam.

During the 6-hour time limit, you will need to complete 250 questions. This provides plenty of time to complete the exam and even provides some time to go back and review your answers. The exam moderator will also keep you informed of how much time you have left to complete the exam.

All questions on the exam are multiple choice, and the exam contains 250 questions. Twenty-five of the questions are for research purposes, so only 225 questions are actually scored for certification. Counting the number of good questions you have answered isn't an indicator of success because of the research questions and because the questions are weighted. Because you are not penalized for wrong questions, you should attempt all the questions, even if you need to guess the answer. The exam questions are developed by an ISC² committee and are always being updated and changed.

In the next section, you learn more about how CISSP test questions look and how they must be answered.

Chapter 1

Multiple-Choice Question Format

All exam questions require you to select a single answer from the given choices. The following multiple-choice question requires you to select a single, correct answer. Following the question is a brief summary of each potential answer and why it is either right or wrong. You will be tasked with selecting the most correct answer. In some cases, more than one answer might appear correct; you must determine which one is most correct.

1. What is the most widely used device to control physical access?
   - ❑ A. Chains
   - ❑ B. Locks
   - ❑ C. Alarms
   - ❑ D. Firewalls

Answer: B. Locks are the most commonly used device to control physical access. Locks have been used since the time of the Egyptians. Answer A is incorrect because chains are not the most commonly used devices for physical access control. Answer C is incorrect because alarms don't prevent access; they only inform you that possible unauthorized access has occurred. Answer D is incorrect because a firewall is used to control logical access.

Exam Strategy

A well-known principle when taking fixed-length exams is to first read the entire exam from start to finish while answering only those questions you feel absolutely sure of. On subsequent passes, you can dive into more complex questions more deeply, knowing how many questions you have left.

Unlike most other exams, this exam is paper based. Each candidate is issued a test booklet and answer sheet before the exam begins. Exam candidates are allowed to write on the exam booklet. You should circle keywords such as *not, maybe, could,* and *should.* Draw an arrow to the right when the question states "from greatest to smallest." Draw an arrow to the left when the question mentions "smallest to greatest." These strategies can help you successfully master the exam.

As you read each question, if you answer only those you're sure of and mark for review those that you're not sure of, you can keep working through a decreasing list of questions as you answer the trickier ones in order.

There's at least one potential benefit to reading the exam completely before answering the trickier questions: Sometimes information supplied in later questions sheds more light on earlier questions. At other times, information you read in later questions might jog your memory about earlier questions. Either way, you'll come out ahead if you defer those questions about which you're not absolutely sure.

Here are some question-handling strategies that apply to fixed-length and short-form tests. Use these tips whenever you can:

➤ When returning to a question after your initial read-through, read every word again; otherwise, you might get confused. Sometimes revisiting a question after turning your attention elsewhere lets you see something you missed, but the strong tendency is to see what you've seen before.

➤ If you return to a question more than twice, try to articulate to yourself what you don't understand about the question, why answers don't appear to make sense, or what appears to be missing. If you chew on the subject a while, your subconscious might provide the details you lack or you might notice a "trick" that points to the right answer. If there is more than one good answer, usually the more general answer that encompasses the other one will take precedence and be the correct answer.

➤ As you work your way through the exam, it's wise to budget your time. Don't forget to leave time to fill in the dots on the answer sheet. Ensure that you do not skip one question on the answer sheet, or all the following answers could be wrong.

➤ If you're not finished when only 5 minutes remain, use that time to guess your way through any remaining questions. Remember, guessing is potentially more valuable than not answering because blank answers are always wrong, but a guess might turn out to be right. If you don't have a clue about any of the remaining questions, pick answers at random or choose all A's, B's, and so on. The important thing is to submit an exam for scoring that has an answer for every question.

When you have completed the exam, take a moment to go back through the questions to compare the answers you have entered on the answer sheet. Make sure you did not miss anything or transcribe something incorrectly.

Question-Handling Strategies

Because of the way the CISSP exam is structured, there is only one correct answer for each question; many times one or two of the answers will be obviously incorrect and two of the answers will be plausible. Take the time to reread the question. Words such as *sometimes*, *not*, *always*, and *best* can make a big difference when choosing the correct answer. Unless the answer leaps out at you, begin the process of answering by eliminating those answers that are most obviously wrong.

Almost always, at least one answer out of the possible choices for a question can be eliminated immediately because it matches one of these conditions:

➤ The answer does not apply to the situation.

➤ The answer describes a nonexistent issue, an invalid option, or an imaginary state.

After you eliminate all answers that are obviously wrong, you can apply your retained knowledge to eliminate further answers. Look for items that sound correct but refer to actions, commands, or features that are not present or not available in the situation that the question describes.

If you're still faced with a blind guess among two or more potentially correct answers, reread the question. Try to picture how each of the possible remaining answers would alter the situation.

Only when you've exhausted your ability to eliminate answers but remain unclear about which of the remaining possibilities is correct should you guess at an answer. An unanswered question offers you no points, but guessing gives you at least some chance of getting a question right; just don't be too hasty when making a blind guess!

Mastering the Inner Game

In the final analysis, knowledge breeds confidence and confidence breeds success. If you study the materials in this book carefully and review all the practice questions at the end of each chapter, you should become aware of those areas where additional learning and study are required.

After you've worked your way through the book, take the practice exams in the back of the book. Taking this test will provide a reality check and help you identify areas to study further. Make sure you follow up and review materials related to the questions you missed on the practice exam before taking the real exam. Only when you've covered that ground and feel comfortable with the whole scope of the practice exam should you set an exam appointment. It's advisable to score 80 percent or better before you attempt the real exam. Otherwise, obtain some additional practice tests and keep trying until you hit the magic number.

Armed with the information in this book and with the determination to augment your knowledge, you should be able to pass the certification exam. However, you need to work at it or you'll spend the exam fee more than once before you finally pass. If you prepare seriously, you should do well. We are confident that you can do it!

Need to Know More?

https://www.isc2.org/cgi-bin/content.cgi?category=539

www.cccure.org/—The CISSP Open Study Guide

Physical Security

Terms you'll need to understand:

✓ Biometric access control
✓ FM-200
✓ Piggyback
✓ Intrusion detection
✓ Halon

Techniques you'll need to master:

✓ Physical security threats
✓ Defense in depth
✓ Fire safety
✓ Fire-detection systems
✓ Requirements for new facilities

Introduction

You probably have a sticker on your car that is required for you to park in the company parking garage. Company policy might require you to get a new photo taken each year for your company ID badge. You might distribute keys for the equipment room to several of your employees. *Physical security* is something that most of us deal with every day.

CISSP candidates studying the physical domain must understand what is involved in choosing a secure site. The candidate must also have knowledge of the methods used to secure the facility and, most important, how to protect its resources and employees. The goal of overall physical security is to deter, delay, detect, assess, and respond.

Physical Security Risks

Physical threats have existed for as long as man has inhabited Earth. In ancient times, a castle simply was not built at any indiscriminate location; careful planning was required. Exterior defenses (such as motes, channels, walls, and barricades) were needed to hold back the marauding hordes. Guards and towers had to be strategically placed to ensure the safety of the castle's inhabitants. As strangers approached, procedures and policies were needed to distinguish between friend or foe and then to pursue the appropriate action with that friend or foe. You had to know when to lower the gate or to boil a pot of hot oil.

In the modern world, a variety of threats to premises security exists. These can be divided into three broad categories: natural disasters, man-made threats, and emergency situations.

Natural Disasters

Natural disasters can come in many forms. Although natural disasters are not something we can prevent, we can develop plans that detail how we would deal with them. As an example, organizations planning to establish a facility in Houston, Texas, might not need to worry about earthquakes; however, hurricanes are an imminent possibility. Therefore, a good understanding of the region and its associated weather-related issues are an important security consideration. These are some of the natural disasters organizations must deal with:

➤ **Hurricanes, typhoons, and tropical cyclones**—These products of Mother Nature are products of the tropical ocean and atmosphere. They are powered by heat from the sea. As they progress across the ocean, they grow in velocity. When they move ashore, they spawn tornadoes and cause high winds and floods.

➤ **Tidal waves/tsunamis**—The word *tsunami* is based on a Japanese word meaning "harbor wave." This natural phenomenon consists of a series of widely dispersed waves that cause massive damage when they come ashore.

➤ **Floods**—Floods can result when the soil has poor retention properties or when the amount of rainfall exceeds the ground's ability to absorb water. Floods are also caused when creeks and rivers overflow their banks.

➤ **Earthquakes**—These are caused from movement of the earth along the fault lines. Areas such as California and Alaska are especially vulnerable because they are on top of a major fault line.

➤ **Tornados**—Tornados are violent storms that form from a thunderstorm. They descend to the ground as a violent rotating column of air. Tornados leave a path of destruction that can extend from the width of a football field to about a mile wide. If you ever see one, steer a wide path around it.

➤ **Fire**—This one leads the list in damage and potential for loss of life. As an example, statistics show that fires in the United States killed more than 4,500 people in 1993. That's a greater loss of life than all other natural disasters that year, including floods, hurricanes, tornadoes, and earthquakes.

Man-Made Threats

Man-made threats are another big concern when thinking about physical security. Not much can be done to prevent floods, hurricanes, or tornados, but man-made threats can be reduced. Man-made threats include terrorism, vandalism, theft, and destruction of company property.

➤ **Terrorism**—To many of us, the actions of terrorists might seem like random acts of violence, but that is not the case. Terrorism is a deliberate use of violence against civilians for political or religious means.

➤ **Vandalism**—Since the Vandals sacked Rome in 455 A.D., the term *vandalism* has been synonymous with the willful destruction of another's property.

➤ **Theft**—Theft of company assets can range from annoying to detrimental. Sure, the CEO's stolen laptop can be replaced, but what about the

data on the laptop? What happens if the company's competitors end up
with that information?

➤ **Destruction**—A former employee thought he would get even with the
company by wiping out an important company database. What will it
cost to recover? Did anyone implement that backup policy?

➤ **Criminal activities**—This includes a wide range of problems. Maybe your
company thought it was getting a real tax break by moving into a lower-
income area. Now, employees don't feel safe walking to their cars at night.
Maybe your web administrator didn't think it would be a problem setting
up a music and movie peer-to-peer download site on the company
network—after all, it's just for fun and a little added pocket money.

Emergency Situations

Unlike natural disasters or man-made threats, these are the events that just
seem to happen, often at highly inopportune times. Although they're incon-
venient, these situations don't usually lead to loss of life. Emergency situations include communication loss, utility loss, and equipment failure.

➤ **Communication loss**—Voice and data communication systems play
a critical role in today's organizations. Communication loss can be the
outage of voice communication systems or data networks. Sure you
leased a redundant T1? How were you supposed to know that both were
terminated at the same junction point across the street? That was, until
someone smashed into that telephone pole on a Saturday night and all
WAN access was lost!

➤ **Utility loss**—Utilities include water, gas, communications systems, and
electrical power. The loss of utilities can bring business to a standstill.
Generators and backup can prevent these problems if they are used. If
you don't think this is a priority, you must not be one of the 50 million
people left without power on August 14, 2003, when the United States
suffered its largest-ever power outage.

➤ **Equipment failure**—Equipment will fail over time. That is why maintenance is so important. A Fortune 1000 study found that 65% of all
businesses that failed to become operational after 1 week never became
operational.

Service-level agreements (SLAs) are one good way to plan for equipment failure. With
an SLA in place, the vendor agrees to repair or replace the covered equipment within
a given period of time.

Requirements for New Site Locations

If you are planning to construct a new facility, it's important to consider all of the threats that were previously discussed. The last thing you want is to build a facility in an area where your employees fear for their personal safety. At the same time, you don't want the facility to feel like a bank vault or be designed like a prison. You need a facility that employees can be comfortable in. Well-designed facilities can be built as both comfortable and secure. Finding the right location is one of the first things you should consider when planning a new facility. The following items list some of the key points to consider:

➤ **Accessibility**—An organization's facility needs to be in a location that people can access. Depending on your business and individual needs, requirements will vary, but items such as roads, freeways, local traffic patterns, and convenience to regional airports need to be considered.

➤ **Climatology and natural disasters**—Mother Nature affects all of us. If you're building in Phoenix, Arizona, you will not have the same weather concerns that someone building a facility in Anchorage, Alaska, will have. Therefore, events such as hurricanes, floods, snowstorms, dust storms, and tornados should be discussed and planned before starting construction.

➤ **Local considerations**—Sure, it seemed like a great deal—the land for the new facility was so cheap just because it was next to a railway. Too bad you didn't know that it's used to haul toxic chemicals and that several derailments have happened over the last several years. Issues such as freight lines, flight paths of airlines, and toxic waste dumps all play into the picture of where you should build a facility.

➤ **Utilities**—You should check that water, gas, and electric lines are adequate for an organization's needs.

➤ **Visibility**—Area population, terrain, and types of neighbors are also concerns. Depending on the type of business, you might need a facility that blends into the neighborhood. You might want to design individual buildings so that it is difficult to identify what type of activity is taking place there. I know of one company that was so concerned about unauthorized personnel eavesdropping and sniffing electrical signals emanating from the facility that it built in a hilly location. Even special fences were used to help cancel out electrical signals leaving the facility.

Location

Location of the facility is an important issue. A good example is the NSA museum outside Baltimore. It's the kind of place every computer geek dreams of going. It's actually behind the main NSA facility in what was a hotel. Rumor has it that this was a favorite hangout of the KGB before the NSA bought the hotel. I use this example to drive home the importance of location. Before construction begins, an organization should be thinking about how the location fits with the organization's tasks and goals. If you're running a covert spy agency next to a hotel that could be used for monitoring and surveillance, there might be a problem. Just as if you manufacture rockets for space shuttles, you might want to be near fire stations and hospitals, in case there's an accident. Just keep in mind that it's about more than just the cost of the property: Cheap property doesn't necessarily mean a good deal.

Construction

After you have chosen a location, your next big task is to determine how the facility will be constructed. In many ways, this is driven by what the facility will be used for and by federal, state, and local laws. Buildings that are used to store the groundskeeper's equipment have different requirements than those used as a clean room for the manufacturer of microchips. Although some things will be locked in and will be out of your control, you must determine others up front. As an example, you'll need to know how various parts of the facility will be used. I once saw a facilities crew trying to install an EMI chamber on the third floor of a building. No one had checked to verify the load-bearing weight of the floor. Concrete floor slabs typically have a rating of 150 pounds per square foot. Had the project continued, there was a good chance that the floor could have collapsed or been damaged. Make sure that the facility is built to support whatever equipment you plan to put in it.

The load is how much weight the walls, floor, and ceiling can support.

Doors, Walls, Windows, and Ceilings

Have you ever wondered why most doors on homes open in, while almost all doors on businesses open out? This design is rooted in security. The door on your home is hinged to the inside. This makes it harder for thieves to remove your door to break in, but it also gives you an easy way to remove the door to bring in that big new leather couch. Years ago, the individuals who designed business facilities had the same thought. Open-in design doesn't work well when people panic. It's a sad fact that the United States has a long and tragic history of workplace fires. In 1911, nearly 150 women and young girls died when they couldn't exit the poultry plant they were working in when it caught fire. Because of this and other tragic losses of life, modern businesses are required to maintain exits that open out. These doors are more expensive because they are harder to install and remove. Special care must be taken to protect the hinges so that they cannot be easily removed. Most are installed with a panic bar that would allow a large crowd to rush through the door— just push, and you're out.

Doors aren't the only thing you need to consider. Most buildings have raised floors, so they need to be constructed in such a way that they are grounded. Walls must be designed to slow the spread of fires, and emergency lighting should be in place to light the way for anyone trying to escape in case of emergency. Other considerations include these:

➤ **Doors**—If doors are electrical-powered, what state are they in if there is a power loss? An unlocked (or disengaged) state allows employees to exit and not be locked in. If a door lock defaults to open when power is disengaged, it is considered fail safe. If the lock defaults closed, it is considered fail secure.

Fail-safe locks are designed to protect employees in case of power loss because they allow employees to exit the facility.

The terms *fail safe* and *fail secure* have very different meanings when discussed in physical security versus logical security. During the exam, read the question carefully to determine in what context the term is being used.

➤ **Ceilings**—These need to be waterproof, have an adequate fire rating, and be reinforced to keep unauthorized personnel from accessing secure areas such as server rooms.

➤ **Electrical and HVAC**—You need to plan for adequate power for the right locations. Rooms that have servers or other heat-producing equipment need additional cooling to protect the equipment. HVAC systems should be tied to fire-suppression equipment; otherwise, HVAC systems can inadvertently provide oxygen and help feed a fire.

Air intakes should be properly protected to protect people from toxin being introduced into an environment. The anthrax threat of 2001 drove home this critical concern.

➤ **Windows**—Interior or exterior windows need to be fixed in place and must be shatter proof. Depending on placement, the windows might need to be either opaque or translucent. Alarms or sensors also might be needed.

➤ **Fire escapes**—These are critical because they provide for the protection of personnel and allow an exit in case of fire. After the collapse of the World Trade Towers, it was discovered that it took individuals three times longer to exit the facility than had been planned. It is critical that fire drills be performed to practice evacuation plans and determine real exit times.

➤ **Fire detection**—Smoke detectors should be used to inform employees of danger. Sprinklers and detectors should be used to reduce the spread of fire. Smoke detectors can be used in many ways to quickly alert individuals to the possibility of danger. Placement of smoke detectors can include under raised floors, above suspended ceilings, in the plenum area, and within air ducts.

The safety of your employees should always be your first concern.

Building Defense in Depth

A layered defense is all about *defense in depth*. With the defense-in-depth approach, each layer has its own defensive mechanisms. Physical security controls are the first line of defense and should be designed so that the breach of any one defensive layer will not compromise the physical security of the organization. CCTV cameras, mantraps, card keys, RFID tags, lighting, guards, dogs, and locks are but a few of the layers of physical security that can be added to build a defense-in-depth defense.

Perimeter Controls

The best way to control premises security is to use fences, gates, and bollards. The amount of control depends on the way in which you deploy these defenses. A 4-foot fence will deter only a causal trespasser, but an 8-foot fence will keep out a determined intruder. Adding a barbed-wire topping is another effective security measure. If you are trying to keep employees in, you should point the barbed wire in. If you are trying to keep the bad guys out, you should point the barbed wire out. Table 2.1 provides more details. If you are really concerned about who's hanging around the perimeter of your facility, you might consider installing a perimeter intrusion and detection assessment system (PIDAS). This special fencing system has sensors to detect intruders. The downside is that a stray deer or grizzly bear might also trigger an alarm.

Table 2.1 Fence Heights	
Height	**Purpose**
3–4 feet high	Will deter only casual trespassers.
6–7 feet high	Considered too tall to easily climb.
8 feet high	Should deter a determined intruder. Three strands of a topping of barbed wire should be pointed out at a 45° angle.

Bollards are another means of perimeter control. Made of concrete or steel, they are used to block vehicular traffic or protect areas where pedestrians might be entering or leaving buildings. After 9/11, these devises have continued to advance far beyond the standard steel poles of the past. Companies now make bollards with electronic sensors to notify building inhabitants that someone has rammed or breached the bollards. Although fences act as a first line of defense, bollards are a close second because they can deter individuals from ramming a facility with a car or truck. Figure 2.1 shows an example of a bollard.

Figure 2.1 Bollards.
Source: www.deltascientific.com/bollards2.htm

Not all of the perimeter controls you might consider building into a new facility design have to look like concrete and steel. Have you ever noticed those majestic ponds located next to many corporate headquarters? Well, don't be lulled into believing they were placed there as a community beautification project. They are merely a form of a barricade or barrier. They are also useful in case of fire because they can serve as an additional water source. Access controls are a critical piece of premise security that can be either natural, such as a body of water, or structural, such as a fence.

Other perimeter-control mechanisms (such as cameras, mantraps, card keys, RFID tags, lighting, guards, dogs, locks, and biometric access controls) are used to monitor the flow of people and personnel. Just as networks use chokepoints, so should physical security controls. Each of these is explained in more depth next.

CCTV Cameras

These devices are effective for surveillance of entrances and critical access points. If employees are not available to monitor live, activity can be recorded and reviewed later. These devices are detective in nature: They don't prevent a crime, but they alert you to one after the fact. If you are considering CCTV systems, worker privacy and blind spots must also be considered.

Mantraps

Mantraps are used to control the flow of individuals into and out of sensitive areas. Turnstiles can also be used to control the flow of individuals into or out of an area. Both are effective in preventing one of the most common types of security breaches: *piggybacking*. Piggybacking, or tailgating, is the act of bypassing authentication by relying on someone else's credentials. It's commonly attempted at parking lot checkpoints or at controlled-entry points where badges or pin codes are required.

Card Keys

Card keys are another widely used form of access control. These keys can be separated into two broad categories: *dumb cards* and *smart cards*. Dumb cards are those that contain no electronics. You can find these in use at many different organizations. An individual's photo is used to verify a person's right to be in a particular area. These photo ID cards are really just a form of identity badge.

The second type of card key could be considered a smart card. Smart cards are much more powerful than the photo card key. Smart card keys can make an entry decision electronically. These devices can be configured in several different ways. Some require only that the user get close to the access-control device. These proximity readers don't require the user to physically insert the card. Others require user activation and, as such, might require the user to input a key code.

What makes these devices particularly high-tech is that they can be part of a total enterprise access-control system. Earlier versions of these cards were field-powered and contained the power supply and electronics onboard. Newer versions are being sold that can act as transponders or purely passive devices. Table 2.2 shows the various types of card keys.

Table 2.2 Card Key Types	
Type of Card	**Attribute**
Active electronic	Can transmit electronic data
Electronic circuit	Has an electronic circuit embedded
Magnetic stripe	Has a stripe of magnetic material
Magnetic strip	Contains rows of copper strips
Optical-coded	Contains a laser-burned pattern of encoded dots
Photo card	Contains a facial photograph of the card holder

Radio Frequency Identification (RFID) Tags

Radio Frequency Identification (RFID) tags are another emerging trend in the field of physical access control. The U.S. military recently conducted trials to test the possibilities of using RFID tags to control vehicle traffic at military locations. RFID tags are extremely small electronic devices composed of a microchip and an antenna. These devices send out small amounts of information when activated.

An RFID tag can be designed in one of several different ways:

➤ **Active**—Active tags have a battery or power source used to power the microchip.

➤ **Passive**—These devices have no battery. They are powered by a RFID reader, which generates an electromagnetic wave that induces a current in the RFID tag.

➤ **Semipassive**—These hybrid devices use a battery to power the microchip, but transmit by harnessing energy from the reader.

Some of these devices are less than half the size of a grain of rice, so their placement possibilities are endless. The Federal Drug Administration (FDA) has approved an RFID tag that will be used to prevent the possibility of wrong-site, wrong-procedure, and wrong-patient surgeries. Government officials have advocated that these devices become standard issue for fire-fighters, police officers, and emergency rescue individuals because their jobs place them in situations in which their identification could be lost or destroyed. Expect to see innovation in this product in the coming years.

Lighting

Lighting is a commonly used form of perimeter protection. Some studies have found that up to 80% of criminal acts at businesses and shopping centers happen in adjacent parking lots. Therefore, it's easy to see why lighting can be such an important concern. Outside lighting discourages prowlers and thieves. The National Institute of Standards and Technologies (NIST) states that, for effective perimeter control, buildings should be illuminated 8 feet high, with 2-foot candle power.

Companies need to practice due care when installing exterior lights. Failure to adequately light parking lots and other high-traffic areas could lead to lawsuits if an employee or visitor is attacked. Just as too little light can be a problem, too much light can lead to a less secure environment. Glare and overlighting can cause problems by creating very dark areas just outside the range of the lighted area. In addition, neighboring businesses or homes might not appreciate residing in such a bright, overlit area. Therefore, exterior lighting involves the balance of too little light versus too much light. Some common types of exterior lights include these:

➤ Floodlights

➤ Streetlights

➤ Searchlights

Guards

Guards can offer the best and worst in the world of protection. Although our increased need for security has driven the demand for more guards, they are only human and their abilities vary. Technology has also driven our need for security guards. As we get more premise control equipment, intrusion-detection systems, and computerized devices, additional guards are required to man and control these infrastructures.

Unlike computerized systems, guards have the ability to make a judgment call and think through how they should handle specific situations. This is called discernment. Just having them in a facility or guarding a site provides a visual deterrence. Guards can also be used in multiple roles so that they can monitor, greet, sign in, and escort visitors.

Before you go out and hire 20 new guards, however, you should also be aware that guards do have some disadvantages. Guards are expensive; they also make mistakes, could be poorly trained, and may sleep on the job, steal company property, or even injure someone.

Dogs

Dogs, much like guards, have been used to secure property throughout time. Although they can be trained and could be loyal, obedient, and steadfast, they are sometimes unpredictable and could bite or harm the wrong person. Because of these factors, dogs are usually restricted to exterior premise control and should be used with caution.

Locks

Locks are one of the most effective and widely used theft deterrents. Locks come in many types, sizes, and shapes, and are one of the oldest forms of theft-deterrent mechanisms: Locks have the highest return on investment. Locks have been used since the time of the Egyptians. It's important to select the appropriate lock for your designated area. Different types of locks provide different levels of protection.

Preset Key Locks

These are easy to install and use. They require a key to open and are sold as latches, cylinders, and deadbolts.

Mobile Security Locks

Employees who are issued laptops should be given a laptop-locking device. Although data security is important, the security of the device should also be considered; it takes only a moment for someone to remove a laptop or other mobile device. This type of lock can help protect physical assets and signal to employees your concern that devices issued to them should be protected.

 Although locks are important to use to secure laptops, it's also important to use encryption because the data is most likely worth more than the hardware.

Programmable Cipher Locks

Programmable locks can use keypads or smart locks to control access into restricted areas. One shortcoming with a keypad device is that bystanders can shoulder-surf and steal pass codes.

To increase security and safety, some of the following items should be considered to make locks more robust:

➤ **Visibility shields**—These are used to prevent bystanders from viewing the combination numbers that are entered into keypad locks.

➤ **Hostage alarms**—These are useful in financial institutions or areas where money transactions take place. They allow employees to silently alert the authorities.

➤ **Delay alarms**—These are useful to alert security that security doors have been held open for long periods of time.

➤ **Master key locks**—This is nothing new for those of us who have spent time in hotels. This option allows a supervisor or housekeeper to bypass the normal lock and gain entry.

Biometric Access Controls

Biometric controls are discussed extensively in Chapter 4, "Access-Control Systems and Methodology." Because they are used for premise control, however, they should be mentioned here. The fascinating thing about biometric controls is that they are based on a physiological attribute or behavioral characteristic of the individual. As an example, one consulting job I had was with a large state agency that took security seriously. This agency had implemented a magnetic strip card control and a biometric finger sensor on the server room doors. This form of two-factor authentication worked well to ensure that the person entering the server room was given access. These are some of the primary types of biometric systems:

➤ Finger scan

➤ Palm scan

➤ Hand geometry

➤ Retina scan

➤ Iris scan

➤ Facial scan

Server Placement

Even with good perimeter control, you must determine where to place high-value assets such as servers and data centers. I once saw a data center that was located outside the company break room. You had to literally walk through the data center to get to the break room. It's not a good idea to have a data center with uncontrolled access or in an area where people will congregate or mill around. Well-placed data centers should not be placed on the top floor of a building because a fire might make it inaccessible. Likewise, you wouldn't want the data center located in the basement because it would be prone to flooding.

A well-placed data center should have limited accessibility, typically no more than two doors. A first-floor interior room is a good location for a data center.

The ceilings should extend all the way up past the drop ceiling, and the access to the room should be controlled. Look for things such as solid-core doors that are hinged to the inside. Additional controls should be used to ensure that unauthorized equipment is not allowed into the data center. Your goal is to make it as hard as possible for unauthorized personnel to gain access to this area. If individuals can gain physical access to your servers, you have no security.

Intrusion Detection

This section discusses intrusion-detection systems (IDS) used in the physical realm. These IDS systems are used for detecting unauthorized physical access. You might have seen IDS sensors around windows or attached to doors and not even realized what they were. Those are two of the most popular types of IDS systems used. These systems can detect the breakage of glass or the opening of doors. Overall, these systems are effective in detecting changes in the environment. Some common type of IDS sensors include these:

➤ **Photoelectric**—These devices use infrared light and are laid out as a grid over an area. If the grid is disturbed, the sensor will detect a change. These changes will trip an alarm so that someone can be notified of a potential breach in security.

 When you encounter intrusion-detection questions on the actual exam, take the time to distinguish whether the question is referencing physical intrusion-detection systems or logical intrusion-detection systems.

➤ **Motion detectors**—You have probably seen this type of sensor on one of the many security lights sold commercially. Motion detectors can be triggered from audio, wave pattern, or capacitance. Audio detectors are triggered by sound, wave patterns detect movement, and capacitance detectors detect motion by a change in capacitance within the sensing device.

➤ **Pressure sensitive**—These devices are sensitive to weight. Most measure a change in resistance to trigger the device. Pressure mats are an example of this type of technology.

Sometimes organizations choose not to use IDS systems because they can produce false positives. Every time there is an alarm, someone must respond and determine whether the event is real. If the IDS has not been tied to a backup power supply, someone can bypass it by killing the power, which could be another problem. There is also the issue of cost. Before these systems are deployed, a risk assessment should be performed to determine the true value of these devices to the organization.

Environmental Controls

Heat can be damaging to computer equipment. That's why most data centers are kept at temperatures of around 70°F. Higher temperatures can reduce the useful life of electronic devices. Temperature should not be your only concern, though. High humidity can cause electronics to corrode, and low humidity increases the risk of static electricity. What might feel like only a small shock to us, can totally destroy electronic components. Grounding devices, such as antistatic wrist bands and antistatic flooring, can be used to reduce the possibility of damage.

Ventilation is also an important concern. Facilities should maintain positive pressurization and ventilation, to control contamination by pushing air outside. This is especially important in case of fires because it ensures that smoke will be pushed out instead of being pulled in the facility, making a bad condition even worse.

Electrical Power

Electrical power is something most of us take for granted, but large portions of the world live without dependable electrical power. Even in areas are subject to line noise or might suffer from electromagnetic interference (EMI). Electrical motors and other electronic devices can cause EMI. You might have noticed that florescent lights can also cause electrical problems; this phenomenon is known as *radio frequency interference (RFI)*. Table 2.3 lists some other power anomalies.

Table 2.3 Power Faults and Descriptions	
Fault	**Description**
Blackout	Prolonged loss of power
Brownout	Power degradation that is low and less than normal
Sag	Momentary low voltage
Fault	Momentary loss of power
Spike	Momentary high voltage
Surge	Prolonged high voltage
Noise	Interference superimposed onto the power line
Transient	Noise disturbances of a short duration
Inrush	Initial surge of power at startup

Luckily, power conditioners, surge protectors, and uninterruptible power supplies can provide the clean power needed to keep business going.

Uninterruptible Power Supply (UPS)

Since computers have become an essential piece of technology, downtime of any significant length of time can be devastating to an organization. Power outages can happen, and businesses must be prepared to deal with the situation. Uninterruptible power supplies are one of the primary means of meeting this challenge. Two categories of UPS exist:

➤ **Online system**—An online system uses AC power to charge a bank of DC batteries. These batteries are held in reserve until power fails. At that time, a power inverter converts the DC voltage back to AC for the computer systems to use. These systems are good for short-term power outages.

➤ **Standby system**—This type of system monitors the power line for a failure. When a failure is sensed, backup power is switched on. This system relies on generators or power subsystems to keep computers running for longer power outages.

Equipment Life Cycle

Even when you have done all the right things, performed preventative maintenance, kept equipment at the right operating temperature, and used surge protectors, equipment will eventually cease to function. That is why many companies choose to maintain service-level agreements (SLAs). An SLA is a contract with a hardware vendor that provides a certain level of protection. For a fee, the vendor agrees to repair or replace the equipment within the contracted time.

You'll also need to know two important numbers when purchasing equipment or attempting to calculate how long the equipment will last. First is the mean time between failure (MTBF), used to calculate the expected lifetime of a device. The higher the MTBF is, the better. The second number you'll need to know is the mean time to repair (MTTR). The MTTR is an estimate of how long it would take to repair the equipment and get it back into use. For MTTR, lower numbers are better.

Fire Prevention, Detection, and Suppression

A fire needs three things: oxygen, heat, and fuel. With those items present, fires can present a lethal threat and can be devastating to people and the facility. Saving human lives should always be your first priority. As a CISSP candidate, it's important to understand that proper precautions, preparation, and training must be performed to help save lives and limit potential damage.

Fire prevention is one of the key items that needs to be addressed to have an effective proactive defense against fires. A big part of prevention is making sure people are trained and know how to prevent possible fire hazards.

You also should make sure that policy defines how employees are trained to deal with fires. Fire drills are another important part of building good policy. Fire drills should be periodic, yet random. Employees should have a designated area to go to that is outside the facility in a safe zone. Supervisors or others should be in charge of the safe zones, where there can be an employee count to ensure that everyone is present and accounted for.

Fire-Detection Equipment

Having plans and procedures to carry out in case of a fire is only part of the overall fire-prevention program. You should make sure you have fire-detection equipment so that employees can be alerted to possible danger. Fire detectors can work in different ways and can be activated by the following:

➤ **Heat**—A heat-activated sensor is triggered when a predetermined temperature is reached or when the temperature rises quickly. The rate-of-rise type of sensor produces more false positives.

➤ **Smoke**—A smoke-activated sensor can be powered by a photoelectric optical detector or by a radioactive smoke-detection device.

➤ **Flame**—A flame-activated sensor is the most expensive of the three types discussed. It functions by sensing either the infrared energy associated with the flame or the pulsation of the flame.

Fire Suppression

Just being alerted to a fire is not enough. Employees need to know what to do and how to handle different types of fires. Fires are rated according to the types of materials that are burning. Whereas it might be acceptable to throw some water on some smoldering paper, it would not be a good idea to try that with an electrical fire. Table 2.4 lists the four fire types and their corresponding suppression methods.

Table 2.4	Fire-Suppression Methods
Class	**Suppression Method**
Class A	Paper or wood fires should be suppressed with water or soda acid.
Class B	Gasoline or oil fires should be suppressed by using CO2, soda acid, or halon.
Class C	Electronic or computer fires should be suppressed by using CO2 or halon.
Class D	Fires caused by combustible metals should be suppressed by applying dry powder or using special techniques.

Halon

During the industrial revolution, asbestos was hailed as a miracle fiber. By the 1920s, it was discovered that it caused major health problems. Sometimes we get ahead of ourselves in believing that products can do no harm. Halon has much the same type of history. It was originally used in computer rooms for fire suppression. In fact, it was considered the perfect fire-suppression method: It mixes easily with air. It doesn't harm computer equipment, and when it dissipates, it leaves no solid or liquid residue.

Unfortunately, over time, some serious problems with halon have been discovered. If it is deployed in concentrations of greater than 10% and in temperatures of 900°F or more, it degrades into hydrogen fluoride, hydrogen bromide, and bromine. This toxic compound is not something that people should be breathing. Halon has also been discovered to be 3–10 times more damaging to the ozone layer than CFCs.

Because of these problems, the Montreal Protocol of 1987 designated halon as an ozone-depleting substance. There are two types of halon:

➤ **Halon 1211**—This type is found in portable extinguishers and is stored as a liquid.

➤ **Halon 1301**—This version is used in fixed flooding systems and is stored as a gaseous agent.

If you currently have a halon fire-suppression system, you can leave it in place, but there are strict regulations on reporting discharges. Laws also govern the removal and disposal of halon fire-suppression systems. If you are considering replacing your halon systems, some common EPA-approved replacements include these:

➤ FM-200

➤ CEA-410

➤ NAF-S-III

➤ FE-13

➤ Argon

➤ Argonite

Water Sprinklers

Water sprinklers are an effective means of extinguishing Class A fires. Water is easy to work with, widely available, and nontoxic. The disadvantage of using sprinkler systems is that water is damaging to electronics. Four variations of sprinkler systems are available:

➤ **Dry pipe**—As the name implies, this sprinkler system maintains no standing water. When it is activated, air flows out of the system and water flows in. The benefit of this type of system is that it reduces the risk of accidental flooding and gives some time to cover or turn off electrical equipment. These systems are also great for cold-weather areas, unmanned warehouses, and other locations where freezing might be possible.

➤ **Wet pipe**—Wet-pipe systems are widely used and are ready for activation. This system is charged and full of water. The next time you are staying in a hotel, take a look around, and you'll probably see this type of system. It typically uses some type of fusible link that allows discharge after the link breaks or melts.

➤ **Preaction**—This is a combination system. Pipes are initially dry and do not fill with water until a predetermined temperature is reached. Even then, the system will not activate until a secondary mechanism triggers. The secondary mechanism might be some type of fusible link like that used in a wet-pipe system.

➤ **Deluge**—This is similar to a dry-pipe system, except that when the system is triggered, there is no holding back the water. A large volume of water will cover a large area quickly.

Exam Prep Questions

1. What's the most commonly used control mechanism?
   - ❏ A. Guards
   - ❏ B. Fences
   - ❏ C. Locks
   - ❏ D. Cameras

2. What height of fence is required to deter determined trespassers?
   - ❏ A. 4 feet
   - ❏ B. 6 feet
   - ❏ C. 8 feet
   - ❏ D. 10 feet

3. What is the first priority upon determining that there is a fire?
   - ❏ A. Removing valuable assets
   - ❏ B. Calling the fire department
   - ❏ C. Alerting employees to evacuate the building
   - ❏ D. Informing senior management

4. Doors with electric locks should default to which of the following in case of a power outage?
   - ❏ A. Engaged
   - ❏ B. Locked
   - ❏ C. Energized
   - ❏ D. Disengaged

5. Halon was replaced with by which of the following?
   - ❏ A. AM-100
   - ❏ B. AM-200
   - ❏ C. FM-100
   - ❏ D. FM-200

6. NIST recommends that buildings be illuminated to what level?
   - ❏ A. 4 feet high, with 1-foot candle power
   - ❏ B. 6 feet high, with 2-foot candle power
   - ❏ C. 8 feet high, with 2-foot candle power
   - ❏ D. 8 feet high, with 4-foot candle power

7. Gasoline or oil fires should be suppressed by which of the following?
   - ❏ A. Water
   - ❏ B. Soda acid
   - ❏ C. Dry powder
   - ❏ D. Cleaning fluid

8. Which of the following water-sprinkler systems will not activate until a secondary mechanism triggers?

   ❑ A. Dry pipe
   ❑ B. Wet pipe
   ❑ C. Preaction
   ❑ D. Deluge

9. Which of the following is a cipher lock?

   ❑ A. Latches
   ❑ B. Keypads
   ❑ C. Cylinders
   ❑ D. Deadbolts

10. Which of the following is described as a power degradation that is low and less than normal?

   ❑ A. Fault
   ❑ B. Sag
   ❑ C. Brownout
   ❑ D. Surge

Answers to Exam Prep Questions

1. Answer: C. Locks are one of the most effective and widely used theft deterrents. All other answers are incorrect because locks are the most widely used and offer the greatest return on initial investment.

2. Answer: C. An 8-foot fence will keep out a determined intruder. The other answers are incorrect because a 4-foot fence will guard against only casual intruders and a 6-foot fence is considered too tall to easily climb. Answer D is not a valid answer.

3. Answer: C. The safety of employees should always be your first concern. All other answers are incorrect: Protecting assets, calling the fire department, and informing senior management should be done only after ensuring the safety of the employees.

4. Answer: D. If doors are electrical-powered, an unlocked (or disengaged) state allows an employee to exit and not be locked in. All other answers are incorrect because they would result in the employee being locked in. This could have tragic results.

5. Answer: D. Halon is a gas that is an effective fire suppressant. It was widely used because it did not leave liquid or solid residue and did not damage computer equipment. The Montreal Protocol of 1987 worked to ban halon in certain countries because it was known to damage the ozone layer. New installations must use alternative fire-suppression methods. FM-200 is the most popular of its replacements.

6. Answer: C. The National Institute of Standards and Technologies (NIST) states that, for effective perimeter control, buildings should be illuminated 8 feet high, with 2-foot candle power.

7. Answer: B. Gasoline or oil fires should be suppressed by using $CO2$, soda acid, or halon. Water is used for paper or wood fires, dry powder is used for metal fires, and cleaning fluid is flammable and should not be used on fires.

8. Answer: C. This is a combination system. Pipes are initially dry and do not fill with water until a predetermined temperature is reached. Even then, the system will not activate until a secondary mechanism triggers. Answers A, B, and D are incorrect because they do not require a secondary mechanism to trigger.

9. Answer: B. Cipher locks use keypads. All the other answers describe preset key locks.

10. Answer: C. Power degradation that is low and less than normal is considered a brownout. All other answers are incorrect: A fault is a momentary loss of power, a sag is momentary low voltage, and a surge is a period of prolonged high voltage.

Need to Know More?

www.usfa.fema.gov/safety/—Fire safety and equipment information

www.deltascientific.com/bollards2.htm—Bollards and other premises-security controls

https://www.denix.osd.mil/denix/Public/News/DLA/Halon/hal1.html—Halon alternatives

http://news.com.com/Photos:+Biometric+systems+stand+guard/2009-1029_3-5566696.html—Biometric systems used by U.S. Homeland Security

www.rfidjournal.com/—Information on RFID technology

www.cccure.org/modules.php?name=Downloads&d_op=viewdownload&cid=10—An excellent source of study materials on the physical security domain

3

Security-Management Practices

Introduction

This chapter helps the reader prepare for the security-management domain. Security management addresses the identification of the organization's information assets. The security-management domain also introduces some critical documents, such as policies, procedures, and guidelines. These documents are of great importance because they spell out how the organization manages its security practices and details what is most important to the organization.

These documents are not developed in a void. Senior management helps point out the general direction, and risk-assessment and risk-analysis activities are used to determine where protective mechanisms should be placed. This chapter also introduces the two ways to calculate risk: qualitatively and quantitatively.

Finally, it's important to not forget the employees. Employees need to be trained on what good security is and what they can do to ensure that good security is always practiced in the workplace. The goal here, as in other domains, is to ensure confidentiality, integrity, and availability of the organization's assets and information. This chapter divides security-management practices into five broad categories:

➤ Risk assessment

➤ Policy

➤ Implementation

➤ Training and education

➤ Auditing the security infrastructure

Before we jump into these topics and look at the ways in which informational assets are protected, let's talk briefly about the risks of poor security management and the role of confidentiality, integrity, and availability.

The Risk of Poor Security Management

Without policies and security-management controls in place, the organization is really saying that anything goes. That opens the organization to a host of risks, both internal and external. Examples of internal threats include leakage of sensitive data, theft, legal liability, and corruption of data. External threats include natural disasters, spyware, viruses, worms, and Trojan programs. This is by no means a complete list, but it should alert you to the many dangers that organizations face each day. Failure to deal with these threats can lead to loss of information assets, reduced profits, civil or criminal suits, or even the demise of the company.

The Role of CIA

The three fundamental items upon which security is based together are known as the CIA triad (see Figure 3.1). You will see these concepts presented throughout this book.

Figure 3.1   CIA security triad.

> ➤ **Confidentiality**—The concept of keeping private information away from individuals who should not have access. Any time there is an unintentional release of information, confidentiality is lost. As an example, if Black Hat Bob can intercept an email between the CEO and the CIO and learn their latest plans, confidentiality has been broken and there is a lapse of security. Other attacks on confidentiality include sniffing, keystroke monitoring, and shoulder surfing.

> ➤ **Integrity**—The concept of integrity means that data is consistent and that it hasn't been modified. This modification can result from access by an authorized or unauthorized individual or process. Integrity must also prevent modification of data while in storage or in transit. For example, if I could access my bank account and change the bank balance by adding a few zeroes . . . well, that's not such a big deal to me, but the bank might not be happy because they would suffer a serious lapse of integrity.

➤ **Availability**—The concept of availability is pretty straightforward. You should have reliable and timely access to the data and resources you are authorized to use. A good example of a loss of availability is a DoS attack. No, it doesn't give the perpetrator access, but it does prevent legitimate users from using the resource.

Which one of these three is most important? Well, that depends. They are all important, but organizations are unique. Different elements of the CIA triad will take the lead in different companies. For example, your local bank might consider integrity the most important, but an organization that does data processing might see availability as the primary concern.

Risk Assessment

A *risk assessment* is the process of identifying and prioritizing risks to the business. The assessment is crucial. Without an assessment, it is impossible to design good security policies and procedures that will defend your company's critical assets. Risk assessment requires individuals to take charge of the risk-management process. These can be either senior management or lower-level employees. If senior management is driving the process, it's considered top-down security, which is the preferred method. After all, senior management knows the goals and objectives of the company and are ultimately responsible. With senior management's support, security will gain added importance. Management can also set the tone and direction of the security program and can define what is most critical.

Bottom-up security refers to a process by which lower-ranking individuals or groups of individuals attempt to implement better security-management practices without the active support of senior management. Bottom-up security places these individuals in a situation that's unlikely to be successful. Without support from senior management, employees typically don't see risk management and good security practices as being that important. Even if these individuals can successfully determine risks and suggest good controls, they'll have a hard time procuring the needed funds for implementation.

Risk Management

Risk management is the act of determining what threats your organization faces, analyzing your vulnerabilities to assess the threat level, and determining how you will deal with the risk. Some of the major parts of risk management include developing the risk-management team, identifying threats and vulnerabilities, placing a value on the organization's assets, and determining how you will deal with the risk you uncover. The following definitions are important to know for risk management:

➤ **Threat**—A natural or man-made event that could have some type of negative impact on the organization.

➤ **Vulnerability**—A flaw, loophole, oversight, or error that can be exploited to violate system security policy.

➤ **Controls**—Mechanisms used to restrain, regulate, or reduce vulnerabilities. Controls can be corrective, detective, preventive, or deterrent.

Before you spend too much time struggling with all these concepts, take a moment to review Figure 3.2, which displays the relationship among threats, vulnerabilities, and controls. Notice that a threat by itself does not represent a danger and is not sufficient for a successful attack. A threat agent is required for an attack to be successful. A threat agent can be described as any circumstance or event that has the potential to cause harm to information assets through destruction, disclosure, or modification. Figure 3.2 uses an example threat of someone hacking a web server. Although it's true that anyone can attempt to attack a web server, the attacker needs a threat agent to be successful. The threat agent is described in Figure 3.2 as unpatched web server software that the attacker can access.

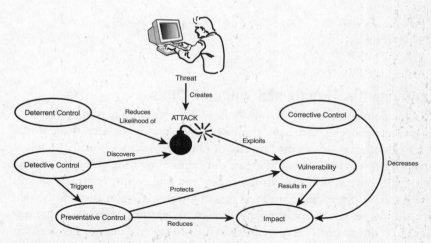

Figure 3.2 Threats, vulnerabilities, and controls.

Risk-Management Team

Don't start thinking that this is a job you are going to take on by yourself. Risk management is a big job. You'll need co-workers and employees from other departments to help. To do an effective job of risk-management analysis, you must involve individuals from all the different departments of the company. Otherwise, you run the risk of not seeing the big picture. It would be hard for any one person to understand the inner workings of all departments.

Sure, as an IT or security administrator, you understand the logical risk the IT infrastructure faces, but do you really have a grasp of the problems HR might have? These might include employee controls, effective termination practices, and control of confidentiality information. Bringing in key employees from other functional areas is required if you expect the risk management process to be successful. Consider employees from the following groups:

➤ Information system security

➤ IT and operations management

➤ System and network administration

➤ Internal audit

➤ Physical security

➤ Business process and information owners

➤ Human resources

➤ Legal

➤ Physical safety

Identifying the Threats and Vulnerabilities

Identifying threats and vulnerabilities is another important part of the risk-management process. Earlier we discussed how a natural or man-made threat can have some type of negative impact on the organization. Now let's look at where threats can come from. Threats can occur as a result of human or natural factors, and can be caused by internal or external events. Figure 3.3 details some common threats to security. This is not meant to be an all-inclusive list, but it should get you thinking about some of the ways in which the organization can be threatened. Threats can also occur because of many other reasons, such as errors in computer code, accidental buffer overflows, or the unintentional actions of employees.

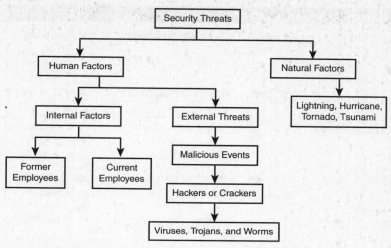

Figure 3.3 Security threats.

Identifying threats, threat agents, and vulnerabilities is just one step of the process. Knowing the values of the assets that you are trying to protect is also important because it would be foolish to exceed the value of the asset by spending more on the countermeasure than the asset is worth. Organizations have only limited funds and resources, so countermeasures must be effectively deployed to guard what has been deemed most critical.

Without placing dollar values or using some other metric to assess these variables, how can you start to analyze the threats, vulnerabilities, and risks the organization faces? One approach is to develop a table such as the one shown in Table 3.1. This helps demonstrate the relationship among threats, vulnerabilities, and risk. For example, an intruder can represent a threat that exposes the organization to theft of equipment because there is no security guard or controlled entrance.

Table 3.1 Threat, Vulnerability, and Risk			
Threat Type	**Threat**	**Exploit/Vulnerability**	**Exposed Risk**
Human factor internal threat	Intruder	No security guard or controlled entrance	Theft
Human factor external threat	Hacker	Misconfigured firewall	Stolen credit card information
Human factor internal threat	Current employee	Poor accountability; no audit policy	Loss of integrity; altered data

(continued)

Table 3.1 Threat, Vulnerability, and Risk *(continued)*			
Threat Type	**Threat**	**Exploit/Vulnerability**	**Exposed Risk**
Natural	Fire	Insufficient fire control	Damage or loss of life
Natural	Hurricane	Insufficient preparation	Damage or loss of life
Malicious external threat	Virus	Out-of-date antivirus software	Virus infection and loss of productivity
Technical internal threat	Hard drive failure	No data backup	Data loss and unrecoverable downtime

Placing a Value on Assets

Now, before you can really manage risk, you must know what's most valuable to the organization. You need to put a value on the organization's assets. You might be thinking that by *value*, we are discussing dollar amounts. That is one way to assess value, called *quantitative assessment*. You also have the choice to perform a *qualitative assessment*. If you choose to perform a qualitative assessment, you won't be dealing with dollar amounts because this is usually scenario driven. Qualitative and quantitative assessment techniques are described more in the following two sections.

Quantitative Assessment

Quantitative assessment deals with numbers and dollar amounts. It attempts to assign a cost (monetary value) to the elements of risk assessment and to the assets and threats of a risk analysis.

To fully complete a quantitative risk assessment, all elements of the process (asset value, impact, threat frequency, safeguard effectiveness, safeguard costs, uncertainty, and probability) are quantified. Therein lies the problem with purely quantitative risk assessment: It is difficult, if not impossible, to assign dollar values to all elements; therefore, some qualitative measures must be applied to quantitative elements. A quantitative assessment requires substantial time and personnel resources. The quantitative assessment process involves the following three steps:

1. **Estimate potential losses (SLE)**—This step involves determining the single loss expectancy (SLE). SLE is calculated as follows:

   Single loss expectancy = Asset value × Exposure factor

   Items to consider when calculating the SLE include the physical destruction or theft of assets, the loss of data, the theft of information, and threats that might cause a delay in processing. The exposure factor is the measure or percent of damage that a realized threat would have on a specific asset.

2. **Conduct a threat analysis (ARO)**—The purpose of a threat analysis is to determine the likelihood of an unwanted event. The goal is to estimate the annual rate of occurrence (ARO). Simply stated, how many times is this expected to happen in one year?

3. **Determine annual loss expectancy (ALE)**—This third and final step of the quantitative assessment seeks to combine the potential loss and rate per year to determine the magnitude of the risk. This is expressed as annual loss expectancy (ALE). ALE is calculated as follows:

Annualized loss expectancy (ALE) = Single loss expectancy (SLE) × Annualized rate of occurrence (ARO)

When performing the calculations discussed in this section, you should include all associated costs, such as these:

➤ Lost productivity

➤ Cost of repair

➤ Value of the damaged equipment or lost data

➤ Cost to replace the equipment or reload the data

When these costs are accumulated and specific threats are determined, the annualized loss expectancy can be calculated. This builds a complete picture of the organization's risk and allows the organization to plan an effective strategy.

Review Table 3.2; we can work through the virus risk example given there. First, you need to calculate the SLE. The SLE requires that you multiply the exposure factor by the asset value:

$9,450 × .17 = $1,650

The asset value is the value you have determined the asset to be worth. The exposure factor is the amount of damage that the risk poses to the asset. For example, the risk-management team might consult with its experts and determine that 17% of its Word documents and data could be destroyed from a virus.

Next, the ARO is calculated. The ARO is the frequency at which this event is expected to happen within a given period of time. For example, the experts might have determined that there is a 90% chance of this event occurring within a 1-year period.

Finally, the ALE is calculated. The ALE is the SLE multiplied by the ARO:

$1,650 \times .9 = $1,485

This third and final step of the quantitative assessment seeks to combine the potential loss and rate per year to determine the magnitude of the risk. You can interpret this figure to mean that the business should expect to lose an average of $1,485 each year due to computer viruses.

Table 3.2   How SLE, ARO, and ALE Are Used

Asset	Risk	Asset Value	Exposure Factor	SLE	Annualized Frequency	ALE
Customer database	Hacked	$432,000	.74	$320,000	.25	$80,000
Word documents and data files	Virus	$9,450	.17	$ 1,650	.9	$1,485
Domain controller	Server failure	$82,500	.88	$ 72,500	.25	$18,125
E-commerce website	DDoS	$250,000	.44	$110,000	.45	$49,500

Automated tools are available that minimize the effort of the manual process. These programs enable users to rerun the analysis with different parameters to answer "what-ifs." They perform calculations quickly and can be used to estimate future expected losses easier than performing the calculations manually.

A lot of math can be involved in a quantitative assessment, but the CISSP exam focuses on the SLE, ALE, and ARO formulas.

Qualitative Assessment

Maybe you are thinking that there has to be another way to perform an assessment. If so, you are right. *Qualitative assessment* is scenario driven and does not attempt to assign dollar values to components of the risk analysis. Purely quantitative risk assessment is hard to achieve because some items are difficult to tie to fixed dollar amounts. Absolute qualitative risk analysis is possible because it ranks the seriousness of threats and sensitivity of assets into grades or classes, such as low, medium, and high. An example of this can be seen in NIST 800-26, a document that uses confidentiality, integrity, and availability as categories of loss and then ranks each loss based on a scale of low, medium, and high. The ranking is subjective:

➤ **Low**—Minor inconvenience that could be tolerated for a short period of time.

➤ **Medium**—Could result in damage to the organization or cost a moderate amount of money to repair.

➤ **High**—Would result in loss of goodwill between the company and clients or employees. Could result in a legal action or fine, or cause the company to lose revenue or earnings.

Table 3.3 displays an example of how this process is performed. As you can see, no dollar amounts are used. Potential loss is only ranked as high, medium, or low.

Table 3.3 Performing a Qualitative Assessment			
Asset	**Loss of Confidentiality**	**Loss of Integrity**	**Loss of Availability**
Customer database	High	High	Medium
Internal documents	Medium	Medium	Low
Advertising literature	Low	Medium	Low
HR records	High	High	Medium

The downside of performing a qualitative assessment is that you are not working with dollar values, so it is sometimes harder to communicate the results of the assessment to management. Another downside is that it is derived from gut feelings or opinions of experts in the company, not always an "exact assessment" that senior management will want to receive from you.

Other types of qualitative assessment techniques include these:

➤ **The Delphi Technique**—A group assessment process that allows individuals to contribute anonymous opinions.

➤ **Facilitated Risk Assessment Process (FRAP)**—A subjective process that obtains results by asking questions. It is designed to be completed in a matter of hours, making it a quick process to perform.

The NSA Information Assurance Methodology (IAM)

The NSA developed the IAM in 1998 in response to Presidential Decision Directive (PDD)-63. PDD-63 mandated that all federal computer systems be assessed to determine their overall security. The purpose of the IAM is to review an organization's INFOSEC posture, identify potential vulnerabilities, and provide recommendations on their elimination or mitigation. It uses the security triad (confidentiality, integrity, and availability) as a basis of assessment.

Handling Risk

Now that you have been introduced to some of the ways to determine risk, you are tasked with making a decision on how to deal with what you have found. Risk can be dealt with in four general ways, either individually or in combination.

➤ **Risk reduction**—Implement a countermeasure to alter or reduce the risk.

➤ **Risk transference**—Purchase insurance to transfer a portion or all of the potential cost of a loss to a third party.

➤ **Risk acceptance**—Deal with risk by accepting the potential cost and loss if the risk occurs.

➤ **Risk rejection**—Pretend that the risk doesn't exist and ignore it. Although this is not a prudent course of action, it is one that some organizations choose to take.

Which is the best way to handle risk? This depends on the cost of the countermeasure, the value of the asset, and the amount by which risk-reduction techniques reduce the total risk. Companies usually choose the one that provides the greatest risk reduction while maintaining the lowest annual cost. These concepts are expressed numerically as the following formulas:

Threat × Vulnerability × Asset value = Total risk

Total risk − Countermeasures = Residual risk

No organization can ever be 100% secure. There will always be remaining risk. The residual risk is the amount that is left after safeguards and controls have been put in place.

NOTE

What's cost-effective? The cost-effectiveness of a safeguard can be measured as follows:

ALE before the safeguard − ALE after the safeguard = Value of the safeguard to the organization

This formula can be used to evaluate the cost-effectiveness of a safeguard or to compare various safeguards to determine which are most effective. The higher the resulting value is, the more cost-effective the safeguard is.

Policies, Procedures, Standards, Baselines, and Guidelines

Security is truly a multilayered process. After an assessment is completed, policies will fall quickly in place because it will be much easier for the organization to determine security policies based on what has been deemed most important from the risk assessments. The assessment should help drive policy creation on items such as these:

➤ Passwords

➤ Patch management

➤ Employee hiring and termination practices

 Low-level checks are for employees starting at low-level jobs. Before they move to a higher-level position, additional checks should be performed.

➤ Backup practices and storage requirements

➤ Security awareness training

➤ Antivirus

➤ System setup and configuration

For security to be effective, it must start at the top of an organization. It must permeate every level of the hierarchy. Senior management must make decisions on what should be protected, how it should be protected, and to what extent it should be protected. These findings should be crafted into written documents.

Before these documents are locked in as policies, they must be researched to verify that they will be compliant with all federal, state, and local laws. These documents should also clearly state what is expected from employees and what the result of noncompliance will be.

Security Policy

Policies are the top tier of formalized security documents. These high-level documents offer a general statement about the organization's assets and what level of protection they should have. Well-written policies should spell out who's responsible for security, what needs to be protected, and what is an acceptable level of risk. They are much like a strategic plan because they outline what should be done but don't specifically dictate how to accomplish the stated goals. Those decisions are left for standards, baselines, and procedures. Security policies can be written to meet advisory, informative, and regulatory needs. Each has a unique role or function.

 The key element in policy is that it should state management's intention toward security.

Advisory Policy

The job of an advisory policy is to ensure that all employees know the consequences of certain behavior and actions. Here's an example advisory policy:

> Illegal copying: Employees should never download or install any commercial software, shareware, or freeware onto any network drives or disks unless they have written permission from the network administrator. *Be prepared* to be held accountable for your actions, including the loss of network privileges, written reprimand, probation, or employment termination if the Rules of Appropriate Use are violated.

Informative Policy

This type of policy isn't designed with enforcement in mind; it is developed for education. Its goal is to inform and enlighten employees. The following is an example informative policy:

> In partnership with Human Resources, the employee ombudsman's job is to serve as an advocate for all employees, providing mediation between employees and management. This job is to help investigate complaints and mediate fair settlements when a third party is requested.

Good policy strikes a balance and is both relevant and understandable. If a policy is too generic, no one will care what it says because it doesn't apply to the company. If a policy is too complex, no one will read it—or understand, it if they did.

Regulatory Policy

These policies are used to make certain that the organization complies with local, state, and federal laws. An example regulatory policy might state:

> Because of recent changes to Texas State law, The Company will now retain records of employee inventions and patents for 10 years; all email messages and any backup of such email associated with patents and inventions will be stored for one year.

Standards

Standards are much more specific than policies. Standards are tactical documents because they lay out specific steps or processes required to meet a certain requirement. As an example, a standard might set a mandatory requirement that all email communication be encrypted. So although it does specify a certain standard, it doesn't spell out how it is to be done. That is left for the procedure.

Baselines

A *baseline* is a minimum level of security that a system, network, or device must adhere to. Baselines are usually mapped to industry standards. As an example, an organization might specify that all computer systems comply with a minimum Trusted Computer System Evaluation Criteria (TCSEC) C2 standard. TCSEC standards are discussed in detail in Chapter 5, "System Architecture and Models."

Guidelines

A *guideline* points to a statement in a policy or procedure by which to determine a course of action. It's a recommendation or suggestion of how things should be done. It is meant to be flexible so it can be customized for individual situations.

 Don't confuse guidelines with best practices. Whereas guidelines are used to determine a recommended course of action, best practices are used to gauge liability. Best practices state what other competent security professionals would have done in the same or similar situation.

Procedures

A procedure is the most specific of security documents. A *procedure* is a detailed, in-depth, step-by-step document that details exactly what is to be done. As an analogy, when my mom sent my wife the secret recipe for a three-layer cake, it described step by step what needed to be done and how. It even specified a convection oven, which my mom stated was an absolute requirement.

Procedures are detailed documents, they are tied to specific technologies and devices (see Figure 3.4). You should expect to see procedures change as equipment changes. As an example, imagine that your company has replaced its CheckPoint firewall with a Cisco PIX. Although the policies and standards dictating the firewalls role in your organization probably will not change, the procedure for configuration of the firewall will.

It's unfortunate that sometimes instead of the donkey leading the cart, the cart leads the donkey. By this, I mean that sometimes policies and procedures are developed as a result of a negative event or an audit. The audit or policy shouldn't be driving the process; the assessment should be. The assessment's purpose is to give management the tools needed to examine all currently identified concerns. From this, management can prioritize the level of exposure they are comfortable with and select an appropriate level of control. This level of control should then be locked into policy.

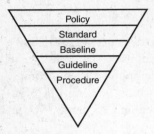

Figure 3.4 Policy structure.

Implementation

You cannot implement what senior management won't support. Sure, you will need the employees to buy into the process, but the biggest element of success depends on making sure that security flows from the top. With senior management leading the way, you can further ensure success by setting up a data-classification scheme so that employees realize the importance of the data they work with. You will also want to consider employee training—without it, how will employees know good security practices? As a final step, you will want to build in security controls because they allow you to monitor the level of compliance.

Data Classification

Organizational information that is proprietary or confidential in nature must be protected. Data classification is a useful way to rank an organization's informational assets. The two most common data-classification schemes are military and public. Companies store and process so much electronic information about their customers and employees that it's critical for them to take appropriate precautions to protect this information. Both military and private data-classification systems accomplish this task by placing information into categories. The first step of this process is to assess the value of the information. When the value is known, it becomes much easier to decide what amount of resources should be used to protect the data. It would make no sense to spend more on protecting something with a lesser value or worth.

Each level of classification that is established should have specific requirements and procedures. The military and commercial data-classification models have predefined labels and levels. When an organization decides which model to use, it can evaluate data placement by using criteria such as the following:

➤ The value of the data

➤ Its age

➤ Laws

➤ Regulations pertaining to its disclosure

➤ Replacement cost

Military Data Classification

The military data-classification system is widely used within the Department of Defense. This system has five levels of classification:

➤ Unclassified

➤ Sensitive

➤ Confidential

➤ Secret

➤ Top secret

Each level represents an increasing level of sensitivity. *Sensitivity* is the desired degree of secrecy that the information should maintain. If an individual holds a confidential clearance, it would mean that he could access unclassified, sensitive, or confidential information for which he has a need to know. His need-to-know would not extend to the secret or top secret levels. The concept of need-to-know is similar to the principle of least privilege, in that employees should have access only to information that they need to know to complete their assigned duties. Table 3.4 provides details about the military and public/private data-classification models.

Public/Private Data Classification

The public or commercial data classification is also built upon a four-level model:

➤ **Public**—This information might not need to be disclosed, but if it is, it shouldn't cause any damage.

➤ **Sensitive**—This information requires a greater level of protection to prevent loss of confidentiality.

➤ **Private**—This information is for company use only, and its disclosure would damage the company.

➤ **Confidential**—This is the highest level of sensitivity, and disclosure could cause extreme damage to the company.

Table 3.4 Commercial and Military Data Classifications	
Commercial Business Classifications	**Military Classifications**
	Top secret
Confidential	Secret
Private	Confidential
Sensitive	Sensitive
Public	Unclassified

 Information has a useful life. Data-classification systems need to build in mechanisms to monitor whether information has become obsolete. If that is the case, it should be declassified or destroyed.

Roles and Responsibility

Just as we have discussed the importance of data classification, it's important to provide a clear division of roles and responsibility. This will be a tremendous help when dealing with any security issues. Everyone should be subject to this policy, including employees, consultants, and vendors. The following list highlights some general areas of responsibility different organizational roles should be held to regarding organizational security. Common roles include owner, data custodian, user, and security auditor:

➤ **Data owner**—Usually a member of senior management. After all, senior management is responsible for the asset and, if it is compromised, can be held responsible. The data owner can delegate some day-to-day duties but cannot delegate total responsibility; senior management is ultimately responsible.

➤ **Data custodian**—This is usually someone in the IT department. The data custodian does not decide what controls are needed, but he or she does implement controls on behalf of the data owner. Other responsibilities include the day-to-day management of the asset. Controlling access, adding and removing privileges for individual users, and ensuring that the proper controls have been implemented are all part of the data custodian's daily tasks.

➤ **User**—This is a role that most of us are familiar with because this is the end user in an organization. Users do have responsibilities: They must comply with the requirements laid out in policies and procedures. They must also practice due care.

➤ **Security auditor**—This is the person who examines an organization's security procedures and mechanisms. How often this process is performed depends on the industry and its related regulations. As an example, the health care industry is governed by the Health Insurance Portability and Accountability Act (HIPAA) regulations and states that audits must be performed yearly. Regardless of the industry, senior management should document and approve the audit process.

Security Controls

The objective of security controls is to enforce the security mechanisms the organization has developed. Security controls can be administrative, technical, or physical. With effective controls in place, risks and vulnerabilities can be reduced to a tolerable level. Security controls are put in place to protect confidentiality, integrity, and availability.

Administrative

Administrative controls are composed of the policies, procedures, guidelines, and baselines an organization develops. Administrative controls also include the mechanisms put in place to enforce and control employee activity and access, such as the following:

➤ **Applicant screening**—A valuable control that should be used during the hiring process. Background checks, reference checks, verification of educational records, and NDAs should all be part of the screening process.

➤ **Employee controls**—Another useful mechanism that can add defense in depth to the organization's administrative controls. Some common employee controls include detailed job descriptions with defined roles and responsibilities. These are procedures that mandate the rotation of duties, the addition of dual controls, and mandatory vacations.

➤ **Termination procedures**—A form of administrative control that should be in place to address the termination of employees. Termination procedures should include exit interviews, review of NDAs, suspension of network access, and checklists verifying that employees have returned all equipment they had in their care, such as remote-access tokens, keys, ID cards, cellphones, pagers, credit cards, laptops, and software.

Technical

Technical controls are the logical mechanisms used to control access, authenticate users, identify unusual activity, and restrict unauthorized access. Some of the devices used as technical controls include firewalls, IDS systems, and authentication devices such as biometrics. Technical controls can be hardware or software.

Physical

Physical controls are the controls that are most typically seen. Examples of physical controls include gates, guards, fences, locks, CCTV systems, turnstiles, and mantraps. Because these controls can be seen, it's important to understand that people might attempt to find ways to bypass them. You've probably seen this at a card key–controlled entrance: One person opens the door, and two or three walk in.

 Because some controls will be highly visible, others should be designed as more covert, to ensure defense in depth.

Training and Education

Right or wrong, employees believe that it is up to employers to provide training. Without proper training, employees are generally unaware of how their actions or activities can affect the security of the organization. One of the weakest links in security is the people who work for the company. Social-engineering attacks prey on the fact that users are uneducated in good security practices; therefore, the greatest defense against these types of attacks is training, education, and security awareness (see Figure 3.5).

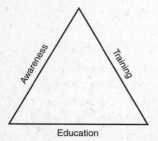

Figure 3.5 Training and education triad.

Besides security awareness, you might find that your employees need more in-depth training in matters of organizational security. This might consist of in-house training programs that teach new employees needed security skills or the decision to send the security staff offsite for a CISSP education program. Regardless of which program your company decides it needs, you can use seven steps to help determine what type of security training to sponsor:

1. Establish organizational technology objectives.

2. Conduct a needs assessment.

3. Find a training program that meets these needs.

4. Select the training methods and mode.

5. Choose a means of evaluating.

6. Administer training.

7. Evaluate the training.

Types of training include the following:

➤ In-house training

➤ Web-based training

➤ Classroom training

➤ Vendor training

➤ On-the-job training

➤ Apprenticeship programs

➤ Degreed programs

➤ Continuing education programs

Training and education are not the same. Training programs are of short duration and usually teach individuals a specific skill. Education is broader based and longer term. Degree programs are examples of education.

Security Awareness

Awareness programs can be effective in increasing employee understanding of security. Security awareness training must be developed differently for the various groups of employees that make up the organization. Not only will the training vary, but the topics and types of questions you'll receive from the participants will also vary. Successful employee awareness programs tailor the message to fit the audience. These are three of the primary groups that security awareness training should be targeted to

➤ **Senior management**—Don't try presenting an in-depth technical analysis to this group. They want to know the costs, benefits, and ramifications if good security practices are not followed.

➤ **Data custodians**—This group requires a more structured presentation on how good security practices should be implemented, who is responsible, and what the individual and departmental cost is for noncompliance.

➤ **Users**—This must align with an employee's daily tasks and map to the user's specific job functions.

 Employee-awareness programs work best when they are run for short periods and changed frequently.

 The goal of security awareness is to increase management's ability to hold employees accountable for their actions and to modify employee behavior toward security.

Auditing Your Security Infrastructure

After all the previous items discussed in this chapter have been performed, the organization's security-management practices will need to be evaluated periodically. This comes in the form of an *audit process*. This is the only way you can verify that the controls put is place are working, that the policies that were written are being followed, and that the training provided to the employees actually works. The audit process can also be used to verify that each individual's responsibility is clearly defined. Employees should know their amount of accountability and what is considered their assigned duties.

 Without sound policies in place, it is not worth doing an audit because there is no adequate baseline on which to base the audit.

Exam Prep Questions

1. Which of the following levels represent the military classification system?
   - ❑ A. Confidential, private, sensitive, and public
   - ❑ B. Top secret, secret, private, sensitive, and public
   - ❑ C. Top secret, confidential, private, sensitive, and unclassified
   - ❑ D. Top secret, secret, confidential, sensitive, and unclassified

2. This method of handling risk works by using a third party to absorb a portion of the risk.
   - ❑ A. Risk reduction
   - ❑ B. Risk transference
   - ❑ C. Risk acceptance
   - ❑ D. Risk rejection

3. You have been asked to calculate the annualized loss expectancy (ALE) for the following variables:

   Single loss expectancy = $25

   Exposure factor = .9

   Annualized rate of occurrence = .4

   Residual risk = $30
   - ❑ A. $9.00
   - ❑ B. $22.50
   - ❑ C. $10.00
   - ❑ D. $14.27

4. Place the following formulas in order:
   - ❑ A. ALE, residual risk, SLE, ARO
   - ❑ B. ALE, ARO, SLE, residual risk
   - ❑ C. ARO, SLE, ALE, residual risk
   - ❑ D. SLE, ARO, ALE, residual risk

5. The downside of performing this type of assessment is that you are not working with dollar values, so it is sometimes harder to communicate the results of the assessment to management.
   - ❑ A. Qualitative
   - ❑ B. Quantitative
   - ❑ C. Numeric mitigation
   - ❑ D. Red team

6. This category of control can include the logical mechanisms used to control access and authenticate users.
   - ❑ A. Administrative
   - ❑ B. Clerical
   - ❑ C. Technical
   - ❑ D. Physical

7. Which of the following formulas represents total risk?
   - ❑ A. Risk × Vulnerability × Asset value = Total risk
   - ❑ B. Threat × Vulnerability × Asset value = Total risk
   - ❑ C. Risk × Value/Countermeasure = Total risk
   - ❑ D. Threat − Vulnerability/Asset value = Total risk

8. Which of the following is a flaw, loophole, oversight, or error that makes an organization susceptible to attack or damage?
   - ❑ A. Risk
   - ❑ B. Vulnerability
   - ❑ C. Threat
   - ❑ D. Exploit

9. This is the most specific of security documents.
   - ❑ A. Procedures
   - ❑ B. Standards
   - ❑ C. Policies
   - ❑ D. Baselines

10. The last thing you want in an organization is that everyone is accountable but no one is responsible. Therefore, the data owner should be which of the following groups?
    - ❑ A. End users.
    - ❑ B. Technical managers.
    - ❑ C. Senior management.
    - ❑ D. Everyone is responsible; therefore, all groups are owners.

Answers to Exam Prep Questions

1. Answer: D. The military data-classification system is widely used within the Department of Defense. This system has five levels of classification: unclassified, sensitive, confidential, secret, and top secret. Each level represents an increasing level of sensitivity.

2. Answer: B. The purchase of insurance to transfer a portion or all of the potential cost of a loss to third party is known as risk transference. All other answers are incorrect: Risk reduction implements a countermeasure, risk acceptance deals with it by accepting the potential cost, and risk rejection pretends it doesn't exist.

3. Answer: C. $25 \times .4 = $10, or Single loss expectancy (SLE) $\times$ Annualized rate of occurrence (ARO) = Annualized loss expectancy (ALE).

4. Answer: D. The quantitative assessment process involves the following steps: Estimate potential losses (SLE), conduct a threat analysis (ARO), determine annual loss expectancy (ALE), and determine the residual risk after a countermeasure has been applied.

5. Answer: A. Qualitative assessment is scenario driven and does not attempt to assign dollar values to components of the risk analysis. Quantitative assessment is based on dollar amounts; both numeric mitigation and red team are distracters.

6. Answer: C. Technical controls can be hardware or software. They are the logical mechanisms used to control access and authenticate users, identify unusual activity, and restrict unauthorized access. Clerical is a nonexistent category, and all other answers are incorrect: Administrative controls are procedural, and physical controls include locks, guards, gates, and alarms.

7. Answer: B. Risk is expressed numerically as follows:

   Threat $\times$ Vulnerability $\times$ Asset value = Total risk

   All other answers do not properly define the formula for total risk.

8. Answer: B. Vulnerability is a flaw, loophole, oversight, or error that makes the organization susceptible to attack or damage. All other answers are incorrect: A risk can be defined as the potential harm that can arise from some present process or from some future event; a threat is an unwanted event that can result in harm to an asset or service; and an exploit takes advantage of a bug, glitch, or vulnerability.

9. Answer: A. A procedure is a detailed, in-depth, step-by-step document that lays out exactly what is to be done. It's a detailed document that is tied to specific technologies and devices. Standards are tactical documents; policies are high-level documents; and baselines are minimum levels of security that a system, network, or device must adhere to.

10. Answer: C. Senior management should be the ultimate owner because
these individuals are responsible for the asset and must answer if a
compromise occurs. Although answer C is the best possible choice, it
is important to realize that, in most cases, the data owner will be a
member of management but might not be the most senior position
within the company. For example, the CFO would be the data owner
for all financial data, the director of human resources would be the data
owner for all HR data, and so on. All other answers are incorrect
because end users, technical managers, and other employees are not
typically the data owners.

Need to Know More?

www.jebcl.com/riskdo/riskdo.htm—Risk assessment do's and don'ts

www.usatoday.com/money/jobcenter/workplace/recruiting/2002-11-20-legal_x.htm—Keeping pre-employment checks legal

http://library.lp.findlaw.com/articles/file/00334/002357/title/Subject/topic/Employment%20Law_At-will%20Employment/filename/employment law_1_454—Self-audits of employment practices

http://csrc.nist.gov/nissc/1997/panels/isptg/pescatore/html/sld001.htm—Building effective security policies

http://searchnetworking.techtarget.com/tip/1,289483,sid7_gci1033304,00.html—Ten traits of effective policy

www.sans.org/resources/policies/—Policy templates and information

www.itl.nist.gov/lab/bulletns/bltnoct03.htm—Building an effective security-awareness program

www.computerworld.com/careertopics/careers/training/story/0,10801,54375,00.html—Methods to build effective security awareness

www.microsoft.com/technet/security/topics/policiesandprocedures/secrisk/srsgch02.mspx—Risk-management guide

Access-Control Systems and Methodology

Terms you'll need to understand:

✓ Dictionary attack
✓ Brute-force attack
✓ Password types
✓ Mandatory access control (MAC)
✓ Discretionary access control (DAC)
✓ Role-based access control (RBAC)
✓ Denial-of-service attack (DoS)
✓ Honeypots
✓ Crossover error rate (CER)

Techniques you'll need to master:

✓ Understand access-control techniques
✓ Understand the goals of penetration testing
✓ Understand the types of intrusion-detection systems
✓ Describe the two types of intrusion-detection systems engines
✓ Be able to differentiate authorization types
✓ Know the advantages of single sign-on technologies

Introduction

Access control is a key component of security. When properly designed, it lets in legitimate users and keeps unauthorized individuals out. Access control has moved far beyond simple usernames and passwords. Modern access-control systems can use physical attributes or biometrics for authentication. Many airports now use biometrics for authentication. Security administrator have more to worry about than just authentication. Many employees now have multiple accounts to keep up with. Luckily, there is a way to consolidate these accounts: single sign-on.

This chapter discusses access-control techniques and the ways to implement control within centralized and decentralized environments. It also discusses some of the threats to access control. Attackers can launch *password-cracking* attacks to try and gain unauthorized access. If they still cannot get into a system, they might attempt to launch *denial-of-service (DoS)* attacks to disrupt availability to legitimate users. That is why access control is also about detective and corrective measures. It's important to have systems to detect misuse or attacks. One such system is an *intrusion-detection system (IDS)*. IDS systems are also discussed in this chapter.

Threats Against Access Control

Access control is probably one of the most targeted security mechanisms. After all, its job is to keep out unauthorized individuals. Attackers can use a variety of tools and techniques to try to bypass or subvert access control.

Password Attacks

Think your passwords are secure? A European Infosec conference performed an impromptu survey and discovered that 74% of those surveyed would trade their passwords for a chocolate bar. Now, the results of this survey might not meet strict scientific standards, but this does prove a valuable point: Many individuals don't practice good password security. Attackers are well aware of this and use the information to launch common password attacks. Attackers typically use one of two methods to crack passwords: a dictionary crack or a brute-force crack.

Dictionary Crack

A *dictionary crack* uses a predefined dictionary to look for a match between the encrypted password and the encrypted dictionary word. Many dictionary files are available, ranging from Klingon to popular movies, sports, and the NFL.

Many times, these cracks can be performed in just a few minutes because individuals tend to use easily remembered passwords. If passwords are well-known, dictionary-based words, dictionary tools will crack them quickly.

Just how do cracking programs recover passwords? Passwords are commonly stored in a hashed format, so most password-cracking programs use a technique called comparative analysis. Each potential password found in a dictionary list is hashed and compared to the encrypted password. If a match is obtained, the password has been discovered. If not, the program continues to the next word, computes its hashed value, and compares that to the hashed password. These programs are comparatively smart because they can manipulate a word and use its variations. For example, take the word *password*. It would be processed as Password, password, PASSWORD, PassWord, PaSSword, and so on. These programs tackle all common permutations of a word. They also add common prefixes, suffixes, and extended characters to try to crack the password. This is called a *hybrid attack*. Using the previous example, these attempts would look like 123password, abcpassword, drowssap, p@ssword, pa44w0rd, and so on. These various approaches increase the odds of successfully cracking an ordinary word or any common variation of it.

Brute-Force Crack

The brute-force attack is a type of encrypted password assault and can take hours, days, months, or years, depending on the complexity of the password and the key combinations used. This type of crack depends on the speed of the CPU's power because the attacker attempts every combination of letters, numbers, and characters.

An alternative to traditional brute-force password cracking is to use a rainbow table. Whereas traditional brute-force password cracking tries one combination at a time, the rainbow table technique precomputes all possible passwords in advance. This is considered a time/memory trade-off technique. When this time-consuming process is complete, the passwords and their corresponding encrypted values are stored in a file called the rainbow table. An encrypted password can be quickly compared to the values stored in the table and cracked within a few seconds.

Emanation Security

Attackers can find other ways to break in besides cracking passwords. They might try to sniff the stray electrical signals that *emanate* from electronic devices. This might sound like science fiction, but the U.S. government was concerned enough about the possibility of this type of attack that it started a program to study it. The program eventually became a standard known as TEMPEST.

TEMPEST is somewhat dated; newer technologies such as white noise and control zones are now used to control emanation security. White noise uses special devices that send out a stream of frequencies that make it impossible for an attacker to distinguish the real information. Control zones are the practice of designing facilities, walls, floors, and ceilings to block electrical signals from leaving the zone.

 A CISSP candidate is expected to know the technologies and techniques implemented to prevent intruders from capturing and decoding information emanated through the airwaves. TEMPEST, white noise, and control zones are the three primary controls.

Denial of Service/Distributed Denial of Service (DoS/DDoS)

Denial-of-service (DoS) attacks consume resources to the point that legitimate access is not possible. Distributed DoS (DDoS) attacks work in much the same way, except that they are launched from many more devices and add a layer between the attacker and the victim. Following are DoS/DDoS attacks:

➤ **Ping of death**—Employs an oversize IP packet.

➤ **Smurf**—Sends a message to the broadcast of a subnet or network so that every node on the network produces one or more response packets.

➤ **Syn flood**—Takes advantage of the maximum number of connection requests that a host can handle at one time. When all possible connections are consumed, no one can access the server for legitimate purposes.

➤ **Trinoo**—A DDoS tool capable of launching User Datagram Protocol (UDP) flood attacks from various channels on a network.

Access-Control Types

One of the main reasons to have a variety of access-control types is to provide the organization with true defense in depth. Each control type provides a different level of protection, and because each level can be tweaked to meet the needs of the organization, the security administrator has a very granular level of control over the security mechanisms. Security mechanisms can serve many purposes, although they are primarily used to prevent, detect, or recover from problems. The best approach is for the organization to focus the bulk of its controls on prevention because this allows the organization to stop a problem before it starts. The three access-control types include administrative, technical, and physical controls.

Administrative Controls

Administrative controls are the policies and procedures implemented by the organization. Preventive administrative controls can include security awareness training, strong password policies, and robust pre-employment checks.

Technical Controls

Technical controls are the logical controls you have put in place to protect the IT infrastructure. Technical controls include strong authentication (biometrics or two-factor), encryption, network segmentation, demilitarized zones (DMZs), and antivirus controls.

Physical Controls

Physical controls are the ones you can most likely see. These controls protect against theft, loss, and unauthorized access. Examples of physical access controls include guards, gates, locks, guard dogs, closed-circuit television (CCTV), and alarms.

Be sure you understand the three types of controls that can be used to limit access—administrative, technical, and physical controls—and what is contained within each set. This is considered required knowledge for the CISSP exam.

Identification, Authentication, and Authorization

Identification, authentication, and authorization are three of the core concepts of access control. Together these items determine who gets into the network and what they have access to. A failure of any of these services can have detrimental results to the security of the organization. *Identification* is the process of identifying yourself to an authentication service. *Authentication* is the process of determining whether a user is who he or she claims to be. *Authorization* is the process of determining whether a user has the right to access a requested resource. These concepts are tied to one additional item: accountability, which is discussed in subsequent chapters. Accountability is the capability to relate specific actions and operations to a unique individual.

Authentication

In network security, authentication is the process of determining the legitimacy of a user or process. Various authentication schemes have been developed over the years. These are some common authentication methods:

➤ **Usernames and passwords**—Typically a name and an alphanumeric password.

➤ **Tokens**—A hardware-based device used for authentication.

➤ **Smart cards**—An intelligent token that been embedded with an integrated circuit chip. It provides not only memory capacity, but computational capability as well.

➤ **Magnetic stripe cards**—A widely used standard that became established in the 1970s. The magnetic strip contains information used to authenticate the user.

➤ **Certificates**—Some authentication methods, such as Protected Extensible Authentication Protocol (PEAP) and Extensible Authentication Protocol (EAP), can use certificates for authentication of computers and users. Certificates can reside on a smart card or can be used by IPSec and Secure Sockets Layer (SSL) for web authentication.

➤ **Biometrics**—Systems that make use of something you are, such as a fingerprint, retina scan, or voice print.

A quick review of this list should illustrate that all these forms of authentication can be distilled into three distinct types:

➤ Something you know—passwords

➤ Something you have—tokens, smart cards, and certificates

➤ Something you are—biometrics

Some experts actually list four categories of authentication: something you know, something you have, something you are, and where you are.

Passwords

Of these three types, probably the most widely used are usernames and passwords. The problem with this method is that passwords as a form of authentication are also one of the easiest to crack. Using passwords makes the network even more vulnerable because most individuals make passwords easy to remember, such as a birthday, an anniversary, or a child's name. Also, people have a limited memory, so the same password is often used to gain access to several different systems. With valid usernames and easily guessed passwords, a network is very close to losing two of the three items that ensure security, confidentiality, and integrity. Programs such as John the Ripper can quickly cycle through huge dictionary files looking for a match. This makes password security an important topic for anyone studying access control: Many times, it is all that stands between an intruder and account access. If you can't make the change to a more robust form of authentication, password policy should at least follow some basic guidelines:

➤ Passwords should not use personal information.

➤ Passwords should be 7 or 14 characters.

➤ Passwords should expire at least every 30 days.

➤ Passwords should never consist of common words or names.

➤ Passwords should be complex and should use upper- and lowercase letters and characters (such as !@#$%^&).

➤ Logon attempts should be limited to a small number of times, such as three to five successive attempts.

A logon limit is also known as a clipping level in CISSP terminology. Remember that a clipping level is the threshold or limit that must be reached before action is taken.

Cognitive Passwords

Cognitive passwords are another interesting password mechanism that has gained popularity. For example, three to five questions might be asked, such as these:

➤ What country were you born in?

➤ What department do you work for?

➤ What's your pet's name?

➤ What is your mother's maiden name?

If you answer all the questions correctly, you are authenticated. Cognitive passwords are widely used during enrollment processes and when individuals call help desks or request other services that require authentication. Cognitive passwords are not without their problems. For example, if your name is Paris Hilton and the cognitive password you're prompted for by T-Mobil is "What's your pet's name?" anyone who knows that your pet's name is Tinkerbell can easily access your account.

One-Time Passwords

One-time passwords are used only once and are valid for only a short period of time. One-time passwords are usually provided through a token device that displays the time-limited password on an LCD screen.

NOTE   A *passphrase* is a type of virtual password. Passphrases function by having someone enter the phrase into the computer. Software converts or hashes that phrase into a stronger virtual password that is harder for an attacker to crack.

Token Device

The tokens described in the previous sections can be synchronous dynamic password tokens or asynchronous password devices. These devices use a Poloniums challenge-response scheme and are form-factored as smart cards, USB plugs, key fobs, or keypad-based units. These devices generate authentication credentials that are often used as one-time passwords. Another great feature of token-based devices is that they can be used for two-factor authentication.

Synchronous

Tokens that are said to be *synchronous* are synchronized to the authentication server. Each individual passcode is valid for only a short period of time. Even if an attacker were able to intercept a token-based password, it would be valid for only a limited time. After that small window of opportunity, it would have no value to an attacker. As an example, RSA's SecurID changes user passwords every 60 seconds.

Asynchronous

Asynchronous token devices are not synchronized to the authentication server. These devices use a challenge-response mechanism. These devices work as follows:

1. The server sends the user a value.

2. The value is entered into the token.

3. The user is prompted to enter a secret passphrase.

4. The token performs a hashing process on the entered value.

5. The new value is displayed on the LCD screen of the token device.

6. The user enters the displayed value into the computer for authentication.

Biometrics

Biometrics is a means of authentication that is based on a behavioral or physiological characteristic that is unique to an individual. Biometrics is a most accurate means of authentication, but it is also more expensive than the other methods discussed. Biometric authentication systems have been slow to mature because many individuals are adverse to the technology. Issues such as privacy are typically raised, although things have started to change somewhat after 9-11. More companies have felt the need for increased security, and biometric authentication systems have been one way to meet the challenge. Biometric systems work by recording information that is very minute and individual to the person. When the biometric system is first used, the system must develop a database of information about the user. This is considered the enrollment period. When enrollment is complete, the system is ready for use. So, if an employee then places his hand on the company's new biometric palm scanner, the scanner compares the ridges and creases found on the employee's palm to the one that is identified as that individual's in the device's database. Whether the employee gains access depends on the accuracy of the system.

Different biometric systems have varying levels of accuracy. The accuracy of a biometric device is measured by the percentage of Type I and Type II errors it produces. Type I errors (false rejection rate) are a measurement of the percentage of individuals who should have gotten in but were not allowed access. Type II errors (false acceptance rate) are the percentage of individuals who got in and should not have been allowed access. Together these two values determine the accuracy of the system. This is determined by mapping the point at which Type I errors equal Type II errors. This point is known as the crossover error rate (CER). The lower the CER, the better—for example, if system A had a CER of 4 and system B had a CER of 2, system B would be the system with the greatest accuracy. Some of the most widely used types of biometric systems include these:

➤ **Finger scan**—Distinguishes one fingerprint from another by examining the configuration of the peaks, valleys, and ridges of the fingerprint. It is the most common type of biometric system used.

➤ **Hand geometry**—Uses the unique geometry of a user's fingers and hand in identification.

➤ **Palm scan**—Uses the creases and ridges of a user for identification.

➤ **Retina pattern**—Uses the person's eye for identification; very accurate.

➤ **Iris recognition**—Another eye-recognition system that matches the person's blood vessels on the back of the eye; also very accurate.

➤ **Voice recognition**—Uses voice analysis for identification.

➤ **Keyboard dynamics**—Analyzes the speed and pattern of typing.

Before attempting the CISSP exam, make sure you understand the difference between Type I and Type II errors and the CER. Type II values are considered to be the most critical error rate to examine, while the CER is considered to be the best measurement of biometric systems accuracy.

Other considerations must be made before deploying a biometric system:

➤ **Employee buy-in**—Users might not like or want to interact with the system. If so, the performance of the system will suffer. For example, a retina scan requires individuals to look into a cuplike device, whereas an iris scanner requires only a quick look into a camera.

➤ **Age, gender, or occupation of the user**—Users who perform physical labor or work in an unclean environment might find finger scanners frustrating.

➤ **The physical status of the user**—Users who are physically challenged or handicapped might find the placement of eye scanners difficult to reach. Those without use of their hands or fingers will be unable to use fingerprint readers, palm scanners, or hand geometry systems.

Strong Authentication

To make authentication stronger, you can combine several of the methods discussed previously. This combination is referred to as multifactor or strong authentication. The most common form of strong authentication is known as two-factor authentication. Tokens combined with passwords form an effective and strong authentication. If you have a bank card, you are familiar with two-factor authentication. Bank cards require two items to successfully access an account: something you have and something you know. These two items, your card and your PIN, grant you access to the account.

The decision to use strong authentication depends on your analysis of the value of the assets being protected. What are the dollar values of the assets being protected? What might it cost the organization in dollars, lost profit, potential public embarrassment, or liability if unauthorized access is successful?

Single Sign-On

Single sign-on is an attempt to address a problem that is common for all users and administrators. Various systems within the organization likely require the user to log on multiple times to multiple systems. Each one of these systems requires the user to remember a potentially different username and password combination. Most of us tire of trying to remember all this information and begin to look for shortcuts. The most common is to just write down the information. Walk around your office, and you might see that many of your co-workers have implemented the same practice. Single sign-on is designed to address this problem by permitting users to authenticate once to a single authentication authority and then access all other protected resources without reauthenticating. Before you run out and decide to implement single sign-on at your organization, you should be aware that it is expensive and if an attacker can gain entry, that person then has access to everything. Kerberos, SESAME, KryptoKnight (by IBM), and NetSP (a KryptoKnight derivative) are authentication server systems with operational modes that can implement single sign-on.

 Thin clients can be considered a type of single sign-on system because the thin client holds no data. All information is stored in a centralized server. Thus, once a user is logged in, there is no reason for that user to reauthenticate.

Kerberos

Kerberos is a network authentication protocol created by the Massachusetts Institute of Technology (MIT) that uses secret-key cryptography. Kerberos has three parts: a client, server, and trusted third party (KDC) to mediate between them. Clients obtain tickets from the Kerberos Key Distribution Center (KDC), and they present these tickets to servers when connections are established. Kerberos tickets represent the client's credentials.

The KDC is a service that runs on a physically secure server. The KDC consists of two components:

➤ **Authentication service**—The authentication service issues ticket-granting tickets (TGTs) that are good for admission to the ticket-granting service (TGS). Before network clients can get tickets for services, they must obtain a TGT from the authentication service.

➤ **Ticket-granting service**—Clients receive tickets to specific target services.

The basic operation of Kerberos is as follows (and is shown in Figure 4.1):

1. The client asks the KDC for a ticket, making use of the authentication service (AS).

2. The client receives the encrypted ticket and the session key.

3. The client sends the encrypted TGT to the TGS and requests a ticket for access to the application server. This ticket has two copies of the session key: One copy is encrypted with the client key, and the other copy is encrypted with the application server key.

4. The TGS decrypts the TGT using its own private key and returns the ticket to the client that will allow it to access the application server.

5. The client sends this ticket, along with an authenticator, to the application server.

6. The application server sends confirmation of its identity to the client.

> Some Kerberos literature uses the term *principal* instead of *client*. Principals can be a user, a process, or an application. Kerberos systems authenticate one principal to another.

Although Kerberos can provide authentication, integrity, and confidentiality, it's not without its weaknesses. One weakness is that Kerberos cannot guarantee availability. Some others are listed here:

➤ Kerberos is time sensitive; therefore, it requires all system clocks to be highly synchronized.

➤ The tickets used by Kerberos, which are authentication tokens, can be sniffed and potentially cracked.

➤ If an attacker targets the Kerberos server, it can prevent anyone in the realm from logging in. It is important to note that the Kerberos server can be a single point of failure.

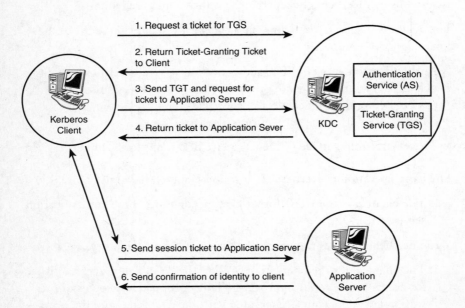

Figure 4.1 Kerberos operation.

SESAME

The Secure European System and Applications in a Multivendor Environment (SESAME) project was developed to address some of the weaknesses found in Kerberos. SESAME incorporates MD5 and CRC32 hashing and two certificates. One of these certificates is used to provide authentication, as in Kerberos, and the second certificate is used to control the access privileges assigned to a client.

Access-Control Models

Access-control models can be divided into two distinct types: centralized and decentralized. Depending on the organization's environment and requirements, typically one methodology works better than the other.

Centralized Access Control

Centralized access-control systems maintain user IDs, rights, and permissions in one central location. RADIUS, TACACS, and DIAMETER are examples of centralized access-control systems. Characteristics of centralized systems include these:

➤ One entity makes all access decisions.

➤ Owners decide what users can access, and the administration supports these directives.

RADIUS

Remote Authentication and Dial-In User Service (RADIUS) is a UDP-based client/server protocol defined in RFCs 2058 and 2059. *RADIUS* provides three services: authentication, authorization, and accounting. It facilitates centralized user administration and keeps all user profiles in one location that all remote services share. Although ISPs have used RADIUS for years, it has become a standard in may other ways. RADIUS is widely used for wireless LAN authentication. The IEEE designed EAP to easily integrate with RADIUS to authenticate wireless users. The wireless user takes on the role of the supplicant, and the access point serves as the client. If the organization has an existing RADIUS server that's being used for remote users, it can be put to use authenticating wireless users, too.

RADIUS functions are as follows (see Figure 4.2):

1. The user connects to the RADIUS client.

2. The RADIUS client requests credentials from the user.

3. The user enters credentials.

4. The RADIUS client encrypts the credentials and passes them to the RADIUS server.

5. The RADIUS server then accepts, rejects, or challenges the credentials.

6. If the authentication was successful, the user is authenticated to the network.

Other centralized authentication methods include TACACS and LDAP.

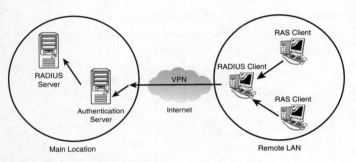

Figure 4.2 RADIUS authentication.

TACACS

Terminal Access Controller Access Control System (TACACS) is available in three variations: TACACS, XTACACS (Extended TACACS), and TACACS+, which features two-factor authentication. TACACS also allows the division of the authentication, authorization, and auditing functions, which gives the administrator more control over its deployment. TACACS has failed to gain the popularity of RADIUS; it is now considered a somewhat dated protocol.

Decentralized Access Control

Decentralized access-control systems store user IDs, rights, and permissions in different locations throughout the network. Characteristics of decentralized systems include these:

➤ Gives control to individuals closer to the resource, such as department managers and occasionally users

➤ Maintains multiple domains and trusts

➤ Does not use one centralized entity to process access requests

➤ Used in database-management systems (DBMS)

> Peer-to-peer in design

> Lacks standardization and overlapping rights, and might include security holes

Data Access Controls

Data access controls are established to control how subjects can access data, what they can access with it, and what they can do with it once accessed. Three primary types of access control are discussed in this section.

Discretionary Access Control (DAC)

The discretionary access control (DAC) model is so titled because access control is left to the owner's discretion. It can be thought of as similar to a peer-to-peer computer network. Each of the users is left in control. The owner is left to determine whether other users have access to files and resources. One significant problem with DAC is that its effectiveness is limited by user's skill and ability. A user who is inexperienced or simply doesn't care can easily grant full access to files or objects under his or her control. These are the two primary components of a DAC:

> **File and data ownership**—All objects within a system must have an owner. Objects without an owner will be left unprotected.

> **Access rights and permissions**—These control the access rights of an individual. Variation exists, but a basic access-control list checks read, write, or execute privileges.

Access rights are controlled through means of an access-control list (ACL). The ACL identifies users who have authorization to specific information. This is a dynamic model that allows data to be easily shared. A sample ACL is shown in Table 4.1. An ACL is a column within the access-control matrix displayed in Table 4.1. A subject's capabilities refer to a row within the matrix and reference what action can be taken.

Table 4.1	Sample Access-Control List			
Subject	**Object 1**	**Object 2**	**Object 3**	**Object 4**
Mike	Full control	Full control	Full control	Full control
Jeff	Read	Read	Read write	No access
Clement	Read	Read write	No access	No access

Mandatory Access Control (MAC)

A MAC model is static and based on a predetermined list of access privileges; therefore, in a MAC-based system, access is determined by the system rather than the user. Figure 4.3 shows the differences between DAC and MAC. The MAC model is typically used by organizations that handle highly sensitive data (such as the DoD, NSA, CIA, and FBI). Systems based on the MAC model use sensitivity labels. Labels such as Top Secret, Secret, or Sensitive are assigned to objects. *Objects* are passive entities that provide data or information to subjects. A *subject* can be a user, system, program, or file. When a subject attempts to access an object, the label is examined for a match to the subject's level of clearance. If no match is found, access is denied. Important items to know about the MAC model include these:

Objects are considered passive entities; subjects are considered active ones.

➤ It's considered a need-to-know system.

➤ It has more overhead than DAC.

➤ All users and resources are assigned a security label.

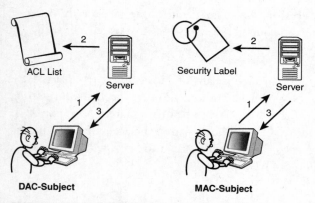

ACL List

Server

Security Label

Server

DAC-Subject

MAC-Subject

Figure 4.3 Differences between DAC and MAC.

Object reuse refers to the reuse of media by individuals who might not have the need to know. This can happen when hard drives are shared, floppies are reused, or media is not properly wiped.

Role-Based Access Control (RBAC)

RBAC enables a user to have certain preestablished rights to objects. These rights are assigned to users based on their roles in the organization. The roles almost always map to the organization's structure. RBAC models are used extensively by banks and other organizations that have very defined roles. One profile might exist for tellers, while another exists for loan officers. Assigning access rights and privileges to a group rather than an individual reduces the burden on administration.

Other Types of Access Controls

Other types of access-control techniques include these:

➤ **Content-dependent access control**—This model is based on the content of the resource. CDAC is primarily used to protect databases that contain potentially sensitive data.

➤ **Lattice-based access control**—This MAC-based model functions by defining boundaries. For example, if you were cleared for secret access, you could read the level below, which is confidential.

➤ **Rule-based access control**—Based on a specific set of rules much like a router ACL, this is considered a variation of the DAC model.

Intrusion-Detection Systems (IDS)

An IDS is designed to function as an access-control monitor. It can monitor network or host activity and record which users attempt to access specific network resources. An IDS can be configured to scan for attacks, track a hacker's movements, alert an administrator to ongoing attacks, and highlight possible vulnerabilities that need to be addressed. IDS systems can be divided into two broad categories: network-based intrusion-detection systems (NIDS) and host-based intrusion-detection systems (HIDS).

IDS systems are like 3-year-olds. They require constant care and nurturing, and don't do well if left alone. I say this because IDS systems take a considerable amount of time to tune and monitor. The two biggest problems with IDS systems are false positives and false negatives. False positives refer to when the IDS has triggered an alarm for normal traffic. For example, if you go to your local mall parking lot, you're likely to hear some car alarms going off that are experiencing false positives. False positives are a big problem because they desensitize the administrator. False negatives are even worse. A false negative occurs when a real attack has occurred and the IDS never picked it up.

Intrusion-prevention systems (IPS) build upon the foundation of IDS and attempt to take the technology a step further. IPS systems can react automatically and actually prevent a security occurrence from happening, preferably without user intervention. IPS is considered the next generation of IDS and can block attacks in real time.

Network-Based Intrusion-Detection Systems (NIDS)

Much like a protocol analyzer operating in promiscuous mode, NIDS capture and analyze network traffic. These devices diligently inspect each packet as it passes by. When they detect suspect traffic, the action taken depends on the particular NIDS. Alarms could be triggered, sessions could be reset, or traffic could be blocked. Among their advantages are that they are unobtrusive, they have the capability to monitor the entire network, and they provide an extra layer of defense between the firewall and the host. Their disadvantages include the fact that attackers can send high volumes of traffic to attempt to overload them, they cannot decrypt or analyze encrypted traffic, and they can be vulnerable to attacks. Things to remember about NIDS include the following:

➤ They monitor network traffic in real time.

➤ They analyze protocols and other relevant packet information.

➤ They integrate with a firewall and define new rules as needed.

➤ They send alerts or terminate offending connection.

Host-Based Intrusion-Detection Systems (HIDS)

HIDS are more closely related to a virus scanner in their function and design because they are application-based programs that reside on the host computer. Running quietly in the background, they monitor traffic and attempt to detect suspect activity. Suspect activity can range from attempted system file modification to unsafe activation of ActiveX commands. Although they are effective in a fully switched environment and can analyze network-encrypted traffic, they can take a lot of maintenance, cannot monitor network traffic, and rely on the underling OS because it does not control core services. Things to remember about HIDS include the following:

➤ They consume some of the host's resources.

➤ They analyze encrypted traffic.

➤ They send alerts when unusual events are discovered.

Signature-Based and Behavior-Based IDS Systems

Signature-based and behavior-based IDS systems are the two primary types of analysis methods used. These two types take different approaches to detecting intrusions.

Signature-based models, also known as rule-based models, rely on a database of known attacks and attack patterns. This system examines data to check for malicious content, which could include fragmented IP packets, streams of SYN packets (DoS), or malformed ICMP packets. Anytime data is found that matches one of these known signatures, it can be flagged to initiate further action. This might include an alarm, an alert, or a change to the firewall configuration. Although signature-based systems work well, their shortcoming is due to the fact that they are only as effective as their most current update. Anytime there is a new or varied attack, the IDS will be unaware of it and will ignore the traffic. The two subcategories of signature-based system include these:

➤ **Model based**—Looks at specific signatures. Snort is an example of this type of design.

➤ **State based**—A more advanced design that has the capability of tracking the state of the traffic and data as it moves between host and target.

A behavior-based IDS observes traffic and develops a baseline of normal operations. Intrusions are detected by identifying activity outside the normal range of activities. As an example, if Mike typically tries to log on only between the hours of 8 a.m. to 5 p.m., and now he's trying to log on 5,000 times at 2 a.m., the IDS can trigger an alert that something is wrong. The big disadvantage of a behavior-based IDS system is that an activity taught over time is not seen as an attack, but merely as normal behavior. These systems also tend to have a high number of false positives. Basic IDS components include the following categories:

➤ **Sensors**—Detect and send data to the system

➤ **Central monitoring system**—Processes and analyzes data sent from sensors

➤ **Report analysis**—Offers information about how to counteract a specific event

➤ **Database and storage components**—Perform trend analysis and store the IP address and information about the attacker

➤ **Response box**—Inputs information from the previously listed components and forms an appropriate response

Carefully read any questions that discuss IDS. Remember that several variables can change the outcome or potential answer. Take the time to underline such words as *network*, *host*, *signature*, and *behavior*, to help clarify the question.

Sensor Placement

Your organization's security policy should detail the placement of your IDS system and sensors. The placement of IDS sensors requires some consideration. IDS sensors can be placed externally, in the DMZ, or inside the network. Your decision to place a sensor in any one or more of these locations will require specific tuning. Without it, the sensor will generate alerts for all traffic that matches a given criteria, regardless of whether the traffic is indeed something that should generate an alert.

False positive alerts are bad, but false negatives are worse because someone was able to perform or attempt unacceptable activity and was not detected.

Penetration Testing

Penetration testing is a series of activities undertaken to identify and exploit security vulnerabilities. Penetration testing can be carried out in several different ways, including zero knowledge, full knowledge, or partial network knowledge. Regardless of what is known about the network, the penetration test team typically starts with basic user access. Its goal is to advance to root or administrator and control the network or systems. Probably the most important step of a penetration test is the approval. Without a signed consent of the network owner, the penetration test team could very well be breaking the law. A generic model of a penetration test is listed here:

1. **Discovery**—Identify and document information about the targeted organization.

2. **Enumeration**—Use intrusive methods and techniques to gain more information about the targeted organization.

3. **Vulnerability mapping**—Map the findings from the enumeration to known and potential vulnerabilities.

4. **Exploitation**—Attempt to gain user and privileged access by launching attacks against known vulnerabilities.

Penetration testing can be performed with the full knowledge of the security staff, as a blind test, or a double-blind test. A blind test is one in which only publicly available information is used. A double-blind test is one in which only publicly available information is used and the security staff is not notified of the event. A double-blind test allows the organization to observe the reactions of the security staff.

These other types of tests should be considered beyond basic penetration tests:

➤ **Application security testing**—Many organizations offer access to core business functionality through web-based applications. This can give attackers a big potential target. Application security testing verifies that the controls over the application and its process flow are adequately designed.

➤ **Denial-of-service (DoS) testing**—The goal of DoS testing is to evaluate the networks susceptibility to DoS attacks.

➤ **War dialing**—War dialing is an attempt to systematically call a range of telephone numbers to identify modems, remote-access devices, and maintenance connections of computers that could exist on an organization's network.

➤ **Wireless network testing**—This form of testing is done to verify the organization's wireless access policies and ensure that no misconfigured devices have been introduced that have caused additional security exposures.

➤ **Social engineering testing**—This form of penetration test refers to techniques using social interaction, typically with the organization's employees, suppliers, and contractors, to gather information and penetrate the organization's systems.

Various guides are available to help the penetration test team members follow a structured methodology for any of the testing scenarios described. The Open Source Security Testing Methodology Manual (OSSTMM) (www.isecom.org) is a good example of a test guide. The Open Web Application Security Project (www.owasp.org) is another source for testing methodologies and tips.

Honeypots

A honeypot is much like an IDS, in that it is another tool for detecting intrusion attempts. A honeypot is really a tool of deception. Its purpose is to fool an intruder into believing that the honeypot is a vulnerable computer. Honeypots usually contain phony files, services, and databases to attract and entrap a hacker. For these lures to be effective, they must adequately persuade hackers that they have discovered a real system. Some honeypot vendors sell products that can simulate an entire network, including routers and hosts that are actually located on a single workstation. Honeypots are effective because real servers can generate tons of traffic, which can make it hard to detect malicious activity. The honeypot can be deployed in such a manner that it is a separate server not being used by production. Because nothing is running on this server except the honeypot, it can easily detect any potential intrusions.

So, honeypots can be configured in such a way that administrators will be alerted to their use and will have time to plan a defense or guard of the real network. However, the downside of honeypots includes the fact that, just like any other security system on the network, they require time and configuration. Administrators must spend a certain amount of time monitoring these systems. In addition, if an attacker can successfully compromise the honeypot, he now has a base of attack from which to launch further attacks.

Exam Prep Questions

1. Which of the following is not a valid defense against emanation leakage?
   - ❑ A. TEMPEST
   - ❑ B. Superzapping
   - ❑ C. White noise
   - ❑ D. Control zones

2. Which of the following biometric systems would be considered the most accurate?
   - ❑ A. Retina scan CER 3
   - ❑ B. Fingerprint CER 4
   - ❑ C. Keyboard dynamics CER 5
   - ❑ D. Voice recognition CER 6

3. What are the two primary components of a DAC?
   - ❑ A. Access rights and permissions, and security labels
   - ❑ B. File and data ownership, and access rights and permissions
   - ❑ C. Security labels and discretionary access lists
   - ❑ D. File and data ownership, and security labels

4. Which of the following is considered a DDoS tool?
   - ❑ A. Trinoo
   - ❑ B. Syn flood
   - ❑ C. Ping of death
   - ❑ D. Smurf

5. When registering for a new service, you were asked the following questions. "What country were you born in? What's your pet's name? What is your mother's maiden name?" What type of password system is being used?
   - ❑ A. Cognitive
   - ❑ B. One-time
   - ❑ C. Virtual
   - ❑ D. Complex

6. Mark has just completed his new peer-to-peer network for the small insurance office he owns. Although he will allow Internet access, he does not want users to log in remotely. Which of the following models most closely matches his design?
   - ❑ A. TACACS+
   - ❑ B. MAC
   - ❑ C. RADIUS
   - ❑ D. DAC

7. Which of the following is the best answer: TACACS+ features what?
   - ❑ A. One-factor authentication
   - ❑ B. Decentralized access control
   - ❑ C. Two-factor authentication
   - ❑ D. Accountability

8. IDS systems are considered what type of control?
   - ❑ A. Logical
   - ❑ B. Administrative
   - ❑ C. Technical
   - ❑ D. Physical

9. RADIUS provides which of the following?
   - ❑ A. Authorization and accounting
   - ❑ B. Authentication
   - ❑ C. Authentication, authorization, and accounting
   - ❑ D. Authentication and authorization

10. One advantage of a honeypot includes:
   - ❑ A. Honeypots don't add costs to network security.
   - ❑ B. Honeypots can lure intruders into getting trapped.
   - ❑ C. Honeypots run on separate servers.
   - ❑ D. Honeypots prevent attacks.

Answers to Exam Prep Questions

1. Answer: B. TEMPEST (answer A), white noise (answer C), and control zones (answer D) are all used for emanation security. Superzapping is using software that bypasses normal security constraints to allow unauthorized access to data.

2. Answer: A. The lower the CER, the better; retina scan CER 3 (answer A) is correct. Fingerprint CER 4 (answer B), keyboard dynamics CER 5 (answer C), and voice recognition CER 6 (answer D) are incorrect because they have higher CERs. The CER is determined by combining Type I and Type II errors. This is determined by mapping the point at which Type I errors equal Type II errors. This point is known as the crossover error rate (CER).

3. Answer: B. The two primary components of a DAC are file and data ownership, and access rights and permissions. With file and data ownership, all objects within a system must have an owner. Objects without an owner will be left unprotected. Access rights and permissions control the access rights of an individual. Variation exists, but a basic access-control list checks read, write, or execute privileges. Answers A, C, and D are incorrect.

4. Answer: A. Trinoo is a DDoS tool that can launch UDP flood attacks from various channels on a network. The ping of death (answer C) is a DoS tool that employs an oversize IP packet. Smurf (answer D) is another DoS tool that sends a message to the broadcast of a subnet or network so that every node on the network produces one or more response packets. A syn flood (answer B) is also considered a DoS tool that manipulates the standard three-way handshake used by TCP.

5. Answer: A. Cognitive passwords are widely used during enrollment processes, when individuals call help desks, or when individuals request other services that require authentication. All other answers are incorrect: One-time passwords (answer B) are associated with tokens, virtual passwords (answer C) are a form of passphrase, and the question does not describe a complex password (answer D).

6. Answer: D. The discretionary access control (DAC) model is so titled because access control is left to the owner's discretion. This can be thought of as being similar to a peer-to-peer computer network. All other answers are incorrect: A MAC model (answer B) is static and based on a predetermined list of access privileges, and both TACACS+ (answer A) and RADIUS (answer C) are used for remote access and do not properly address the question.

7. Answer: C. TACACS+ features two-factor authentication. All other answers are incorrect: TACACS+ offers more than one-factor authentication (answer A); it is a centralized, not decentralized, access-control

system (answer B); and although it offers accountability (answer D), it also offers authorization.

8. Answer: C. The three access-control types include administrative (answer B), technical (answer C), and physical (answer D) controls. Administrative controls are the policies and procedures implemented by the organization. Technical controls are put in place to protect the IT infrastructure. Technical controls include IDS systems, encryption, network segmentation, and antivirus controls. Physical controls are most likely seen as guards, gates, and alarms.

9. Answer: C. RADIUS provides three services: authentication, authorization, and accounting. RADIUS facilitates centralized user administration and keeps all user profiles in one location that all remote services share. Answers A, B, and D are incorrect because they do not fully answer the question.

10. Answer: B. When deployed at vulnerable points on the network, honeypots can lure intruders into thinking that it's an opportunity to break into a network; subsequently, they get trapped during the intrusion attempt. Answers A and C are actually disadvantages, and answer D is incorrect because honeypots do not prevent attacks.

Need to Know More?

www.honeypots.net—Honeypot resources

www.owasp.org/index.html—The Open Web Application Security Project

www.cccure.org/Documents/Ben_Rothke/Access%20Control.ppt—Access-control information

www.itsecurity.com/papers/camelot.htm—Getting a grip on access control

www.microsoft.com/windows2000/techinfo/administration/radius.asp—RADIUS best practices

www.antsight.com/zsl/rainbowcrack/—Rainbow tables, advanced password-cracking techniques

www.nwfusion.com/news/2005/021405ids.html—Why IPS is better than IDS

http://project.honeynet.org—The Honeynet Project

http://searchsecurity.techtarget.com/content/0,290 959, sid14_gci1011764,00
.html—Cognitive passwords

5

System Architecture and Models

Terms you'll need to understand:

✓ Buffer overflows
✓ Security modes
✓ Rings of protection
✓ Trusted Computer System Evaluation Criteria (TCSEC)
✓ Information Technology System Evaluation Criteria (ITSEC)
✓ System vulnerabilities
✓ Common Criteria
✓ Reference monitor
✓ Trusted computing base
✓ Open and closed systems

Techniques you'll need to master:

✓ Understanding confidentiality models, such as Bell-LaPadula
✓ Identifying integrity models, such as Biba and Clark-Wilson
✓ Understanding common flaws and security issues associated with system-architecture designs
✓ Distinguishing between certification and accreditation

Introduction

The systems architecture and models domain deals with system hardware and the software that interacts with it. This chapter discusses the standards for securing these systems and protecting confidentiality, integrity, and availability. You are introduced to the trusted computer base and the ways in which systems can be evaluated to assess the level of security.

To pass the CISSP exam, you need to understand system hardware software models, and how models of security can be used to secure systems. Standards such as Common Criteria, Information Technology System Evaluation Criteria (ITSEC), and Trusted Computer System Evaluation Criteria (TCSEC) are covered on the exam.

Common Flaws in the Security Architecture

Just as in other chapters of this book, this one starts by reviewing potential threats and vulnerabilities. The purpose of placing these sections at the beginning of each chapter is to drive home the point that we live in a world of risk. As security professionals, we need to be aware of these threats to security and understand how the various protection mechanisms discussed throughout the chapter can be used to raise the level of security. Doing this can help build real defense in depth.

Buffer Overflow

Buffer overflows occur because of poor coding techniques. A *buffer* is a temporary storage area that has been coded to hold a certain amount of data. If additional data is fed to the buffer, it can spill over or overflow to adjacent buffers. This can corrupt these buffers and cause the application to crash or possibly allow an attacker to execute his own code that he has loaded onto the stack.

As an example, Eeye Digital Security discovered a vulnerability with Microsoft's ISAPI filter extension used for Web-based printing back in 2001. The vulnerability occurred when a buffer of approximately 420 bytes was sent to the HTTP host for a .printer ISAPI request. As a result, attackers could take control of the web server remotely and make themselves administrator.

The point here is that the programmer's work should always be checked for good security practices. Due diligence is required to prevent buffer flows.

All data that is being passed to a program should be checked to make sure that it matches the correct parameters.

Back Doors

Back doors are another potential threat to the security of systems and software. *Back doors*, which are also sometimes referred to as maintenance hooks, are used by programmers during development to allow easy access to a piece of software. A back door can be used when software is developed in sections and developers want a means of accessing certain parts of the program without having to run through all the code. If back doors are not removed before the release of the software, they can allow an attacker to bypass security mechanisms and hack the program.

Asynchronous Attacks

Asynchronous attacks are a form of attack that typically targets timing. The objective is to exploit the delay between the time of check (TOC) and the time of use (TOU). These attacks are sometimes called *race conditions* because the attacker races to make a change to the object after it has been changed but before the system uses it.

As an example, if a program creates a date file to hold the amount a customer owes and the attacker can race to replace this value before the program reads it, he can successfully manipulate the program. In reality, it can be difficult to exploit a race condition because a hacker might have to attempt to exploit the race condition many times before succeeding.

Covert Channels

A *covert channels* is a means of moving information in a manner in which it was not intended. Covert channels are a favorite of attackers because they know that you cannot deny what you must permit. The term was originally used in TCSEC documentation to refer to ways of transferring information from a higher classification to a lower classification. Covert channel attacks can be broadly separated into two types:

➤ **Covert timing channel attacks**—Timing attacks are difficult to detect and function by altering a component or by modifying resource timing.

➤ **Covert storage channel attacks**—These attacks use one process to write data to a storage area and another process to read the data.

Here is an example of how covert channel attacks happen in real life. Your organization has decided to allow ping traffic into and out of your network. Based on this knowledge, an attacker has planted the Loki program on your network. Loki uses the payload portion of the ping packet to move data into and out of your network. Therefore, the network administrator sees nothing but normal ping traffic and is not alerted, all while the attacker is busy stealing company secrets. Sadly, many programs can perform this type of attack.

 The CISSP exam expects you to understand the two types of covert channel attacks.

Incremental Attacks

The goal of an incremental attack is to make a change slowly over time. By making such a small change over such a long period of time, an attacker hopes to remain undetected. Two primary incremental attacks include data diddling, which is possible if the attacker has access to the system and can make small incremental changes to data or files, and a salami attack, which is similar to data diddling but involves making small changes to financial accounts or records.

 The attacks discussed are items that you can expect to see on the exam.

Computer System Architecture

At the core of every computer system is the CPU and hardware that make it run. These are the physical components that interact with the OS and applications to do the things we need done. Let's start at the heart of the system and work our way out.

Central Processing Unit (CPU)

The CPU is the heart of the computer system. The CPU consists of an arithmetic logic unit (ALU), which performs arithmetic and logical operations, and a control unit, which extracts instructions from memory and decodes and executes the requested instructions. Two basic designs of CPUs are manufactured for modern computer systems:

➤ **Reduced Instruction Set Computing (RISC)**—Uses simple instructions that require a reduced number of clock cycles

➤ **Complex Instruction Set Computing (CISC)**—Performs multiple operations for a single instruction

The CPU requires two inputs to accomplish its duties: instructions and data. The data is passed to the CPU for manipulation, where it is typically worked on in either supervisor or problem state. In problem state, the CPU works on the data with nonprivileged instructions. In supervisor state, the CPU executes privileged instructions.

 A superscalar processor is one that can execute multiple instructions at the same time, whereas a scalar processor can execute only one instruction at a time. You will need to know this distinction for the exam.

The CPU can be classified in one of several categories, depending on its functionality. Both the hardware and software must be supported to use these features. These categories include the following:

➤ **Multiprogramming**—Can interleave two or more programs for execution at any one time.

➤ **Multitasking**—Can perform one or more tasks or subtasks at a time.

➤ **Multiprocessor**—Supports one or more CPUs. As an example, Windows 98 does not support the multiprocessor, whereas Windows 2003 does.

The data that CPUs work with is usually part of an application or program. These programs are tracked by a process ID, or PID. Anyone who has ever looked at Task Manager in Windows or executed a ps command on a Linux machine has probably seen a PID number. Fortunately, most programs do much more than the first C code you probably wrote that just said, "Hello World." Each line of code or piece of functionality that a program has is known as a thread.

The data that the CPU is working with must have a way to move from the storage media to the CPU. This is accomplished by means of the bus. The bus is nothing more than lines of conductors that transmit data between the CPU, storage media, and other hardware devices.

Storage Media

The CPU uses memory to store instructions and data. Therefore, memory is an important type of storage media. The CPU is the only device that can directly access memory. Systems are designed that way because the CPU has a high level of system trust. Memory can have either physical or logical addresses. Physical addressing refers to the hard-coded address assigned to the memory. Applications and programmers writing code use logical addresses. Not only can memory be addressed in different ways, but there are also different types of memory. Memory can be either nonvolatile or volatile. Examples of both are given here:

➤ Read-only memory (ROM) is nonvolatile memory that retains information even if power is removed. Types of ROM include Erasable Programmable Read-Only Memory (EPROM), Electrically Erasable Programmable Read-Only Memory (EEPROM), Flash memory, and programmable logic devices (PLD). ROM is typically used to load and store firmware.

➤ Random access memory (RAM) is volatile memory. If power is lost, the data is destroyed. Types of RAM include static RAM, which uses circuit latches to represent binary data, and dynamic RAM, which must be refreshed every few milliseconds.

Secondary Storage

Although memory plays an important part in the world of storage, other long-term types of storage are also needed. One of these is sequential storage. Anyone who has owned an IBM PC with a tape drive knows what sequential storage is. Tape drives are a type of sequential storage that must be read sequentially from beginning to end. Another well-known type of secondary storage is direct-access storage. Direct-access storage devices do not have to be read sequentially; the system can identify the location of the information and go directly to it to read the data. Hard drives are an example of a sequential storage device: They are used to hold data and software. Software is the operating system or an application that you've installed on a computer system.

Virtual Memory and Virtual Machines

Modern computer systems have developed other ways in which to store and access information. One of these is virtual memory. Virtual memory is the combination of the computer's primary memory, RAM, and secondary storage, the hard drive. By combining these two technologies, the OS can make the CPU believe that it has much more memory than it actually does. When RAM is depleted, the CPU begins saving data onto the computer's hard drive. This information is saved in pages that can be swapped back and forth between the hard drive and RAM, as needed. Individuals who have opened more programs on their computers than they've had enough memory to support are probably familiar with the operation of virtual memory.

Closely related to virtual memory are virtual machines. VMWare and VirtualPC are the two leading contenders in this category. A virtual machine enables the user to run a second OS within a virtual host. For example, a virtual machine will let you run another Windows OS, Linux x86, or any other OS that runs on x86 processor and supports standard BIOS booting. Virtual machines are used primarily for development and system administration, and to reduce the number of physical devices needed.

Security Mechanisms

Although a robust architecture is a good start, real security requires that you have security mechanisms in place to control processes and applications. Some good security mechanisms are described in the following sections.

Process Isolation

Process isolation is required to maintain a high level of system trust. To be certified as a multilevel security system, process isolation must be supported. Without process isolation, there would be no way to prevent one process from spilling over into another process's memory space, corrupting data or possibly making the whole system unstable. Process isolation is performed by the operating system; its job is to enforce memory boundaries.

For a system to be secure, the operating system must prevent unauthorized users from accessing areas of the system to which they should not have access. Sometimes this is done by means of a virtual machine. A virtual machine allows the user to believe that they have the use of the entire system, but in reality, processes are completely isolated. To take this concept a step further, some systems that require truly robust security also implement hardware isolation. This means that the processes are segmented not only logically, but also physically.

 NOTE   Java uses a form of virtual machine because it uses a sandbox to contain code and allows it to function only in a controlled manner.

Operation States

When systems are used to process and store sensitive information, there must be some agreed-upon methods for how this will work. Generally, these concepts were developed to meet the requirements of handling sensitive government information with categories such as sensitive, secret, and top secret.

The burden of handling this task can be placed upon either administration or the system itself.

Single-state systems are designed and implemented to handle one category of information. The burden of management falls upon the administrator, who must develop the policy and procedures to manage this system. The administrator must also determine who has access and what type of access the users have. These systems are dedicated to one mode of operation, so they are sometimes referred to as dedicated systems.

Multistate systems depend not on the administrator, but on the system itself. They are capable of having more than one person log in to the system and access various types of data, depending upon the level of clearance. As you would probably expect, these systems are not inexpensive. Multistate systems can operate as a compartmentalized system. This means that Mike can log into the system with a secret clearance and access secret-level data, while Carl can log in with top-secret level access and access a different level of data. These systems are compartmentalized and can segment data on a need-to-know basis.

Unfortunately, things don't always operate normally; they sometimes go wrong, and a system failure can occur. A system failure could potentially compromise the system. Efficient designs have built-in recovery procedures to recover from potential problems:

➤ **Fail-safe**—If a failure is detected, the system is protected from compromise by termination of services.

➤ **Fail-soft**—A detected failure terminates the noncritical process, and the system continues to function.

Protection Rings

So how does the operating system know who and what to trust? It relies on rings of protection. Rings of protection work much like your network of family, friends, coworkers, and acquaintances. The people who are closest to you, such as your spouse and family, have the highest level of trust. Those who are distant acquaintances or are unknown to you probably have a lower level of trust. It's much like the guy I met in Times Square trying to sell me a new Rolex for $100—I had little trust in him and the supposed Rolex!

In reality, the protection rings are conceptual. Figure 5.1 shows an illustration of the protection ring schema.

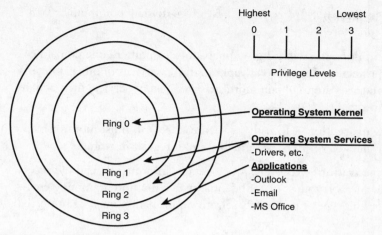

Figure 5.1 Rings of protection.

The protection ring model provides the operating system with various levels at which to execute code or restrict its access. It provides much greater granularity than a system that just operates in user and privileged mode. As you move toward the outer bounds of the model, the numbers increase and the level of trust decreases.

➤ **Layer 0** is the most trusted level. The operating system kernel resides at this level. Any process running at layer 0 is said to be operating in privileged mode.

➤ **Layer 1** contains nonprivileged portions of the operating system.

➤ **Layer 2** is where I/O drivers, low level operations, and utilities reside.

➤ **Layer 3** is where applications and processes operate. Items such as FTP, DNS, Telnet, and HTTP all operate at this level. This is the level at which individuals usually interact with the operating system. Applications operating here are said to be working in user mode.

Trusted Computer Base

The trusted computer base (TCB) is the sum of all the protection mechanisms within a computer and is responsible for enforcing the security policy. This includes hardware, software, controls, and processes. The TCB is responsible for confidentiality and integrity. It monitors four basic functions:

➤ **Input/output operations**—I/O operations are a security concern because operations from the outermost rings might need to interface with rings of greater protection. These cross-domain communications must be monitored.

➤ **Execution domain switching**—Applications running in one domain or level of protection often invoke applications or services in other domains. If these requests are to obtain more sensitive data or service, their activity must be controlled.

➤ **Memory protection**—To truly be secure, the TCB must monitor memory references to verify confidentiality and integrity in storage.

➤ **Process activation**—Registers, process status information, and file access lists are vulnerable to loss of confidentiality in a multiprogramming environment. This type of potentially sensitive information must be protected.

An important component of the TCB is the reference monitor, an abstract machine that is used to implement security. The reference monitor's job is to validate access to objects by authorized subjects. The reference monitor is implemented by the security kernel, which is at the heart of the system and handles all user/application requests for access to system resources. A small security kernel is easy to verify, test, and validate as secure. However, in real life, the security kernel is usually not that small because processes located inside can function faster and have privileged access. To avoid these performance costs, Linux and Windows have fairly large security kernels and have opted to sacrifice size in return for performance gains. No matter what the size is, the security kernel must

➤ Control all access

➤ Be protected from modification or change

➤ Be verified and tested to be correct

Security Models of Control

Security models of control are used to determine how security will be implemented, what subjects can access the system, and what objects they will have access to. Simply stated, they are a way to formalize security policy. Security models of control are typically implemented by enforcing integrity or confidentiality.

Integrity

Integrity is a good thing. It is one of the basic elements of the security triad, along with confidentiality and availability. Integrity plays an important role in security because it can verify that unauthorized users are not modifying data, that authorized users don't make unauthorized changes, and that data remains internally and externally consistent. Two security models of control that address integrity include Biba and Clark-Wilson.

Biba

The Biba model was the first model developed to address the concerns of integrity. Originally published in 1977, this lattice-based model has two defining properties:

➤ **Simple Integrity Property**—This property states that a subject at one level of integrity is not permitted to read an object of lower integrity.

➤ **Star * Integrity Property**—This property states that an object at one level of integrity is not permitted to write to an object of higher integrity.

Biba addresses integrity only, not availability or confidentiality. It also assumes that internal threats are being protected by good coding practices and, therefore, focuses on external threats.

Remember that the Biba model deals with integrity. As such, writing to an object of a higher level might endanger the integrity of the system.

Clark-Wilson

The Clark-Wilson model was created in 1987. It differs from previous models because it was developed with the intention to be used for commercial activities. This model dictates that the separation of duties must be enforced, subjects must access data through an application, and auditing is required. It also differs from the Biba model in that subjects are restricted. This means a subject at one level of access can read one set of data, whereas a subject at another level of access has access to a different set of data.

Confidentiality

Although integrity is an important concept, confidentiality was actually the first to be addressed in a formal model. This is because the Department of Defense (DoD) was concerned about the confidentiality of information. The DoD divides information into categories, to ease the burden of managing who has access to what levels of information. DoD information classifications include confidential, secret, and top secret.

Bell-LaPadula

The Bell-LaPadula model was actually the first formal model developed to protect confidentiality. This is a state machine that enforces confidentiality. A *state machine* is a conceptual model that monitors the status of the system to prevent it from slipping into an insecure state. Systems that support the state machine model must have all their possible states examined to verify that all processes are controlled. The Bell-LaPadula model uses mandatory access control to enforce the DoD multilevel security policy. For a subject to access information, he must have a clear "need to know" and meet or exceed the information's classification level.

The Bell-LaPadula model is defined by the two following properties:

➤ **Simple Security Property (ss Property)**—This property states that a subject at one level of confidentiality is not allowed to read information at a higher level of confidentiality. This is sometimes referred to as "no read up."

➤ **Star * Security Property**—This property states that a subject at one level of confidentiality is not allowed to write information to a lower level of confidentiality. This is also known as "no write down."

Review the Bell-LaPadula Simple Security and Star * Security models closely; they are easy to confuse with Biba's two defining properties.

Know that the Bell-LaPadula model deals with confidentiality. As such, reading information at a higher level than what is allowed would endanger confidentiality.

Take-Grant Model

The Take-Grant model is another confidentiality-based model that supports four basic operations: take, grant, create, and revoke. This model allows subjects with the take right to remove take rights from other subjects. Subjects possessing the grant right can grant this right to other subjects. The create and revoke operations work in the same manner: Someone with the create right can give the create right to others, and those with the revoke right can remove that right from others.

Brewer and Nash Model

The Brewer and Nash model is similar to the Bell-LaPadula model and is also called the Chinese Wall model. It was developed to prevent conflict of interest (COI) problems. As an example, imagine that your security firm does security work for many large firms. If one of your employees could access information about all the firms that your company has worked for, he might be able to use this data in an unauthorized way. Therefore, the Chinese Wall model would prevent a worker consulting for one firm from accessing data belonging to another, thereby preventing any COI.

Other Models

Although not as popular, other security models of control exist:

➤ **Noninterference model**—As its name states, this model's job is to make sure that objects and subjects of different levels don't interfere with the objects and subjects of other levels.

➤ **Information-flow model**—This model is the basis of design of both the Biba and Bell-LaPadula models. Information-flow models are considered a type of state machine. The Biba model is designed to prevent information from flowing from a low security level to a high security level. This helps protect the integrity of sensitive information. The Bell-LaPadula model is designed to prevent information from flowing from a high security level to a lower one. This protects confidentiality. The real goal of any information-flow model is to prevent the unauthorized, insecure information flow in any direction.

➤ **Graham Denning model**—This model uses a formal set of protection rules for which each object has an owner and a controller.

➤ **Harrison-Ruzzo-Ullman model**—This model details how subjects and objects can be created, deleted, accessed, or changed.

Spend some time reviewing all the models discussed in this section. Make sure you know which models are integrity based and which are confidentiality based; you will need to know this distinction for the exam.

Open and Closed Systems

Open systems accept input from other vendors and are based upon standards and practices that allow connection to different devices and interfaces. The goal is to promote full interoperability whereby the system can be fully utilized.

Closed systems are proprietary. They use devices that are not based on open standards and are generally locked. They lack standard interfaces to allow connection to other devices and interfaces.

An example of this can be seen in the U.S. cellphone industry. Cingular and T-Mobile cellphones are based on the worldwide Global System for Mobile Communications (GMS) standard and can be used overseas easily on other networks by simply changing the SIM module. These are open-system phones. Other phones, such as Sprint, use Code Division Multiple Access (CDMA), which does not have worldwide support.

Documents and Guidelines

The documents and guidelines discussed in the following sections were developed to help evaluate and establish system assurance. These items are important to the CISSP candidate because they provide a level of trust and assurance that these systems will operate in a given and predictable manner. A trusted system has undergone testing and validation to a specific standard. Assurance is the freedom of doubt and a level of confidence that a system will perform as required every time it is used.

The Rainbow Series

The rainbow series is aptly named because each book in the series has a different color of label. This 6-foot-tall stack of books was developed by the National Computer Security Center (NCSC), an organization that is part of the National Security Agency (NSA). These guidelines were developed for the Trusted Product Evaluation Program (TPEP), which tests commercial products against a comprehensive set of security-related criteria. The first of these books was released in 1983 and is known as the Orange Book. Because it addresses only standalone systems, other volumes were developed to increase the level of system assurance.

The Orange Book: Trusted Computer System Evaluation Criteria

The Orange Book's official name is the Trusted Computer System Evaluation Criteria (TCSEC). As noted, it was developed to evaluate standalone systems. Its basis of measurement is confidentiality, so it is similar to the Bell-LaPadula model. It is designed to rate systems and place them into one of four categories:

➤ A: Verified protection. An A-rated system is the highest security division.

➤ B: Mandatory security. A B-rated system has mandatory protection of the TCB.

➤ C: Discretionary protection. A C-rated system provides discretionary protection of the TCB.

➤ D: Minimal protection. A D-rated system fails to meet any of the standards of A, B, or C, and basically has no security controls.

 The Canadians have their own version of the Orange Book, known as The Canadian Trusted Computer Product Evaluation Criteria (CTCPEC). It is seen as a more flexible version of TCSEC.

The Orange Book not only rates systems into one of four categories, but each category is also broken down further. For each of these categories, a higher number indicates a more secure system, as noted in the following:

➤ A is the highest security division. An A1 rating means that the system has verified protection and supports mandatory access control (MAC).

　➤ A1 is the highest supported rating. Systems rated as such must meet formal methods and proof of integrity of TCB. Examples of A1 systems include the Gemini Trusted Network Processor and the Honeywell SCOMP.

➤ B is considered a mandatory protection design. Just as with an A-rated system, those that obtain a B rating must support MAC.

　➤ B1 (labeled security protection) systems require sensitivity labels for all subjects and storage objects. Examples of B1-rated systems include the Cray Research Trusted Unicos 8.0 and the Digital SEVMS.

　➤ For a B2 (structured protection) rating, the system must meet the requirements of B1 and support hierarchical device labels, trusted path communications between user and system, and covert channel analysis. An example of a B2 system is the Honeywell Multics.

　➤ Systems rated as B3 (security domains) must meet B2 standards and support trusted path access and authentication, automatic security analysis, and trusted recovery. An example of a B3-rated system is the Federal XTS-300.

➤ C is considered a discretionary protection rating. C-rated systems support discretionary access control (DAC).

　➤ Systems rated at C1 (discretionary security protection) don't need to distinguish between individual users and types of access.

　➤ C2 (controlled access protection) systems must meet C1 requirements plus must distinguish between individual users and types of access.

C2 systems must also support object reuse protection. A C2 rating is common; products such as Windows NT and Novell NetWare 4.11 have a C2 rating.

➤ Any system that does not comply with any of the other categories or that fails to receive a higher classification is rated as a D-level (minimal protection) system. MS-DOS is a D-rated system.

The CISSP exam will not expect you to know what systems meet the various Orange Book ratings; however, it will expect you to know where MAC and DAC are applied.

The Red Book: Trusted Network Interpretation

The Red Book's official name is the Trusted Network Interpretation. Its purpose is to address the deficiencies of the Orange Book. Although the Orange Book addresses only confidentiality, the Red Book examines integrity and availability. It also is tasked with examining the operation of networked devices.

Information Technology Security Evaluation Criteria (ITSEC)

ITSEC is a European standard that was developed in the 1980s to evaluate confidentiality, integrity, and availability of an entire system. ITSEC designates the target system as the Target of Evaluation (TOE). The evaluation is actually divided into two parts: One part evaluates functionality, and the other evaluates assurance. There are 10 functionality (F) classes and 7 assurance (E) classes. Assurance classes rate the effectiveness and correctness of the system. Table 5.1 shows these ratings and how they correspond to the TCSEC ratings.

Table 5.1 ITSEC Functionality Ratings and Comparison to TCSEC		
(F) Class	**(E) Class**	**TCSEC Rating**
NA	E0	D
F1	E1	C1
F2	E2	C2
F3	E3	B1

(continued)

Table 5.1 ITSEC Functionality Ratings and Comparison to TCSEC (*continued*)		
(F) Class	**(E) Class**	**TCSEC Rating**
F4	E4	B2
F5	E5	B3
F5	E6	A1
F6	—	TOEs with high integrity requirements
F7	—	TOEs with high availability requirements
F8	—	TOEs with high integrity requirements during data communications
F9	—	TOEs with high confidentiality requirements during data communications
F10	—	Networks with high confidentiality and integrity requirements

Common Criteria

With all the standards we have discussed, it would be easy to see how someone might have a hard time determining which one is the right choice. The International Standards Organization (ISO) had these same thoughts. Therefore, they decided that because of the various standards and ratings that existed, there should be a single global standard.

In 1997, the ISO released the Common Criteria (ISO 15408), which is an amalgamated version of TCSEC, ITSEC, and the CTCPEC. Common Criteria is designed around TCB entities. These entities include physical and logical controls, startup and recovery, reference mediation, and privileged states. Common Criteria categorizes assurance into one of seven increasingly strict levels of assurance. These are referred to as *Evaluation Assurance Levels (EAL)*. EALs provide a specific level of confidence in the security functions of the system being analyzed. The system being analyzed and tested is known as the *Target of Evaluation (TOE)*, which is just another name for the system that is being subjected to the security evaluation. The assurance requirements and specifications to be used as the basis for evaluation are known as the *Security Target (ST)*. A description of each of the seven levels of assurance follows:

➤ EAL 0: Inadequate assurance

➤ EAL 1: Functionality tested

➤ EAL 2: Structurally tested

➤ EAL 3: Methodically checked and tested

➤ EAL 4: Methodically designed, tested, and reviewed

➤ EAL 5: Semiformally designed and tested

➤ EAL 6: Semiformally verified designed and tested

➤ EAL 7: Formally verified designed and tested

Common Criteria defines two types of security requirements: *functional* and *assurance*. Functional requirements define what a product or system does. They also define the security capabilities of the product. Assurance requirements define how well the product is built. Assurance requirements give confidence in the product and show the correctness of its implementation.

 The Common Criteria seven levels of assurance and its two security requirements are required test knowledge.

British Standard 7799

The BS 7799 was developed in England to be used as a standard method to measure risk. Because the document found such a wide audience and was adopted by businesses and organizations, it evolved into ISO 17799 in December 2000. This is a comprehensive standard in its coverage of security issues and is divided into 10 sections:

➤ Security Policy

➤ Security Organization

➤ Asset Control and Classification

➤ Environmental and Physical Security

➤ Employee Security

➤ Computer and Network Management

➤ Access Controls

➤ System Development and Maintenance

➤ Business Continuity Planning

➤ Compliance

Compliance with 7799 is an involved task and is far from trivial for even the most security conscious of organizations.

System Validation

No system or architecture will ever be completely secure; there will always be a certain level of risk. Security professionals must understand this risk and be comfortable with it, mitigate it, or offset it to a third party. All the documentation and guidelines already discussed dealt with ways to measure and assess risk. These can be a big help in ensuring that the implemented systems meet our requirements. However, before we begin to use the systems, we must complete two additional steps.

U.S. federal agencies are required by law to have their IT systems and infrastructures certified and accredited. Although you shouldn't expect to see this information on the exam, it is worth knowing if you plan to interact with any agencies that require their use. Depending on the agency, one of the following methodologies is typically used:

➤ **Defense Information Technology Systems Certification and Accreditation Process (DITSCAP)**—Typically used for defense agencies, but can be used by civilian firms

➤ **National Information Assurance Certification and Accreditation Process (NIACAP)**—A certification process developed by the National Security Telecommunications and Information System Security Instruction

➤ **National Institute of Standards and Technology (NIST)**—A certification process that is based on Special Publication 800-37 and can be used by government and civilian industries

All of these methodologies look at much more than your standard penetration test. In reality, they are more like an audit. They must validate that the systems are implementing, configuring, and operating as expected and meet all security policies and procedures.

Certification and Accreditation

Certification is the process of validating that systems we implement are configured and operating as expected. It also validates that the systems are connected to and communicate with other systems in a secure and controlled manner, and that they handle data in a secure and approved manner. The certification process is a technical evaluation of the system that can be carried out by independent security teams or by the existing staff. Its goal is to uncover any vulnerabilities or weaknesses in the implementation.

The results of the certification process are reported to the organization's management for mediation and approval. If management agrees with the findings of the certification, the report is formally approved. The formal approval of the certification is the *accreditation process*. Management usually issues this in a formal written approval that the certified system is approved for use and specified in the certification documentation. If changes are made to the system, it is reconfigured; if there are other changes in the environment, a recertification and accreditation process must be repeated. The entire process is periodically repeated at intervals depending on the industry and the regulations they must comply with. As an example, Section 404 of Sarbanes-Oxley requires an annual evaluation of internal systems that deal with financial controls and reporting systems.

Exam Prep Questions

1. Which of the following best describes a superscalar processor?
   - ❑ A. A superscalar processor can execute only one instruction at a time.
   - ❑ B. A superscalar processor has two large caches that are used as input and output buffers.
   - ❑ C. A superscalar processor can execute multiple instructions at the same time.
   - ❑ D. A superscalar processor has two large caches that are used as output buffers.

2. Which of the following are developed by programmers and used to allow the bypassing of normal processes during development?
   - ❑ A. Back doors
   - ❑ B. Traps
   - ❑ C. Buffer overflows
   - ❑ D. Covert channels

3. Carl has noticed a high level of TCP traffic in and out of the network. After running a packet sniffer, he discovered malformed TCP ACK packets with unauthorized data. What has Carl discovered?
   - ❑ A. Buffer-overflow attack
   - ❑ B. Asynchronous attack
   - ❑ C. Covert-channel attack
   - ❑ D. DoS attack

4. Which of the following types of CPUs can perform multiple operations from a single instruction?
   - ❑ A. DITSCAP
   - ❑ B. RISC
   - ❑ C. NIACAP
   - ❑ D. CISC

5. Which of the following standards evaluates functionality and assurance separately?
   - ❑ A. TCSEC
   - ❑ B. TNI
   - ❑ C. ITSEC
   - ❑ D. CTCPEC

6. Which of the following was the first model developed that was based on confidentiality?
   - ❑ A. Bell-LaPadula
   - ❑ B. Biba
   - ❑ C. Clark-Wilson
   - ❑ D. Take-Grant

7. Which of the following models is integrity based and was developed for commercial applications?

❏ A. Information-flow

❏ B. Clark-Wilson

❏ C. Bell-LaPadula

❏ D. Brewer-Nash

8. Which of the following does the Biba model address?

❏ A. Focuses on internal threats

❏ B. Focuses on external threats

❏ C. Addresses confidentiality

❏ D. Addresses availability

9. Which model is also known as the Chinese Wall model?

❏ A. Biba

❏ B. Take-Grant

❏ C. Harrison-Ruzzo-Ullman

❏ D. Brewer-Nash

10. Which of the following examines integrity and availability?

❏ A. Orange Book

❏ B. Brown Book

❏ C. Red Book

❏ D. Purple Book

Answers to Exam Prep Questions

1. Answer: C. A superscalar processor can execute multiple instructions at the same time. Answer A describes a scalar processor; it can execute only one instruction at a time. Answer B does not describe a superscalar processor because it does not have two large caches that are used as input and output buffers. Answer D is incorrect because a superscalar processor does not have two large caches that are used as output buffers.

2. Answer: A. Back doors, also referred to as maintenance hooks, are used by programmers during development to give them easy access into a piece of software. Answer B is incorrect because a trap is a message used by the Simple Network Management Protocol (SNMP) to report a serious condition to a management station. Answer C is incorrect because a buffer overflow occurs because of poor programming. Answer D is incorrect because a covert channel is a means of moving information in a manner in which it was not intended.

3. Answer: C. A covert channel is a means of moving information in a manner in which it was not intended. A buffer overflow occurs because of poor programming and usually results in program failure or the attacker's ability to execute his code; thus, answer A is incorrect. An asynchronous attack deals with performing an operation between the TOC and the TOU (so answer B is incorrect), whereas a DoS attack affects availability, not confidentiality (making answer D incorrect).

4. Answer: D. The Complex Instruction Set Computing (CISC) CPU can perform multiple operations from a single instruction. Answer A is incorrect because DITSCAP is the Defense Information Technology Systems Certification and Accreditation Process. Answer B describes the Reduced Instruction Set Computing (RISC) CPU, which uses simple instructions that require a reduced number of clock cycles. Answer C is incorrect because NIACAP is the National Information Assurance Certification and Accreditation Process, an accreditation process.

5. Answer: C. ITSEC is a European standard that evaluates functionality and assurance separately. All other answers are incorrect because they do not separate the evaluation criteria. TCSEC is also known as the Orange Book, TNI is known as the Red Book, and CTCPEC is a Canadian assurance standard; therefore, answers A, B, and D are incorrect.

6. Answer: A. Bell-LaPadula was the first model developed that is based on confidentiality. It uses two main rules to enforce its operation. Answers B, C, and D are incorrect. Biba and Clark-Wilson both deal with integrity, whereas the Take-Grant model is based on four basic operations.

7. Answer: B. Clark-Wilson was developed for commercial activities. This model dictates that the separation of duties must be enforced, subjects must access data through an application, and auditing is required. Answers A, C, and D are incorrect. The information-flow model addresses the flow of information and can be used to protect integrity or confidentiality. Bell-LaPadula is an integrity model, and Brewer-Nash was developed to prevent conflict of interest.

8. Answer: B. The Biba model assumes that internal threats are being protected by good coding practices and, therefore, focuses on external threats. Answers A, C, and D are incorrect. Biba addresses only integrity, not availability or confidentiality.

9. Answer: D. The Brewer-Nash model is also known as the Chinese Wall model and was specifically developed to prevent conflicts of interest. Answers A, B, and C are incorrect because they do not fit the description. Biba is integrity based, Take-Grant is based on four modes, and Harrison-Ruzzo-Ullman defines how access rights can be changed, created, or deleted.

10. Answer: C. The Red Book examines integrity, availability, and networked components. Answer A is incorrect because the Orange Book deals with confidentiality. Answer B is incorrect because the Brown Book is a guide to understanding trusted facility management. Answer D is incorrect because the Purple Book deals with database management.

Need to Know More?

www.multicians.org/protection.pdf—Protection rings

www.cs.ucsb.edu/~jzhou/security/overflow.html—Smashing the stack for fun and profit

www.radium.ncsc.mil/tpep/library/rainbow/NCSC-TG-030.html—Covert-channel attacks

www.javaworld.com/javaworld/jw-08-1997/jw-08-hood.html—Java security

http://developer.novell.com/research/appnotes/1996/june/netnotes/03.htm—How Windows and Novell measure up to TCSEC standards

www.governmentsecurity.org/articles/RainbowSeriesLibraryTheOneThe Only.php—The Rainbow Series

http://infoeng.ee.ic.ac.uk/~malikz/surprise2001/spc99e/article2/—The Bell-LaPadula model

www.iso17799software.com/—ISO 17799

6

Telecommunications and Network Security

Terms you'll need to understand:

✓ Denial of service (DoS)
✓ Address Resolution Protocol (ARP)
✓ Domain Name Service (DNS)
✓ Firewalls
✓ Network Address Translation (NAT)
✓ IP Security (IPSec)
✓ The Open Systems Interconnect (OSI) model
✓ Transmission Control Protocol/Internet Protocol (TCP/IP)
✓ Local area networks (LAN)
✓ Wide area networks (WAN)

Techniques you'll need to master:

✓ Understand the various types of attacks against networks
✓ Understand the differences between LAN and WAN topologies
✓ Describe and define the OSI model and its layers
✓ Describe the four layers of the TCP/IP stack
✓ Understand the function and purpose of VPNs

Introduction

The telecommunications and network security domain addresses communications and network security. Mastery of this domain requires you to fully understand voice and data communications, as well as the countermeasures that can be implemented to protect these systems.

If you have spent some time working in this segment of IT security management, you might need only a quick review of the material. If your work has led you to concentrate in other domains, you will want to spend some time here reviewing the content because this is a large domain with many potential exam questions.

To be fully prepared for the exam, you will need to understand the data communication process and how it relates to network security. Knowledge of remote access, the use of firewalls, network equipment, and network protocols is also required. Being adept in network security also requires that you understand the techniques used for preventing network-based attacks.

Threats to Network Security

Many threats to network security exist. Attackers are opportunistic and typically take the path of least resistance. This means they choose the most convenient route and exploit the most well-known flaw. Threats to network security can include denial-of-service attacks, disclosure, and destruction or alteration of information.

DoS Attacks

Many times denial-of-service (DoS) attacks are a last-ditch effort by malicious users to bring down a network. The thought process is that if they cannot have access to the network, no one else should, either. Some common DoS attacks include these:

➤ **Ping of death**—An oversize packet is illegal but possible when fragmentation is used. When the fragments are reassembled at the other end into a complete packet, it can cause a buffer overflow on some systems.

➤ **Smurf**—Uses a spoofed ping packet addressed to the broadcast address, with the source address listed as the victim. It floods the victim with ping responses.

➤ **Teardrop**—Sends packets that are malformed, with the fragmentation off-set value tweaked so that the receiving packets overlap. These overlapping fragments crash or lock up the receiving system, thereby causing a denial of service.

➤ **Land**—Sends a packet with the same source and destination port and IP address. The receiving system typically does not know how to handle these malformed packets, so the system freezes or locks up, thereby causing a denial of service.

➤ **SYN flood**—Instead of targeting the Internet Control Message Protocol (ICMP) or Internet Protocol (IP), a SYN flood disrupts the Transmission Control Protocol (TCP) by sending a large number of fake packets with the SYN flag set. This fills the buffer on the victim's system and prevents it from accepting legitimate connections.

Disclosure Attacks

Disclosure attacks seek to gain access to systems and information that should not be available to unauthorized individuals. As a CISSP candidate, you should be aware of these attacks and their potential effects. They include the following:

➤ **Sniffing**—This rather passive form of attack requires that the attacker gain some type of access to the network. This is easy to perform if the network is using hubs. The goal is to uncover sensitive information. This is made possible by the fact that many protocols, such as the File Transfer Protocol (FTP), Telnet, and the Simple Mail Transfer Protocol (SMTP), send usernames and passwords in clear text.

➤ **ARP poisoning**—This attack usually is done to redirect traffic on a switch. Because switches do not send all traffic to all ports like a hub, attackers must use ARP poisoning techniques to put themselves in the middle of a data exchange. When this has been achieved, the attack can attempt a series of attacks, including sniffing and interception of confidential information.

➤ **DNS spoofing**—Much like ARP poisoning, this attack attempts to poison the domain name service (DNS) process. Individuals who succeed have their fake DNS entry placed into the victim's DNS cache. Victims then can be redirected to the wrong Internet sites.

➤ **Pharming attack**—Pharming exploits are another type of attack that misuses the DNS protocol. Normally DNS is responsible for translating web addresses into IP addresses. Pharming attacks hijack the DNS and force it to redirect Voice over IP (VoIP) or other traffic to a location of the attacker's choice. This allows the attacker to get control of VoIP calls. This means that your phone call might no longer be private and could be monitored.

➤ **Phishing attack**—This social-engineering attack attempts to lure victims into disclosing confidential information. The attacker typically attempts to trick the victim by sending a fake email that appears to be from a legitimate bank or e-commerce vendor. The supplied link to the organization's website appears real but is actually hosted by the attackers.

➤ **War dialing**—This old-school attack is based on the premise that if the attacker can successfully connect to the victim's modem, he might be able to launch an attack. War-dialing programs work by dialing a predetermined range of phone numbers, in hopes of finding one that is connected to an open modem. The threat of war dialing is that the compromised host acts as a gateway between the network and the Internet.

➤ **War driving**—The practice of war driving, flying, boating, or walking around an area is to find wireless access points. Many individuals that perform this activity look specifically for unsecured wireless networks to exploit. The primary threat is that these individuals might then have a direct connection to your internal network or unrestricted Internet access.

➤ **Spyware**—Spyware includes a broad category of illicit programs that can be used to monitor Internet activity, redirect you to specific sites, or barrage you with pop-up ads. Spyware is usually installed on a computer by some form of browser hijacking or when a user downloads a computer program that has the spyware bundled with it. Spyware typically works by tracking and sending data and statistics via a server installed on the victim's computer. Spyware programs can result in a loss of confidentiality.

➤ **Viruses/worms**—These programs are created specifically to invade computers and networks and wreak havoc on them. Some display only cryptic messages on the victim's machine, whereas others are capable of disclosing information, altering files, or informing others so that they can victimize your computer. The big difference between viruses and worms is that viruses cannot replicate themselves. Worms are self-replicating and can spread so quickly that they clog networks and cause denial of service.

Destruction, Alteration, or Theft

The destruction, alteration, or theft of data represents a serious threat to the security of the organization. These attacks cut to the heart of the organization by compromising a network and accessing items such as databases that contain credit card information, for example. Even if regulatory requirements do not hold the organization liable, there is still the possibility of a serious public relations problem if one of these attacks occurs:

➤ **Database attacks**—These attacks target an organization's database. Although the techniques vary, the results are the same: Malicious users can run their code on the victim's database server or steal information for the server. This can be a serious threat to the integrity or confidentiality of the organization.

➤ **Cellphone attacks**—It's not hard to believe that Americans now spend more time talking on their cellphones than they do land lines. With so many cellphones in use, there are numerous ways in which attackers can try to exploit their vulnerabilities. One is through the practice of cloning. Cellphones have an electronic serial number (ESN) and a mobile identification number (MIN). Attackers can use snifferlike equipment to capture these numbers from your phone and install them in another. The attacker then can sell or use this cloned phone.

Tumbling is another form of cellphone attack. Specially modified phones tumble and shift to a different pair of ESN/MIN numbers after each call. This technique makes the attacker's phone appear to be a legitimate roaming cell phone. First-generation (1G) cellphones were vulnerable to this attack. Today most cellphones are second- (2G) and third- (3G) generation phones.

➤ **Data diddling**—This form of attack works by changing data as it is being keyed in or processed by a computer. It can include canceling debts without proper authority or assigning a large hourly pay increase to your salary. Trying to track down the problem is difficult, and it could be months before the attack is uncovered.

➤ **Identity theft**—FBI statistics list identity theft as one of the fastest-growing white-collar crimes. Identity theft is the deliberate assumption of another person's identity, usually to gain access to that person's finances or to use his or her identity and credit history to purchase goods or services, or to establish credit or receive loans under the victim's name. This form of attack can endanger the integrity and confidentiality of the victim's credit history.

➤ **Password cracking**—This type of attack targets an organization's passwords. These passwords could belong to anyone from the CEO to the help-desk technician. Techniques include guessing, shoulder surfing, and dictionary, hybrid, and brute-force attacks. Dictionary password cracking pulls words from dictionaries and word lists to attempt to discover a user's password. Hybrid attacks use dictionaries and word lists, and then prepend and append characters and numbers to dictionary words in an attempt to crack the user's password. Brute-force attacks use random numbers and characters to crack a user's password.

➤ **Privilege escalation**—Some computer operations require special privilege to complete their tasks. These operations can be executed as administrator, system, or root. Attackers look at the code that executes the operations in search of errors or other bugs. By injecting their code into these programs, they can sometimes execute their commands, giving them control of the computer.

➤ **Salami attack**—This financial crime works by taking small amounts of money over an extended period. For the attacker to be successful, he must remove an amount so small that it will go unnoticed.

➤ **Software piracy**—This illegal activity occurs when individuals or corporations distribute software outside its legal license agreement. Not only is software piracy morally wrong, but there are also significant financial and legal penalties. Individuals who distribute pirated software can face felony charges and be jailed for up to 5 years.

➤ **Session hijacking**—This attack allows an attacker to take over an existing connection. It is an effective attack because most TCP services perform only authentication at the beginning of the session. So in this case, the attacker simply waits until authentication is complete and then jumps in and takes control. Applications such as FTP and Telnet are vulnerable to this attack.

➤ **Spamming**—Spam is unsolicited bulk mail. One of the real dangers of spam is that your organization's mail servers could be tricked into forwarding SPAM if they are not properly secured. Spammers don't want to send junk mail from their own domains so they troll the Internet looking for open mail relays, which they then use to send junk mail.

LANs and Their Components

A local area network (LAN) is a critical component of a modern data network. A LAN is comprised of one or more computers, a communication protocol, a network topology, and cabling or a wireless network to connect the systems.

A LAN is best defined as computers or other devices that communicate over a small geographical area such as the following:

➤ A section of a one-story building

➤ The whole floor of a small building

➤ Several buildings on a small campus

LAN Communication Protocols

More than 80% of all LANs use the Ethernet protocol as a means of communication. The Ethernet specification describes how data can be sent between computers in physical proximity. The DIX (Digital, Intel, and Xerox) group first released Ethernet in 1975. Since its introduction, the IEEE Standards Committee has introduced several variations of the Ethernet II protocol, including these:

➤ IEEE 802.3

➤ IEEE 802.3 with Logical Link Control (LLC)

➤ IEEE 802.3 with Subnetwork Access Protocol (SNAP)

Although the CISSP exam will not delve very far into the specifics of Ethernet, it is interesting to note the size and structure of these frames. An Ethernet frame is from 64 to 1,518 bytes. The Ethernet frame itself uses 18 bytes for control information; therefore, the data in an Ethernet frame can be between 46 and 1,500 bytes long.

The second most popular LAN networking protocol is Token Ring, which functions by arranging all the systems in a circle. A special packet, known as a token, travels around the circle. If any one device needs to send information, it must capture the token, attach a message to it, and then let it continue to travel around the network.

Network Topologies

The design layout of a network is its topology. Before a network can be installed, a topology must be chosen to match its needs and intended use. Common topologies include bus, star, and ring; each is discussed next.

Bus Topology

A bus topology consists of a single cable with multiple computers or devices attached to it. This cable is terminated on each end. In large environments, this is impractical because the medium has physical limitations. These problems can run the range from low speeds to network outages: One break can bring down the entire network (see Figure 6.1).

Figure 6.1 Bus topology.

Star Topology

This is the oldest of the three primary network topologies and was originally used in telephone systems. The design of a star network consists of multiple computers or devices attached to a central hub. Wires radiate outward from the hub in a starlike pattern. Although this scheme uses the most cable, a break will most like affect only one computer. This is the most widely used LAN topology (see Figure 6.2).

Figure 6.2 Star topology.

Ring Topology

The ring topology is characterized by the fact that there are no endpoints or terminators. Its layout is that of a continuous loop of cable in which all networked computers are attached. Token Ring and Fiber Distributed Data Interface (FDDI) networks use a ring topology (see Figure 6.3).

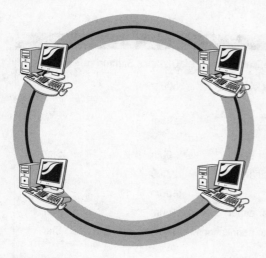

Figure 6.3 Ring topology.

LAN Cabling

Even with a defined topology, it is necessary to determine what type of cable will connect the various devices. Cables carry the electrical signal between the devices. One of two transmissions methods is used: baseband or broadband. Baseband transmissions use a single channel to communicate. Ethernet uses a baseband transmission scheme. Broadband uses many channels and frequencies. Two good examples of broadband are cable television and digital subscriber lines (DSL).

Many types of cables can be used for network communications, including coaxial (coax), twisted-pair, and fiber:

➤ **Coaxial cable**—Coax cable consists of a single solid-copper wire core that uses a braided shield for the second conductor. Both conductors are covered with a plastic or insulative coating. Although it was widely used in the early days of networking, its usage has waned.

➤ **Twisted pair**—If you're in an office, you will probably notice that twisted-pair wiring is being used to connect your computer to a wall jack located nearby. The most common connector is the RJ-45. Twisted pair can be purchased in a multitude of varieties, one of which is unshielded twisted pair (UTP). UTP is unshielded copper wire insulated in plastic that is twisted together. Not only is it easy to work with, but it also is generally inexpensive. The primary drawback to copper cabling is that it is vulnerable to being tapped and emanates electrical energy, which could possibly be intercepted. Table 6.1 specifies many common table types, lengths, and topologies.

Table 6.1 Cable Specification			
Ethernet Name	**Cable Specifications**	**Distance Supported**	**Topology**
10BASE-5	50-ohm, thick coaxial (Thicknet)	500m	Bus
10BASE-2	50-ohm, RG-58 A/U (Thinnet)	185m	Bus
10BASE-T	Cat3 UDP (or better)	100m	Star
10BASE-FL	Multimode fiber optic	2,000m	Star
100BASE-TX	Cat5 UTP	100m	Star
100BASE-T4	Cat3 UTP (or better)	100m	Star
100BASE-FX multimode fiber optic	Multiple-fiber connections	136 meters	Star
100BASE-FX multimode fiber optic	One-fiber connection	160 meters	Star

For the exam, you will want to know that plenum-grade cable is coated with a fire-retardant coating and is designed to be used in crawlspaces, in false ceilings, and below raised floors in a building. This special coating is designed to not give off toxic gasses or smoke as it burns, to help ensure the safety of occupants in case of fire.

➤ **Fiber-optic cable**—Whereas twisted pair and coax rely on copper wire for data transmissions, fiber uses glass. These strands of glass carry light waves that represent the data being transmitted. Basically two types of fiber cables are in use. They are constructed differently to handle different types of light:

➤ **Multimode fiber**—Typically used in LANs and powered by LEDs

➤ **Single-mode fiber**—Typically used in WANs and powered by laser light

You will want to remember that fiber is more secure than copper cable because it does not radiate signals and is extremely difficult to tap.

802.11 Wireless Networking

When is a cable not a cable? When you use wireless for connectivity. Wireless networks have become popular because of their low cost and convenience. It's so much easier to plug in a *wireless access point (WAP)* than to run 1,000 feet of cable. Currently, the standard for wireless networks is 802.11 wireless, which is handled by the Institute of Electrical and Electronic Engineers (IEEE). Although it is not quite as robust as a wired network, 802.11 wireless equipment is generally fast and efficient. There are three primary types:

➤ **802.11a**—This version operates in the 5.15–5.35GHz to 5.725–5.825GHz frequency range and can support speeds of up to 54Mbps.

➤ **802.11b**—Operates in the 2.4000–2.2835GHz frequency range and can reach speeds of up to 11Mbps.

➤ **802.11g**—This popular standard operates in the 2.4GHz frequency range and can support speeds up to 54Mbps.

In North America, 802.11 supports 11 channels. The channel designates the frequency on which the network will operate. European units support 13 channels. Most wireless devices broadcast by using spread-spectrum technology. This method of transmission transmits data over a wide range of radio frequencies. Spread-spectrum technologies include frequency-hopping spread spectrum, an older technology, and sequence spread spectrum. Spread spectrum lessens noise interference and allows data rates to speed up or slow down, depending on the quality of the signal. Obstructions such as walls, doors, and other solid objects tend to block or reduce signal strength.

Unfortunately, many end users who are moving to wireless don't have any appreciation of the security measures they should employ. Using wireless requires little more than powering up the access point and plugging in an active RJ-45 jack.

So, what are some of the technologies used to protect wireless? Originally, there was Wired Equivalent Privacy (WEP), which the IEEE implemented at the data link layer. WEP encrypts data with the RC4 encryption algorithm. The key was limited to 40 bits because of export rules that existed during the late 1990s when the 802.11 protocol was being developed. This provides a very limited level of encryption that is relatively easy to compromise by someone with even a modest understanding of the problem. One way the industry responded to this potential problem was by incorporating 802.1x into many wireless devices. 802.1x provides port-based access control. When used in conjunction with extensible authentication protocol

(EAP), it can be used to authenticate devices that attempt to connect to a specific LAN port.

WEP's sucessor was WiFi Protected Access (WPA). WPA uses Temporal Key Integrity Protocol (TKIP). TKIP scrambles the keys using a hashing algorithm and adds an integrity-checking feature that verifies that the keys haven't been tampered with. In 2004, the IEEE approved the next upgrade to wireless security, WPA2. It is officially known as 802.11.i. This wireless security standard makes use of the Advanced Encryption Standard (AES). Don't be surprised to see key sizes of up to 256 bits, which is a vast improvement over the original 40-bit encryption WEP used.

War driving is the practice of driving around, finding, mapping, and possibly connecting to open wireless networks. Tools such as Netstumbler, Kismit, and AirSnort are used to aid the wardriver.

Bluetooth

Bluetooth technology is designed for short-range wireless communication between mobile and handheld devices. Bluetooth started to grow in popularity in the mid- to late 1990s. Bluetooth was envisioned as a technology that would facilitate for the growth of *personal area networks (PANs)*, which allow a variety of personal and handheld electronic devices to communicate. For example, in a PAN, a cellphone could communicate with a personal digital assistant (PDA) and a laptop. Bluetooth will allow these devices to communicate as they come in range of each other or are activated. The three classifications of Bluetooth are as follows:

➤ **Class 1**—This classification has the longest range (up to 100m) and has 100mW of power.

➤ **Class 2**—Although this classification is not the most popular, it allows transmission of up to 20m and has 2.5mW of power.

➤ **Class 3**—This is the most widely implemented classification. It supports a transmission distance of 10m and has 1mW of power.

Although Bluetooth does have some built-in security features, it has been shown to be vulnerable to attack. At a recent DEFCON security conference, security professionals demonstrated ways to sniff Bluetooth transmissions from up to a half-mile away. Bluetooth operates at a frequency of 2.45GHz and divides the bandwidth into narrow channels to avoid interference with other devices that use the same frequency.

WANS and Their Components

Wide area networks (WANs) are considerably different than LANs. Organizations usually own their own LANs, but WAN services are typically leased; it's not feasible to have your network guy run a cable from New York to Dallas. WANs are concerned with the long-haul transmission of data and connect remote devices; the Internet is a good example of a WAN. WAN data transmissions typically cost more per megabyte than LAN transmissions. WAN technologies can be divided into two broad categories: *packet switching* and *circuit switching*.

Packet Switching

Packet-switched networks share bandwidth with other devices. Packet-switched networks divide data into packets and frames. These packets are individually routed among various network nodes at the provider's discretion. They are considered more resilient than circuit-switched networks and work well for on-demand connections with bursty traffic. Each packet takes the most expedient route, which means they might not all arrive in order or at the same time. Packet switching is a form of connectionless networking.

X.25

X.25 is one of the original packet-switching technologies. Although it is not fast, with speeds up to 56Kbps, it is reliable and works over analog phone lines.

Frame Relay

Frame Relay is a virtual circuit-switched network. It is a kind of streamlined version of X.25. Frame Relay controls bandwidth use with a *committed information rate (CIR)*. The CIR specifies the maximum guaranteed bandwidth that the customer is promised. The customer can send more data than is specified in the CIR if additional bandwidth is available. If there is additional bandwidth, the data will pass; otherwise, the data is marked discard eligibility (DE) and is discarded. Frame Relay can use *permanent virtual circuits (PVCs)* or *switched virtual circuits (SVCs)*. A PVC is used to provide a dedicated connection between two locations. A SVC works much like a phone call, in that the connection is set up on a per-call basis and is disconnected when the call is completed. Switched virtual circuits are good for teleconferencing, for phone calls, and when data transmission is sporadic.

Asynchronous Transfer Mode (ATM)

ATM is a cell-switching-based physical-layer protocol. It supports high-bandwidth data needs and works well for time-sensitive applications. Because the switching process occurs in hardware, delays are minimized. ATM uses a fixed 53-byte cell size. ATM can be implemented on LANs or WANs.

ATM is being surpassed by newer technologies, such as *Multiprotocol Label Switching Architecture (MPLS)*. MPLS designers recognized that data didn't need to be converted into 53-byte cells. MPLS packets can be much larger than ATM cells. MPLS can provide traffic engineering and allows VPNs to be created without end-user applications.

Voice over IP (VoIP)

VoIP is carried on packet-switched networks in IP packets. Networks that have been configured to carry VoIP treat voice communications as just another form of data. Companies are moving to VoIP because of major cost savings. However, using VoIP is not without risks; as a network service, it is vulnerable in some of the same ways as other data traffic. Attackers can intercept the traffic, hack the VoIP server, or launch a DoS attack against the VoIP server and cause network outages. Another consideration is that the vulnerabilities of the operating system that the VoIP application is running on are inherited.

Circuit Switching

Circuit switching comes in either analog or digital configurations. Today the most common form of circuit switching is the *Plain Old Telephone Service (POTS)*, but *Integrated Services Digital Network (ISDN)*, *T-carriers*, and *digital subscriber line (DSL)* are also options.

Plain Old Telephone Service (POTS)

POTS is a voice-grade analog telephone service used for voice calls and for connecting to the Internet and other locations via modem. Modem speeds can vary from 9600bps to 56Kbps. Although the POTS service is relatively inexpensive and widely available, it offers only low data speeds.

Integrated Services Digital Network (ISDN)

ISDN is a communication protocol that operates similarly to POTS, except that all digital signaling is used. Although it was originally planned as a replacement for POTS, it was not hugely successful. ISDN uses separate frequencies called *channels* on a special digital connection. It consists of B channels used for voice, data, video, and fax services, and a D channel used for signaling by the service provider and user equipment. Keeping the D signaling data separate makes it harder for attackers to manipulate the service. The D channel operates at a low 16Kbps; the B channels operate at a speed up to 64Kbps. By binding the B channels together, ISDN can achieve higher speeds. ISDN is available in two levels: Basic Rate Interface (BRI) 128Kbps and Primary Rate Interface (PRI) 1.544Mbps.

T-Carriers

T-carrier service is used for leased lines. A leased line is locked in between two locations. It is very secure, but users pay a fixed monthly fee for this service, regardless of use. The most common T-carrier is a T1. A T1 uses time-division multiplexing and consists of 24 digital signal 0 (DS0) channels. Each DS0 channel is capable of transmitting 64Kbps of data; therefore, a T1 can provide a composite rate of 1.544Mbps. T3s are the next available choice. A T3 is made up of 672 DS0s and has a composite data rate of 45Mbps. For those who don't need a full T1 or a full T3, fractional service is available. A fractional T-line is just a portion of the entire carrier. Table 6.2 details common T-carrier specifications and contrasts them with POTS, ISDN, and DSL.

Table 6.2	T-Carrier Specifications	
Service	**Characteristics**	**Maximum Speed**
POTS dial-up service	Switch line; widely used	56Kbps
ISDN BRI digital	Requires a terminal adaptor; can be costly	128Kbps
ISDN PRI digital	Requires a terminal adaptor; can be costly	1.54Mbps
DSL	Typically asymmetric; downloads faster than uploads	up to 52Mbps
T1	Dedicated leased line; 24 bundled phone lines	1.54Mbps
T3	Dedicated leased line; 28 bundled T1s	44.736Mbps

Digital Subscriber Line (DSL)

DSL is another circuit-switching connectivity option. Most DSLs are asymmetric, which means that the download speed is much faster than the upload speed. The theory is that you usually download more than you upload.

DSL modems are always connected to the Internet; therefore, you do not have to dial in to make a connection. As long as your computer is powered on, it is connected to the Internet and is ready to transmit and receive data. This is the primary security concern of DSL. Unlike the usual lengthy connection time used for dial-up service, no waiting time is involved. An advantage of the DSL is that it maintains more of a fixed speed than cable modems typically do. Table 6.3 details the different DSL types.

Table 6.3	DSL Types and Speeds		
Name	Data Rate	Mode	Distance
IDSL (Internet digital subscriber line)	160Kbps	Duplex	18,000 ft., 24AWG
HDSL (High-data-rate digital subscriber line)	1.544Mbps 2.048Mbps	Duplex Duplex	12,000 ft., 24 AWG
SDSL (Symmetric digital subscriber line)	1.544Mbps 2.048Mbps	Duplex Duplex	10,000 ft., 24 AWG
ADSL (Asymmetrical digital subscriber line)	1.5–9Mbps 16–640Kbps	Down Up	9,000–18,000 ft., 24 AWG
VDSL (Very-high-data-rate digital subscriber line)	13–52Mbps 1.5–2.3Mbps	Down Up	1,000–4,500 ft., 24 AWG

Cable Modems

Cable Internet access refers to the delivery of Internet access over the cable television infrastructure. The Internet connection is made through the same coaxial cable that delivers the television signal to your home. The coaxial cable connects to a special cable modem that demultiplexes the TCP/IP traffic. This always-on Internet connection is a big security issue if no firewall is used. One of the weaknesses of cable Internet access is that there is a shared amount of bandwidth among many users. Cable companies control the maximum data rate of the subscriber by capping the maximum data rate. Some unscrupulous individuals attempt to uncap their line to obtain higher speeds. *Uncappers* are almost always caught and can be prosecuted because cable Internet providers check for this daily.

Another lingering concern is that of the loss of confidentiality. Individuals have worried about the possibility of sniffing attacks. Most cable companies have addressed this issue by implementing the Data Over Cable Service Interface Specification (DOCSIS) standard. The DOCSIS standard specifies encryption and other security mechanisms that prevent sniffing and protect privacy.

Network Models and Standards

Network models and standards play an important role in the telecommunications industry. You have already seen how standards for services such as DSL, ATM, 802.11 wireless, Bluetooth, and others make it much easier for developers to design interoperable equipment, ease the burden of networking, and develop security solutions. Two of the most widely discussed network models are discussed in the following sections. In case you haven't guessed, these are the Open Systems Interconnect (OSI) model and the Transmission Control Protocol/Internet Protocol (TCP/IP) model.

OSI Model

The International Standards Organization (ISO) developed the Open Systems Interconnect (OSI) model in 1984. The model is based on a specific hierarchy in which each layer builds upon the output of each adjacent layer. It is described in ISO 7498. Today it is widely used as a guide in describing the operation of a networking environment. What was once considered the universal communications standard now serves as a teaching model for all other protocols.

The OSI model is designed so that control is passed down from layer to layer. Information is put into the application layer and ends at the physical layer. Then it is transmitted over the medium—wire, coax, wireless—toward the target device and then back up the stack to the application. The seven layers of the OSI model are the application, presentation, session, transport, network, data link, and physical layers. Most people remember this order by using one of the many acronyms that have been thought up over the years. My favorite one is based on the popular television show *American Idol*: "**P**eople **D**on't **N**eed **T**o **S**ee **P**aula Abdul." For a better understanding of how the OSI model works, we'll start at the bottom of the stack and work our way up. The OSI model is shown on Figure 6.4.

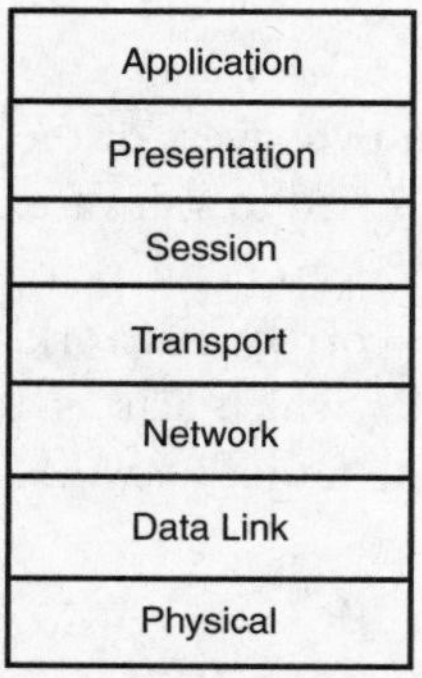

Application
Presentation
Session
Transport
Network
Data Link
Physical

Figure 6.4   OSI model.

Physical Layer

Layer 1 is known as the physical layer. At Layer 1, bit-level communication takes place. The bits have no defined meaning on the wire, but the physical layer defines how long each bit lasts and how it is transmitted and received. Physical-layer components include these:

➤ Copper cabling

➤ Fiber cabling

➤ Wireless system components

➤ Wall jacks and connectors

➤ Ethernet hubs

Data Link Layer

Layer 2 is known as the data link layer. It is focused on traffic within a single LAN. The data link layer is responsible for formatting and organizing the data before sending it to the physical layer. The data link layer organizes the data into frames. A *frame* is a logical structure in which data can be placed. When a frame reaches the target device, the data link layer is responsible for stripping off the data frame and passing the data packet up to the network layer. Data-link–layer components include these:

➤ Bridges

➤ Switches

➤ NIC cards

➤ MAC addresses

Network Layer

Layer 3 is known as the network layer. Whereas the bottom two layers of the OSI model are associated with hardware, the network layer is tied to software. This layer is concerned with how data moves from network A to network B; it makes sure frames from the data link layer reach the correct network. The network layer is the home of the Internet Protocol (IP), which acts as a postman in determining the best route from the source to the target network. Network-layer components include the following:

➤ Routers

➤ Firewalls/packet filters

Transport Layer

Layer 4 is known as the transport layer. Whereas the network layer routes information to its destination, the transport layer ensures completeness by handling end-to-end error recovery and flow control. Transport-layer protocols include these:

➤ TCP, a connection-oriented protocol. It provides reliable communication through the use of handshaking, acknowledgments, error detection, and session teardown.

➤ UDP (User Datagram Protocol), a connectionless protocol. It offers speed and low overhead as its primary advantage.

Session Layer

Layer 5 is known as the session layer. Its purpose is to allow two applications on different computers to establish and coordinate a session. A session is simply a name for a connection between two computers. When a data transfer is complete, the session layer is responsible for tearing down the session. Session-layer protocols include these:

➤ Remote Procedure Call

➤ Structured Query Language

Presentation Layer

Layer 6 is known as the presentation layer. The presentation layer performs a job similar to that of a waiter in a restaurant: Its main purpose is to deliver and present data to the application layer. In performing its job, the data must be formatted in a way that the application layer can understand and interpret the data. The presentation layer is skilled in translation because its duties include encrypting data, changing, or converting the character set and handling protocol conversion.

Encapsulation is the process of adding headers to user data as it is handed from each layer to the next lower layer.

Application Layer

Layer 7 is known as the application layer. Recognized as the top layer of the OSI model, this layer serves as the window for application services. This is the layer we, as users, work with. We send email or surf the Web and many times never think about all the underling processes that make it possible. Layer 7 is not the application itself, but rather the channel through which applications communicate.

TCP/IP

TCP/IP is the foundation of the Internet as we know it today. Its roots can be traced back to standards adopted by the U.S. government's Department of Defense (DoD) in 1982. TCP/IP is similar to the OSI model, but it consists of only four layers: the network access layer, the Internet layer, the host-to-host layer, and the application layer.

It is of critical importance to remember that the TCP/IP model was originally developed as a flexible, fault-tolerant network. Security was not the driving concern. The network was designed to these specifications to withstand a nuclear strike that might destroy key routing nodes. The designers of this original network never envisioned the Internet we use today. Therefore, most of TCP/IP is insecure, and many of the security mechanisms in use today are add-ons to the original protocol suite.

Network Access Layer

The network access layer loosely corresponds to Layers 1 and 2 of the OSI model. Some literature separates this layer into two and references them as physical access and data link. Whether viewed as one layer or two, this portion of the TCP/IP network model is responsible for the physical delivery of IP packets via frames.

Ethernet is the most commonly used LAN frame type. Ethernet frames are addressed with MAC addresses, which identify the source and destination devices. MAC addresses are 6 bytes long and are unique to the NIC card in which they are burned. Programs are available that allow attackers to spoof MAC addresses.

Internet Layer

The Internet layer maps to OSI Layer 3. This layer contains the information needed to make sure that data can be routed through an IP network and that the network can differentiate hosts. Currently, most organizations use IPv4. IPv6 is its planned replacement, with better security and support for 128-bit IP addresses instead of the current 32-bit addresses. IPv4 uses a logical address scheme or IP address. Whereas MAC addresses are considered a physical address, an IP address is considered a logical address. IP addresses are laid out in dotted-decimal notation format. The IPv4 address format is four decimal numbers separated by decimal points. Each of these decimal numbers is 1 byte in length, to allow numbers to range from 0 to 255.

➤ **Class A networks**—Consist of up to 16,777,214 client devices. Their address range can extend from 1 to 126.

➤ **Class B networks**—Host up to 65,534 client devices. Their address range can extend from 128 to 191.

➤ **Class C networks**—Can have a total of 245 devices. Their address range can extend from 192 to 223.

➤ **Class D networks**—Reserved for multicasting. Their address range can extend from 224 to 239.

➤ **Class E networks**—Reserved for experimental purposes. Their addresses range from 240 to 254.

Not all of the addresses shown can be used on the Internet. Some addresses are reserved for private use and are considered nonroutable. These addresses include the following:

➤ Class A: 10.0.0.0

➤ Class B: 172.16.0.0 to 172.31.0.0

➤ Class C: 192.168.0.0 to 192.168.255.0

IP security issues include fragmentation, source routing, and DoS attacks, such as a teardrop. The Internet layer contains not only the Internet Protocol (IP), but also Internet Control Message Protocol (ICMP), Address Resolution Protocol (ARP), and the Internet Group Management Protocol (IGMP). ICMP and IGMP are IP support, error, and diagnostic protocols that handle problems such as error messages and multicast messages. ARP is used to resolve unknown MAC addresses to known IP addresses.

IP addresses are required because physical addressees are tied to the physical topology used. Some LANs use Ethernet, but others are connected to ATM or Token Ring networks. Because no common format or structure exists, the IP protocol is used to bind these dissimilar networks together.

Internet Control Message Protocol (ICMP)

One of the protocols residing at the Internet layer is ICMP. Its purpose is to provide feedback used for diagnostics or to report logical errors. Even though ICMP resides at the Internet layer, it is a separate protocol and is distinctly different from IP.

All ICMP messages follow the same basic format. The first byte of an ICMP header indicates the type of ICMP message. The following byte contains the code for each particular type of ICMP. Eight of the most common ICMP types are shown in Table 6.4.

Table 6.4	ICMP Types and Codes	
Type	**Code**	**Function**
0/8	0	Echo Response/Request (Ping)
3	0–15	Destination Unreachable
4	0	Source Quench
5	0–3	Redirect
11	0–1	Time Exceeded
12	0	Parameter Fault
13/14	0	Time Stamp Request/Response
17/18	0	Subnet Mask Request/Response

One of the most common ICMP types is a ping. Although ICMP can be very helpful, it is also valued by attackers and can be manipulated and used for a variety of attacks, including the ping of death, Smurf, timestamp query, netmask query, source routing, and redirects.

Address Resolution Protocol (ARP)

ARP's two-step resolution process is performed by first sending a broadcast message requesting the target's physical address. If a device recognizes the address as its own, it issues an ARP reply containing its MAC address to the original sender. The MAC address is then placed in the ARP cache and used to address subsequent frames. Proxy ARPs can be used to extend a network and allow one device to communicate with a device on an adjunct node. Attackers can manipulate ARP because it is a trusting protocol. Bogus ARP responses are accepted as valid, which can allow attackers to redirect traffic on a switched network. ARP attacks play a role in a variety of man-in-the-middle attacks, spoofing, and session-hijack attacks.

 Remember that ARP is unauthenticated. Therefore, an attacker can send unsolicited ARP replies, poison the ARP table, and spoof another host.

Host-to-Host Layer

The host-to-host layer corresponds to OSI Layers 4 and 5. The host-to-host layer provides end-to-end delivery. Two primary protocols are located at the host-to-host layer: the Transmission Control Protocol (TCP) and User Datagram Protocol (UDP).

TCP

TCP enables two hosts to establish a connection and exchange data reliably. TCP does this by performing a three-step handshake before data is sent. During the data-transmission process, TCP guarantees delivery of data by using sequence and acknowledgment numbers. At the completion of the data-transmission process, TCP performs a four-step shutdown that gracefully concludes the session. At the heart of TCP is a 1-byte flag field. Flags help control the TCP process. Common flags include synchronize (SYN), acknowledgment (ACK), push (PSH), and finish (FIN). See Figure 6.5 for additional details on the flags and the startup/shutdown process. TCP security issues include TCP sequence number attacks, session hijacking, and SYN flood attacks.

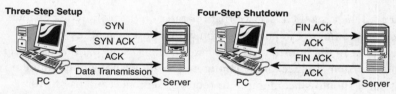

Figure 6.5 TCP operation.

UDP

UDP performs none of the handshaking processes that we see performed with TCP. So although that makes it considerably less reliable than TCP, it does offer the benefit of speed. It is ideally suited for data that requires fast delivery and is not sensitive to packet loss but is easier to spoof by attackers because it does not use sequence and acknowledgment numbers. Figure 6.6 details the operation of UDP.

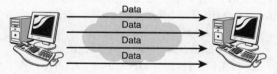

Figure 6.6 UDP operation.

Application Layer

The application layer sits at the top of the protocol stack and maps loosely to OSI Layers 6 and 7. This layer is responsible for application support. Applications are typically mapped not by name, but by their corresponding port. Ports are placed into TCP and UDP packets so the correct application can be passed to the required protocols. Although applications can be made to operate on nonstandard ports, the established port numbers serve as the de facto standard. There are approximately 65,000 ports, divided into well-known ports (0–1024), registered ports (1024–49151), and dynamic ports (49152–65535). Some well-known applications and their associated ports are as follows:

➤ **File Transfer Protocol (FTP)**—FTP is a TCP service and operates on ports 20 and 21. This application is used to move files from one computer to another. Port 20 is used for the data stream and transfers the data between the client and the server. Port 21 is the control stream and is used to pass commands between the client and the FTP server. Attacks on FTP target misconfigured directory permissions and compromised or sniffed clear-text passwords. FTP is one of the most commonly hacked services.

➤ **Telnet**—Telnet is a TCP service that operates on port 23. Telnet enables a client at one site to establish a session with a host at another site. The program passes the information typed at the client's keyboard to the host computer system. Telnet can be configured to allow anonymous connections, but it should be configured to require usernames and passwords. Unfortunately, even then, Telnet sends them in clear text. When a user is logged in, he or she can perform any allowed task. Applications such as Secure Shell (SSH) should be considered as a replacement.

➤ **Simple Mail Transfer Protocol (SMTP)**—This application is a TCP service that operates on port 25. It is designed for the exchange of electronic mail between networked systems. Messages sent through SMTP have two parts: an address header and the message text. All types of computers can exchange messages with SMTP. Spoofing and spamming are two of the vulnerabilities associated with SMTP.

➤ **Domain Name Service (DNS)**—This application operates on port 53 and performs address translation. DNS converts fully qualified domain names (FQDNs) into numeric IP addresses, or IP addresses into FQDNs. This system works similar to a phone directory, which enables users to remember domain names (such as examcram2.com) instead of IP addresses (such as 114.112.18.23). DNS uses UDP for DNS queries and TCP for zone transfers. DNS is subject to poisoning and, if misconfigured, can be solicited to perform a full zone transfer.

➤ **Trivial File Transfer Protocol (TFTP)**—TFTP operates on port 69. It is considered a down-and-dirty version of FTP because it uses UDP to cut down on overhead. It not only does so without the session management offered by TCP, but it also requires no authentication, which could pose a big security risk. It is used to transfer router-configuration files and to configure cable modems for cable companies.

➤ **Hypertext Transfer Protocol (HTTP)**—HTTP is a TCP service that operates on port 80. This application is one of the most well known. HTTP has helped make the Web the popular protocol it is today. The HTTP connection model is known as a stateless connection. HTTP uses a request-response protocol in which a client sends a request and a server sends a response. Attacks that exploit HTTP can target the server, a browser, or scripts that run on the browser. Nimda is an example of code that targeted a web server.

➤ **Simple Network Management Protocol (SNMP)**—SNMP is a UDP service and operates on ports 161 and 162. It was envisioned to be an efficient and inexpensive way to monitor networks. The SNMP protocol allows agents to gather information, including network statistics, and report back to their management stations. Most large corporations have implemented some type of SNMP management. Some of the security problems that plague SNMP are caused by the fact that community strings can be passed as clear text and that the default community strings (public/private) are well known. SNMP version 3 is the most current and offers encryption for more robust security.

Network Equipment

Telecommunications equipment is all the hardware used to move data between networked devices. This equipment can be used in a LAN or WAN. This is important to know not only from a networking standpoint, but also to better implement security solutions and pass the CISSP exam.

Hubs

Hubs are one of the most basic networking devices. A hub allows all the connected devices to communicate with one another. A hub is logically a common wire to which all computers have shared access.

Hubs have fallen out of favor because of their low maximum throughput. Whenever two or more systems attempt to send packets at the same time on the same hub, there is a collision. As utilization increases the number of collisions skyrockets and the overall average throughput decreases.

Bridges

Another somewhat outdated piece of equipment is a bridge. Bridges are semi-intelligent pieces of equipment that have the capability to separate collision domains. Bridges examine frames and look up the MAC address. If the device tied to that MAC address is determined to be local, the bridge blocks the traffic. One of the big problems with bridges is that, by default, they pass broadcast traffic. Too much broadcast traffic can effectively flood the network and cause a broadcast storm.

 Don't spend too much time worrying about hubs and bridges—just know their basic purpose and that they have been replaced by switches.

Switches

A switch performs in much the same way as a hub; however, switches are considered intelligent devices. Switches segment traffic by observing the source and destination MAC address of each data frame.

The switch stores the MAC addresses by placing them in a lookup table, which is located in random access memory (RAM). This lookup table also contains the information needed to match each MAC address to the corresponding port it is connected to. When the data frame enters the switch, it finds the target MAC address in the lookup table and matches it to the switch port the computer is attached to. The frame is forwarded to only that switch port; therefore, computers on all other ports never see the traffic. Some advantages of a switch are as follows:

➤ Provides higher-layer independence

➤ Provides higher throughput than a hub

➤ Provides virtual LAN (VLAN) capability

➤ Can be configured for full duplex

Not all switches are made the same. Switches can process an incoming frame in three ways:

➤ **Store-and-forward**—After the frame is completely inputted into the switch, the destination MAC is analyzed to make a block or forward decision.

➤ **Cut-through**—This faster design is similar to the store-and-forward switch, but it focuses on examining only the first 6 bytes.

➤ **Fragment Free**—This is a Cisco design that has a lower error rate.

Routers

Routers reside at Layer 3 of the OSI model. Routers are usually associated with the IP protocol, which, as previously discussed, sends blocks of data that have been formatted into packets. IP is considered a "best effort" protocol, and IP packets are examined and processed by routers. Routers are used to join similar or dissimilar networks. A router's primary purpose is to forward IP packets toward their destination through a process known as routing. Whereas bridges and switches examined the physical frame, routers focus on what information is found in the IP header. One important item in the IP header that routers examine is the IP address. IP addresses are considered a logical address. Routers can also be used to improve performance by limiting physical broadcast domains, act as a limited type of firewall by filtering with *access control lists (ACLs)*, and ease network management by segmenting devices into smaller subnets instead of one large network. The security of the router is paramount. A compromised router can have devastating consequences, especially if it is being used for other services, such as IPSec, a virtual private network (VPN) termination point, or a firewall.

Each time a router is presented with packets, the router must examine the packets and determine the proper interface to forward the packets to. Not all routing protocols that routers work with function in the same manner. Routing protocols can be divided into two broad categories:

➤ Algorithms based on distance-vector protocols

➤ Algorithms based on link-state protocols

Distance-vector protocols are based on Bellman-Ford algorithms. The basic methodology of a distance-vector protocol is to find the best route by determining the shortest path. The shortest path is commonly calculated by hops. Distance-vector routing is also called *routing by rumor*. The Routing Information Protocol (RIP) is probably the most common distance-vector protocol in use. One major shortcoming of distance-vector protocols is that the path with the lowest number of hops might not be the optimal route; the path with the lowest hop count could have considerable less bandwidth than a route with a higher hop count.

Distance-vector protocols such as RIP can be spoofed and are subject to redirection. It also easy for attackers to sniff RIP updates. RIP sends out complete routing tables every 30 seconds.

Link-state protocols are based on Dijkstra algorithms. Unlike distance-vector protocols, link-state protocols determine the best path with metrics such as delay or bandwidth. When this path is determined, the router informs other routers of its findings. This is how reliable routing tables are developed and routing tables reach convergence.

Link-state routing is considered more robust than distance-vector routing protocols. Open Shortest Path First (OSPF) is probably the most common link-state routing protocol; many times, it is used as a replacement for RIP.

Common routing protocols include these:

➤ **Routing Information Protocol (RIP)**—Legacy UDP-based routing protocol that does not use authentication and determines path by hop count.

➤ **Open Shortest Path First (OSPF)**—An improved link-state routing protocol that offers authentication.

➤ **Border Gateway Protocol (BGP)**—The core routing protocol used by the Internet. It is based on TCP and is used to connect autonomous systems.

Access Methods and Remote Connectivity

Well-designed networks will always require authentication and access control. You might be internal to the organization or on the road in a hotel. Being outside the organization raises other concerns besides proper authentication, such as confidentiality and privacy. This section discusses an array of topics, including the Password Authentication Protocol (PAP), the Challenge Handshake Authentication Protocol (CHAP), virtual private networks (VPNs), and IP Security (IPSec).

Point-to-Point Protocol (PPP)

PPP is the most commonly used protocol for dial-up connections. It can run on a line of any speed, from POTS to T1. Developed in 1994 by the IETF, PPP is a replacement to Serial Line IP (SLIP). SLIP is capable of carrying only IP and had no error detection, whereas PPP supports many types of authentication, including PAP, CHAP, and EAP.

Password Authentication Protocol (PAP)

This authentication protocol uses a two-way handshake to authenticate a client to a server when a link is initially established. PAP is vulnerable because it sends the password in clear text, which makes it highly vulnerable to sniffing attacks.

Challenge Handshake Authentication Protocol (CHAP)

CHAP is an improved version of the PAP protocol. It uses a three-way handshake to authenticate both the client and the server. The server uses MD5 to encrypt the challenge with the password stored in its database. The client is also sent the challenge, which it combines with the entered password. This hashed value is returned to the server for comparison. No plain text ever crosses the network. MS-CHAP is an improved version of CHAP that goes a step further by storing the clear-text password in an encrypted form.

Extensible Authentication Protocol (EAP)

EAP makes PPP more robust by adding the capability to implement different types of authentication mechanisms, including digital certificates, token cards, and MD5-Challenge. EAP is used in by 802.11i wireless LAN security protocols such as WPA to authenticate an end user or device. When used in this manner, the wireless access point initiates the EAP protocol. EAP can then negotiate an encryption key, called the *pair-wise master key (PMK)*. When the key has been established, it can be used by the Advanced Encryption Standard (AES) or the Temporal Key Integrity Protocol (TKIP) to encrypt the communication session.

EAP can be implemented in many different ways, including EAP-MD5, EAP-TLS, EAP-SIM, LEAP, PEAP-MSCHAP, and PEAP-GTC. The goal is not for you to memorize each of these in detail, but to understand that, as a CISSP, you must be able to select the appropriate protocol, depending on the policy established for authentication strength.

Virtual Private Networks (VPNs)

VPNs are used to connect devices through the public Internet. Their primary benefit is that they offer a cost advantage over private lines and T1s by providing the same capabilities as a private network at a much lower cost. The big concern with a VPN is privacy; after all, you're sending your company's traffic over the public Internet. Three protocols are used to provide VPN functionality and security: the Point-to-Point Tunneling Protocol (PPTP), the Layer 2 Tunneling Protocol (L2TP), and Internet Security (IPSec).

When an appropriate protocol is defined, the VPN traffic can be tunneled through the Internet. Two types of tunnels can be implemented:

➤ **LAN-to-LAN tunnels**—Users can tunnel transparently to each other on separate LANS.

➤ **Client-to-LAN tunnels**—Mobile users can connect to the corporate LAN.

Having a tunnel is just one part of establishing communication. Another important concept is that of authentication. Almost all VPNs use digital certificates serve as the primary means of authentication. X.509 v3 is the de facto standard. X.509 specifies certificate requirements and their contents. Much like that of a state driver's license office, the Certificate Authority guarantees the authenticity of the certificate and its contents. These certificates act as an approval mechanism.

Just as with other services, organizations need to develop policies to define who will have access to the VPN and how the VPN will be configured. It's important that VPN policies be designed to map to the organization's security policy. Senior management must approve and support this policy.

Remote Authentication Dial-in User Service (RADIUS)

RADIUS was designed for dial-up users and typically used a modem pool to connect to the organization's network. Because of the features RADIUS offers, it is now used for more than just dial-up users. Enterasys uses it for secure network products, and WAPs and 802.11i also widely use it. A RADIUS server contains usernames, passwords, and other information to validate the user. RADIUS is a well-known UDP-based authentication and accountability protocol. Information is passed to RADIUS using PAP or CHAP. The RADIUS client then encrypts the information and sends it to the RADIUS server to be authenticated.

Terminal Access Controller Access Control System (TACACS)

TACACS is an access-control protocol used to authenticate a user logging onto a network. TACACS is a UDP-based protocol that provides authentication, authorization, and accountability. It was originally used in Cisco devices. TACACS is very similar to RADIUS. When TACACS receives an authentication request, it forwards the received username and password to a central database. This database verifies the information received and returns it to TACACS to allow or deny access based on the results. The fundamental reason TACACS did not become popular is because TACACS is a proprietary solution from Cisco, and its use would require the payment of royalties. TACACS+, which is neither proprietary nor compatible with TACACS, was introduced in 1990. TACACS+ is TCP based and offers extended two-factor authentication.

IPSec

IPSec was developed to provide security for IP packets. Without IPSec, someone could capture, read, or change the contents of data packets and then send them back to the unsuspecting target. The current version of IP, IPv4, supports IPSec as an add-on; IPv6 has IPSec built in. IPSec offers its users several levels of cryptographic security:

➤ **Authentication header (AH)**—Protects data against modification; does not provide privacy

➤ **Encapsulating security payload (ESP)**—Provides privacy and protects against malicious modification

➤ **Internet key exchange (IKE)**—Allows secret keys to be exchanged securely before communications begin

Because IPSec can be applied below the application layer, any application can use it. IPSec has two modes of operation:

➤ **Transport mode**—Functions as a host-to-host connection involving only two machines, which protects just the payload.

➤ **Tunnel mode**—Protects the payload and the header. In this configuration, IPSec acts as a gateway; traffic for any number of client computers can be carried.

Message Privacy

New technologies make it possible to monitor all types of information that one individual might send to another. *Carnivore* is one example of such a technology. This controversial program was developed by the Federal Bureau of Investigation (FBI) to give the U.S. government the ability to monitor the Internet and email activities of suspected criminals.

Some Internet applications have little or no built-in security. *Instant messaging (IM)* is a good example. Many corporations allow or use IM, but it was built for chatting, not security. Most IM applications lack encryption capabilities, have insecure password management, and have features that actively work to bypass firewalls. IM can be vulnerable to sniffing attacks, can be used to spread viruses and worms, and can be targeted for buffer overflow attacks.

Standard email is also very insecure. Sending an email message is much like sending a postcard to Mom through the U.S. Mail. Anyone who happens to see the card during transit can read the message you sent her from your trip to Niagara Falls. If you need a little privacy, you must use encryption. Using encryption is the equivalent of sending a letter: The sealed envelope will prevent the casual snoop from learning about your trip to Niagara Falls. Email protection mechanisms include Pretty Good Privacy (PGP), Secure Multipurpose Internet Mail Extensions (S/MIME), and Privacy Enhanced Mail (PEM).

PGP

Phil Zimmerman initially developed Pretty Good Privacy (PGP) in 1991 as a free email security application. It is as close to military grade encryption as a private individual can get and works well at securing email. Unlike public key infrastructure (PKI), PGP works by using a web of trust. Users distribute and sign their own public keys. Unlike the PKI certificate authority, this web of trust requires users to determine how much they trust the other parties they exchange keys with. PGP is a hybrid cryptosystem, in that it uses both public and private encryption. Some of the algorithms PGP can use include Triple DES and Twofish for symmetric encryption, and Diffie-Hellman, Digital Signature Standard (DSS), and RSA for asymmetric encryption.

S/MIME

Secure Multipurpose Internet Mail Extensions (S/MIME) secures email by using X.509 certificates for authentication. The public key cryptographic standard is used to provide encryption. It can work in one of two modes: signed and enveloped. Signing mode provides integrity and authentication. Enveloped mode provides confidentiality, authentication, and integrity.

Privacy Enhanced Mail (PEM)

PEM is an older email security standard. It provides encryption, authentication, and X.509 certificate-based key management.

Network Access Controls

Security should be implemented in layers to erect several barriers against attackers. One good example of a network access control is a firewall. The firewall can act as a choke point to control traffic as it ingresses and egresses the network. Another network access control is the DMZ, which establishes a safe zone for internal and external users to meet.

Firewalls

It's a sad fact that we need firewalls. Just as in the real world, some individuals enjoy destroying other people's property. A *firewall* is a computer, router, or software component implemented to control access to a protected network. It enables organizations to protect their network and control traffic.

Packet Filters

Packet filters are devices that filter traffic based on IP addresses. Savvy hackers use spoofing tools and other programs that are easily available on the Internet to bypass packet filters. The first firewalls ever implemented were packet filters. These devices inspect the TCP/IP headers and make a decision based on a set of predefined rules. Packet filters simply drop packets that do not conform to the predefined rule set. These devices are considered stateless. Packet filters are configured by compiling an access control list (ACL). ACLs can include IP addresses, protocol types, TCP ports, and UDP ports.

NAT

Network Address Translation (NAT) was originally developed because of the explosive growth of the Internet and the increase in home and business networks; the number of available IP addresses is simply not enough. NAT allows a single device, such as a router, to act as an agent between the Internet and the local network. This device or router provides a pool of addresses to be used by your local network. Only a single, unique IP address is required to represent this entire group of computers. The outside world is unaware of this division and thinks that only one computer is connected. NAT can provide a limited amount of security because it can hide internal addresses from external systems. When *private addressing* is used, NAT is a requirement. Otherwise, packets with private IP addresses cannot be routed to external IP addresses, and external traffic cannot be routed into the NAT'ed network. RFC 1918 defines the three ranges of private addresses on the 10.0.0.0, 172.16.0.0, and 192.168.0.0 network ranges.

Common types of NAT include these:

➤ **Static NAT**—Uses a one-to-one mapping between public and private IP addresses.

➤ **Dynamic NAT**—Uses a pool of public addresses. When internal devices need Internet connectivity, they are mapped to the next available public address. When the communication session is complete, the public address is returned to the pool.

➤ **Port Address Translation (PAT)**—Most home networks using DSL or cable modems use this type of NAT. It is designed to provide many internal users Internet access through one external address.

Stateful Firewalls

Stateful firewalls keep track of every communication channel by means of a state table. Because of this, they are considered an intelligent firewall. They're part of the third generation of firewall design. Packet filters do not have this capability. Remember that models addressed here, such as stateful inspection and proxies, are theoretical, so most vendors products will not match perfectly to one design.

Proxy Servers

By definition, the word *proxy* means "to stand in place of." Therefore, a *proxy* is a hardware or software device that can perform address translation and that communicates with the Internet on behalf of the network. The real IP address of the user remains hidden behind the proxy server. The proxy server can also be configured to filter higher-layer traffic to determine whether the traffic is allowed to pass. Proxy servers offer increased security because they don't allow untrusted systems to have a direct connection to internal computers. Proxy servers function as follows: They accept packets from the external network, copy the packets, inspect them for irregularities, change the addresses to the correct internal device, and then put them back on the wire to the destination device. Other types of proxies include these:

➤ **Application-level proxy**—Not all proxies are made the same. Application-level proxies inspect the entire packet and then make a decision based on what was discovered while inspecting the contents. This method is very thorough and slow. For the application-level proxy to work correctly, it must understand the protocols and applications it is working with.

 An application proxy provides a high level of security and offers a very granular level of control. Its disadvantages include that it could break some applications and can be a performance bottleneck.

➤ **Circuit-level proxy**—A circuit-level proxy closely resembles a packet-filtering device, in that it makes decisions on addresses, ports, and protocols. It does not care about higher-layer applications, so it works for a wider range of protocols but doesn't provide the depth of security that an application-level proxy does.

➤ **SOCKS**—SOCKS takes the proxy servers concept to the next level. SOCKS must be deployed as a client and server solution. It provides a secure channel between the two devices. It examines individual applications to determine whether they are allowed access. Common SOCKS applications include these:

➤ **FTP**—Blocks or allows files to be transferred into or out of the network

➤ **HTTP**—Blocks or allows Internet access

➤ **SMTP**—Blocks or allows email

Demilitarized Zone (DMZ)

In the computer world, the DMZ prevents outsiders from getting direct access to internal services. DMZs are typically set up to allow external users access to services within the DMZ. Basically, shared services such as Internet, email, and DNS might be placed within a DMZ. The DMZ provides no other access to services located within the internal network. If an attacker is able to penetrate and hack computers within the DMZ, no internal computers would be accessible. Usually the computers placed in the DMZ are *bastion hosts*. A bastion host is a computer that has had all unnecessary services and applications removed; it has been hardened against attack. To add security to the devices in the DMZ, a *screened host* sometimes is used. A screened host is a firewall that is being partially shielded by a router acting as a packet filter. This furthers the concept of defense in depth.

Exam Prep Questions

1. Your PBX has been hacked. Which of the following groups could be responsible?
   - ❑ A. Hackers
   - ❑ B. Phreakers
   - ❑ C. War drivers
   - ❑ D. War dialers

2. You just overheard two people discussing ways to steal electronic serial numbers (ESNs). What type of attack are they discussing?
   - ❑ A. Bank card hacking
   - ❑ B. Modem hacking
   - ❑ C. PBX hacking
   - ❑ D. Cellphone hacking

3. Your boss has asked that you implement IPSec to secure the contents and the header information of traffic. Which of the following matches that description?
   - ❑ A. Transport mode
   - ❑ B. IKE mode
   - ❑ C. Tunnel mode
   - ❑ D. Encrypted mode

4. What is a mechanism for converting internal IP addresses found in IP headers into public addresses for transmission over the Internet?
   - ❑ A. ARP
   - ❑ B. DNS
   - ❑ C. DHCP
   - ❑ D. NAT

5. Clement has implemented PEM. What is he trying to protect?
   - ❑ A. IP traffic
   - ❑ B. TCP traffic
   - ❑ C. Email traffic
   - ❑ D. VPN traffic

6. The transport layer of the OSI model corresponds to which TCP/IP layer?
   - ❑ A. Application layer
   - ❑ B. Internet layer
   - ❑ C. Host-to-host layer
   - ❑ D. Network access layer

7. Which of the following is considered an updated standard to the WEP protocol?
   - ❑ A. WPA
   - ❑ B. SMLI
   - ❑ C. PGP
   - ❑ D. POP

8. Which of the following closely resembles a packet-filtering device as it makes decisions on addresses, ports, and protocols?
   - ❑ A. Stateless firewall
   - ❑ B. Circuit proxy
   - ❑ C. Application proxy
   - ❑ D. Stateful firewall

9. This protocol is considered a forerunner to Frame Relay and works over POTS lines.
   - ❑ A. SMDS
   - ❑ B. ATM
   - ❑ C. X.25
   - ❑ D. T-carrriers

10. RADIUS provides which of the following?
    - ❑ A. Authentication and accountability
    - ❑ B. Authorization and accountability
    - ❑ C. Authentication and authorization
    - ❑ D. Authentication, authorization, and accountability

11. Which of the following is a cell-switched technology?
    - ❑ A. DSL
    - ❑ B. T1
    - ❑ C. ISDN
    - ❑ D. ATM

12. Which of the following is considered a third-generation firewall?
    - ❑ A. Packet filter
    - ❑ B. Circuit proxy
    - ❑ C. Application proxy
    - ❑ D. Stateful firewall

Answers to Exam Prep Questions

1. Answer: B. Phreakers practice the art of phone hacking. Answer A is incorrect as hackers do not typically target phone systems. Answer C is incorrect as war drivers are individuals that target wireless systems. Answer D is incorrect as war dialers are individuals that target modems.

2. Answer: D. Cellphone hackers scan for electronic serial numbers (ESNs) and mobile identification numbers (MINs). These are used to clone phones. Answer A is incorrect because bank card hacking would most likely target a database. Answer B is incorrect because the individuals that target modems are known as war dialers. Answer C is incorrect because PBX hacking is performed by phreakers.

3. Answer: C. Tunnel mode protects the payload and the header. Transport mode just protects the payload, so answer A is incorrect. There is no IKE mode or encrypted mode, so answers B and D are incorrect.

4. Answer: D. NAT allows a single device, such as a router, to act as an agent between the Internet and the internal network. ARP is used for physical address resolution, so answer A is incorrect. DNS is used for IP address resolution, so answer B is incorrect. DHCP is used to assign dynamic addresses, so answer C is incorrect.

5. Answer: C. PEM provides encryption, authentication, and X.509 certificate-based key management. PEM is used to protect email. Answer A is incorrect because IPSec, not PEM, is used to protect IP traffic. Answer B is incorrect because although measures can be taken to protect TCP, PEM is not one of them. Answer D is incorrect because protocols associated with VPNs include PPTP, L2TP, and IPSec, not PEM.

6. Answer: C. The TCP/IP host-to-host layer corresponds to the transport layer of the OSI model, which is Layer 4. All other answers are incorrect because those layers do not map to the transport layer. Answer A, the application layer of the TCP/IP model, corresponds to Layers 6 and 7 of the OSI model. Answer B is incorrect because the TCP/IP Internet layer loosely corresponds to Layer 3 of the OSI model. Answer D is incorrect because the network access layer loosely corresponds to Layers 1 and 2 of the OSI model.

7. Answer: A. The replacement for WEP is WI-FI Protected Access (WPA). WPA uses the Temporal Key Integrity Protocol for more robust security. SMLI (answer B) is incorrect because it is a firewall technology. PGP (answer C) is an email-protection mechanism, and POP (answer D) is associated with email, so neither of these is correct.

8. Answer: B. Circuit-level proxies closely resemble packet-filtering devices because they examine addresses, ports, and protocols. Stateless firewalls are packet-filtering devices and application proxies, and stateful firewalls examine higher-level content, so answers A, C, and D are incorrect.

9. Answer: C. X.25 predates Frame Relay. Although it is not fast, it is reliable and works over analog phone lines. SMDS is a high-speed MAN/WAN packet-switched protocol, so answer A is incorrect. ATM is a modern protocol that offers high speed and various classes of service, so answer B is incorrect. T-carriers are a circuit-switched technology, so answer D is incorrect.

10. Answer: C. RADIUS is a client/server protocol used to authenticate dial-in users and authorize access. The other answers are incorrect because they do not meet the specification of RADIUS.

11. Answer: D. ATM is a cell-switched technology. DSL, T1, and IDDN are not based on cell-switching technology and, therefore, are incorrect.

12. Answer: D. Stateful firewalls are considered intelligent firewalls and are third-generation devices. Circuit and application proxies are second-generation devices, and packet filters are first-generation devices, so answers A, B, and C are incorrect.

Need to Know More?

http://pclt.cis.yale.edu/pclt/COMM/TCPIP.HTM—An introduction to TCP/IP

https://secure.linuxports.com/howto/intro_to_networking/c4412.htm—An introduction to the ISO Model

www.telephonetribute.com/phonephreaking.html—Phone phreaking

www.untruth.org/~josh/security/radius/radius-auth.html—The RADIUS authentication protocol

http://searchnetworking.techtarget.com/tip/1,289483,sid7_gci838703,00.html—Protecting network assets from attack

7

Applications and Systems-Development Security

Terms you'll need to understand:

✓ Tuple
✓ Polyinstantiation
✓ Inference
✓ Certification
✓ Accreditation
✓ Database
✓ Malware
✓ Buffer overflow

Techniques you'll need to master:

✓ Identifying the system development life cycle
✓ Understanding database design
✓ Stating the steps of the development life cycle
✓ Recognizing the different types of failure states
✓ Recognizing the four primary types of databases

Introduction

Well-written applications are the key to good security. As such, this chapter focuses on the security requirements that are needed when developing applications. Although this chapter won't make you into a programmer, it will help you understand the steps required to build robust and secure applications.

To become certified as a CISSP, ISC² expects test candidates to understand how to develop secure applications, know the steps of the system development life cycle, have knowledge of database design and structure, and be able to recognize and respond to malicious code and system vulnerabilities.

Malicious Code

Just as in other chapters, this one starts off by looking at some of the threats. As a CISSP, you will be responsible for identifying risk and vulnerabilities, and then finding ways to minimize the impact that could happen if a threat agent gives rise to a threat that exploits a vulnerability.

Malicious code is a threat. The computer you are using likely has antivirus software loaded on it, to detect and prevent computer viruses, which are one type of malicious code. Many types of malicious code exist, but generally, malicious code can be defined as any program that is specifically written to damage, penetrate, or break a system. This genre of software can include Trojans, denial-of-service tools, remote-access Trojans, logic bombs, viruses, worms, and back doors.

Viruses and Worms

Viruses and worms are nothing new; they have been around since the dawn of the computer era. What has changed through the years is the way in which viruses infect systems. There are three broad categories of propagation:

➤ **Master boot record infection**—This form is the oldest of malicious code techniques. It functions by attacking the master boot record of floppy disks or the hard drive. This was effective in the days when everyone passed around floppy disks.

➤ **File infection**—A slightly newer form of virus that relies on the user to execute the file. Extensions such as .com and .exe are typically used. Some form of social engineering is usually used to get the user to execute the program.

➤ **Macro infection**—The most modern type of virus began appearing in the 1990s. Macro viruses exploit scripting services installed on your computer. Most of you probably remember the "I Love You" virus, a prime example of a macro infector.

 Many antivirus programs work by means of file signature. File signature programs examine boot sectors, files, and sections of program code that are known to be vulnerable to viral programs. Although the programs are efficient, they are only as good as their last update. They must be updated regularly to detect the most recent type of computer viruses.

Worms, unlike viruses, require no interaction on the user's part to replicate and spread. One of the worst worms to be released on the Internet was the RTM worm. It was developed by Robert Morris back in 1998 and was meant to be only a proof of concept. Its accidental release brought home the fact that these types of code can do massive damage to the Internet.

Today these are the biggest changes to viruses and worms:

➤ The means by which they spread.

➤ The new methods of how they attack.

➤ The new types of payloads. The payload of some viruses might do nothing more than display a message on your screen at a certain data and time, whereas others could destroy your hard drive.

Nimda: A New Type of Worm

Nimda is a good example of how viruses and worms have changed in the last few years. Nimda actually had the capability to infect a computer when infected email was read or even previewed. A user did not have to open an attachment. Nimda also had the capability to modify pages on a web server so that any computer accessing those pages might also become infected.

When Nimda first attacked, it had several ways in which to propagate itself from the web server that had not previously been seen. Nimda sent out random http "Get requests" looking for other unpatched Microsoft web servers to infect. Nimda also scanned the hard drive once every 10 days for email addresses. These addresses were used to send copies of itself to other victims. Nimda used its own internal mail client, making it difficult for individuals to determine who really sent the infected email. If all that isn't enough, Nimda also had the capability to add itself to executable files to spread itself to other victims.

Who created Nimda? Well, that it still unknown. Antivirus experts are left with only a few clues. One of them is in the code. It stated, "Concept Virus (CV) V.5, Copyright(C) 2001 R.P.China." What is known is that Nimda infected at least 1.2 million computers and caused untold monetary damage.

Buffer Overflow

Buffer overflow attacks are used by individuals to gain access to systems or to elevate their privilege. Buffer overflows occur when programmers use unsecured functions or don't enforce limits on buffers. Basically, the programmer is not practicing good coding techniques. If an attacker can find this vulnerable code, he can attempt to inject and run his malicious code on that system. If the original code executed with administrator or root rights, those privileges are granted to the attacker. The end result is that, many times, the attacker will gain a command prompt on the system under attack. When this occurs, the attacker has complete control.

Denial of Service (DoS)

DoS attacks are usually intended to disable or disrupt computer services or resources. Although this sometimes can be accidental, it is most often a deliberate act. DoS attacks are sometimes used in a final act of desperation when an attacker cannot gain access to a system. DoS is also occasionally used in blackmail attempts: "Meet my demands or I will shut down your network." Because specific DoS attacks have been discussed in other chapters, only the names of common attacks are provided in the following list:

➤ Smurf

➤ Fraggle

➤ Teardrop

➤ Ping of death

➤ Land

➤ SYN attack

Distributed Denial of Service (DDoS)

One step above the DoS attack is the DDoS attack. DDoS is similar to DoS, in that the goal of the attack is a disruption of service. However, it is more powerful, in that it uses a large number of previously compromised systems to direct a coordinated attack against the target. These systems, known as zombies, wait until the attacker signals the attack. A DDoS attack can be devastating because of the tremendous amount of traffic generated. DDoS attack tools include these:

➤ Trinoo

➤ Shaft

➤ Tribal Flood Network

➤ TFN 2K

➤ Stacheldraht

Malformed Input (SQL Injection)

Application developers should never assume that users will input the correct data. A user who is bent on malicious activity will attempt to stretch the protocol or application in an attempt to find possible vulnerabilities. An example is an order quantity field on a web page that accepts negative values. Buyers typically don't order negative quantities of an item. Attackers think outside the box, and so should programmers when developing applications. Parameter problems are best solved by implementing pre-validation and post-validation control.

Databases are a common target of malformed input. An attacker can attempt to insert database or SQL commands to disrupt the normal operation of the database. This could cause the database to become unstable and leak information. This type of attack is known as SQL injection. The attacker searches for web pages in which to insert SQL commands. Attackers use logic such as 1 = 1 -- or a single quote, such as ' to test the database for vulnerabilities. Responses such as the one shown in the following code give the attacker the feedback needed to know that the database is vulnerable to attack.

```
Microsoft OLE DB Provider for ODBC Drivers error '80040e07'
[Microsoft][ODBC SQL Server Driver][SQL Server]Syntax error converting
the nvarchar value 'sa_login' to a column of data type int.
/index.asp, line 5
```

Although knowing the syntax and response used for a database attack is not required exam knowledge, it is useful to know as you attempt to secure your infrastructure. Other security issues that can be tied directly to input validation include these:

➤ Client-side validation

➤ Cross-site scripting

➤ Direct OS commands

➤ Path traversal

➤ Unicode encoding

➤ URL encoding

All of these issues can be addressed by performing proper input validation.

Spyware

Many of us have dealt with programs such as adware, browser hijackers, sur-veillance programs, or web bugs. Although spyware programs are nothing new, they continue to grow in virulence and sophistication. There is some debate as to whether these programs are aggressive marketing gone too far or a real invasion of privacy.

Spyware programs are typically installed when the user downloads a free piece of software that contains spyware in the installation package. Vendors justify these programs by declaring that spyware programs allow them to offer their products for free and that if users do not want to install the spyware, they can refrain from installing their programs by opting to purchase a for-pay copy that doesn't include the spyware.

Other spyware programs are less up front about giving you an option to install and might be loaded onto your computer by just visiting a website with a browser that is vulnerable. Spyware programs have become rather advanced. Some have incorporated concepts such as Alternate Data Streams (ADS). This hacker technique allows the spyware distributor to stream one file behind another. A quick search of the drive will find no trace of the offending executable because there is no entry in the File Allocation Table (FAT), where the directory listing of all files is kept. Removing these pro-grams requires one or more specialized tools, such as HijackThis. Other defenses against spyware include changing to an alternate browser, staying current on your patch management, and not downloading or installing adware-supported programs.

Back Doors and Trapdoors

Many times back-door programs are used to access and control a computer. These programs are associated with Trojans and other malicious code that can be used to trick the user into installing them. Once installed, these programs operate on high-order or unused ports to communicate with the attacker. Many of the programs give the attacker complete control of the victim's com-puter and allow him or her to execute programs, access the Registry, turn on the camera and mic, control the browser, and start and stop applications. Common back-door programs include these:

➤ Back Orifice

➤ SubSeven

➤ NetBus

➤ Beast

Trapdoors, unlike back doors, are used by programmers as a secret entry point into a program. These can be used to allow someone to gain functionality to the program without going through the usual security procedures. Programmers find these useful during application development; however, they should be removed before the code is finalized.

Change Detection

One of the ways in which malicious code can be detected is through the use of change-detection software. This software can detect changes to system and configuration files. Most of these programs work by storing a hashing algorithm of the original file in a database. Periodically, the file is rechecked and the hashed values are compared. If the two values do not match, the program can trigger an alert to signal that there might have been a compromise.

Checksums and hashed values are widely used. Most software vendors list the fingerprints of their programs on their websites because this give customers a way to ensure they have the authentic file. Popular programs that perform this function include Tripwire and MD5sum.

Failure States

As previously discussed, buffer overflows are one way in which an attacker can attempt to compromise application security; therefore, it is important that the developer exam the ways in which the application can fail and attempt to contain the damage. Well-coded applications have built-in recovery procedures, such as the following:

➤ **Fail safe**—If a failure is detected, the system is protected from compromise by termination of services or disabling of the system.

➤ **Fail soft**—A detected failure terminates the noncritical process or application while the system continues to function.

 Applications that recover to a fail-open state allow an attacker to bypass security controls and easily compromise the system. Systems that fail-open are typically undesirable because of the security risk.

The System Development Life Cycle

A framework for system development can make the development process much easier and more structured. Many different models exist; although some have more steps than the others, overall the goal is the same: to control the process and add security at each level of the process. Two examples of this include NIST 800-64, "Security Considerations in the Information System Development Life Cycle," and NIST 800-14, "Generally Accepted Principles and Practices for Securing Information Technology Systems." NIST 800-14 separates the development into five distinct steps:

1. Project initiation

2. Development/acquisition

3. Implementation

4. Operation/maintenance

5. Disposal

Project Initiation

This step of the process usually includes a meeting with everyone who is involved with the project. This is a good opportunity to make sure everyone gets a chance to meet and that everyone understands the goals of the project. A plan must be developed to map the process and develop deadlines and submission dates.

A sensitivity assessment should also be conducted. This should help identify the type of information that will be processed and its level of sensitivity. Discussions should be held to determine the level of risk involved in handling this data and to establish the results from its accidental exposure. These items must be completed before the system design specifications are locked in.

Development and Acquisition

In this step, the system is designed, developed, programmed, and acquired. Programmers work to develop the application code. Security should be the focus here, as the programmers work to ensure that input and output controls, audit mechanisms, and file-protection schemes are used. Examples of input controls include dollar counts, transaction counts, error detection, and correction. Example output controls include validity checking and authorizing controls. It's important that programmers don't assume that systems are always installed and operated in trusted environments.

Acceptance Testing/Implementation

This step occurs when the application coding is complete. The acceptance testing and implementation should not be performed by the programmers. Testing should be performed by a different group of individuals. These tasks are usually assigned to auditors or quality assurance engineers. The important concept here is separation of duties. If the code is built and verified by the same individuals, errors can be missed and security functions can be bypassed.

When the issues and concerns have been worked out between the QA engineers and the programmers, the application is ready for deployment.

Operations/Maintenance

At this step, the application is prepared for release into its intended environment. Certification and accreditation are the final steps involved in accepting the application and agreeing that it is ready for use.

 Certification is a technical evaluation and analysis of the security features and safeguards of a system, to establish the extent to which the security requirements are satisfied and vendor claims are verified.

 Accreditation is the formal process of management's official approval of the certification, that the application or system operates as specified in the environment it was designed to be used in.

Disposal

This step of the process is reached when the application or system is no longer needed. Those involved in this step of the process must consider the disposal of the application, archiving of any information or data that might be needed in the future, disk sanitization (to ensure confidentiality), and the disposal of equipment. This is an important step that is sometimes overlooked.

Disposal Is a Big Problem

Computer forensics investigators at the University of Glamorgan in England examined more than 100 drives purchased at random on eBay. Only two of the drives contained no data. All of the remaining drives contained various amounts of residual information. One contained psychological reports on school children, and several others contained confidential information.

If hard drives are not destroyed, they should be wiped and sanitized. One standard is Department of Defense standard 5220.22-M. It recommends overwriting all addressable locations with a character, its complement, and then a random character to verify that the residual data has been cleared and sanitized.

Software-Development Methods

So, what is the most important concept of software development? Finding a good process and sticking to it. Several proven software-development process are detailed next.

The Waterfall Model

Probably the most well-known software-development process is the waterfall model. This model operates as the name suggests: Developers are limited to going back only one stage; therefore, the process flows logically from one stage to the next. An advantage of this method is that it provides a sense of order and is easily documented. The primary disadvantage is that it does not work large and complex projects.

The Spiral Model

This model was developed in 1988 by Barry Boehm. Each phase of the spiral model starts with a design goal and ends with the client review. The client can be either internal or external, and is responsible for reviewing the progress. Analysis and engineering efforts are applied at each phase of the project. An advantage of the spiral model is that it takes risk much more seriously. Each phase a of the project contains its own risk assessment. Each time a risk assessment is performed, estimated costs to complete and schedules are revised and then a decision is made to continue or cancel the project. The disadvantage of this method is that it is much slower and takes longer to complete.

Joint Application Development (JAD)

JAD is a process that was developed at IBM in 1977. Its purpose is to accelerate the design of information technology solutions. An advantage of JAD is that it helps developers work effectively with users to develop applications that work. A disadvantage is that it requires users, expert developers, and technical experts to work closely together throughout the entire process. Projects that are good candidates for JAD include some of the following characteristics:

➤ Involve a group of users whose responsibilities cross department or division boundaries

➤ Considered critical to the future success of the organization

➤ Involve users who are willing to participate

➤ Developed in a workshop environment

➤ Use a facilitator who has no vested interest in the outcome

Rapid Application Development (RAD)

RAD is a fast application-development process that was created to deliver fast results. RAD is not suitable for all projects. An advantage of RAD is that it works well for projects that are on strict time limits and must be developed quickly. However, this can also be a disadvantage if the quick decisions lead to poor design and product. That is why you won't see RAD used for things such as shuttle launches or other highly critical systems. Two of the most popular RAD systems for Microsoft Windows are Delphi and Visual Basic.

Computer-Aided Software Engineering (CASE)

CASE enhances the software development life cycle by using software tools and automation to perform systematic analysis, design, development, and implementation of software products. Its advantage is that it is useful for large, complex projects that involve multiple software components and a lot of people. Its disadvantages include that it requires building and maintaining software tools, and training developers to understand how to use the tools effectively. CASE can be used for tasks such as these:

➤ Modeling real-world processes and data flow that will pass through the application

➤ Developing data models to better understand the process

➤ Developing a process and functional descriptions of the model

➤ Producing databases and procedures for their management

 Prototyping is the process of building a proof-of-concept model that can be used to test various aspects of a design and verify its marketability. Prototyping is widely used during the development process.

Change Management

Change management is a formalized process. Its purpose is to control modifications made to systems and programs, and to analyze the request, examine its feasibility and impact, and develop a timeline to implement approved changes. The change-management process gives all concerned parties an opportunity to voice opinions and concerns before changes are made.

These are the six steps for change management:

1. Define change-management processes and practices.

2. Receive change requests.

3. Plan and document the implementation of changes.

4. Implement and monitor the changes. Develop a means of backing out of proposed changes, if necessary.

5. Evaluate and report on implemented changes.

6. Modify the change-management plan, if necessary.

Programming Languages

Programming languages are used to convert sets of instructions into a vocabulary that a computer can understand. The goal is to compile instructions into a format that will allow the computer to complete a specific task (see Figure 7.1). Over the years, these languages have evolved into generations:

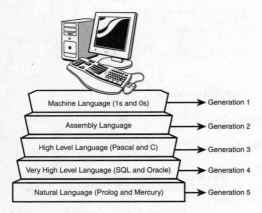

Machine Language (1s and 0s)	→ Generation 1
Assembly Language	→ Generation 2
High Level Language (Pascal and C)	→ Generation 3
Very High Level Language (SQL and Oracle)	→ Generation 4
Natural Language (Prolog and Mercury)	→ Generation 5

Figure 7.1 Programming languages.

1. Generation 1: Machine language, the native language of a computer.

2. Generation 2: Assembly language, human-readable notation that translates easily into machine language.

3. Generation 3: High-level language—programming languages such as C+ and FORTRAN.

4. Generation 4: Very high-level language, typically those used to access databases. SQL is an example of a fourth-generation language.

5. Generation 5: Natural language. These are categorized by their use of inference engines and natural language processing. Mercury and Prolog are two examples of fifth-generation languages.

After the code is written, it must be translated into a format that the computer will understand. These are the three most common methods:

➤ **Assembler**—A program translates assembly language into machine language.

➤ **Compiler**—A compiler translates a high-level language into machine language.

➤ **Interpreter**—Instead of compiling the entire program, an interpreter translates the program line by line. Interpreters have a fetch-and-execute cycle. An interpreted language is much slower than a compiled or assembly language.

Hundreds of different programming languages exist. Many have been written to fill a specific niche or market demand. Examples of common programming languages include these:

➤ **Active X**—This language forms a foundation for higher-level software services, such as transferring and sharing information among applications. ActiveX controls are a Component Object Model (COM) technology.

➤ **COBOL**—Common Business Oriented Language is a third-generation programming language used for business finance and administration.

➤ **C, C-Plus, C++**—The C programming language replaced B and was designed by Dennis Ritchie. C was originally designed for UNIX and is very popular and widely used.

➤ **FORTRAN**—This language features an optimized compiler that is widely used by scientists for writing numerically intensive programs.

➤ **HTML**—Hypertext Markup Language is a markup language that is used to create web pages.

➤ **Java**—This is a relatively new language, developed in 1995 by Sun Microsystems.

➤ **Visual Basic**—This programming language was designed to be used by anyone, and it makes it possible to develop practical programs quickly.

Object-Oriented Programming

Object-oriented programming (OOP) is a modular form of programming that supports object technology. It allows pieces of software to be reused and interchanged between programs. This method of programming has been widely embraced because it is more efficient and results in lower programming costs. Because it makes use of modules, a programmer can easily modify an existing program. New modules can be inserted into the program that inherit features from existing objects. Objects that share a particular structure and behavior are said to belong to a particular class. Code from one class can be passed down to another through the process of inheritance. Java and C++ are two examples of OOP languages.

Object-Oriented Considerations

Some of the major concerns and issues of OOP include these:

➤ **Encapsulation**—This is the act of hiding the functionality of a process inside classes. It allows a developer to separate distinct parts of code so there is no direct interaction between the various parts.

➤ **Polymorphism**—Technically, this means that one thing has the capability to take on many shapes. In OOP, it is used to invoke a method on a class without having to care about how the job gets done. The results will be different because variables within the object itself might be different. Even though the same methods are being passed to different objects, the results will not be the same.

➤ **Polyinstantiation**—Users at different security levels will see different information about the same object. This is widely used by the government and military and can be used to protect sensitive or secret information. Without polyinstantiation, an attacker might be able to use inference to determine secret information.

CORBA

Common Object Request Broker Architecture (CORBA) is vendor-independent middleware. Its purpose is to tie together different vendor products so they can seamlessly work together over distributed networks. The heart of the CORBA system is the Object Request Broker (ORB). The ORB simplifies the process of a client requesting server objects. The ORB finds the object; transparently activates it, if necessary; and then delivers the requested object back to the client.

Database Management

Databases are important to business, government, and individuals because they provide a way to catalog, index, and retrieve related information and facts. They are widely used. If you have booked a reservation on a plane, looked up the history of a used car you were thinking about buying, or researched the ancestry of your family, you have most likely used a database to accomplish this function. Databases can be centralized or distributed, depending on the database-management system (DBMS) that has been implemented. The DBMS allows the database administrator to control all aspects of the database, including its design, functionality, and security. Database types include these:

➤ **Hierarchical database-management system**—This form of database links structures in a tree structure. Each record can have only one owner and because of this, a restriction hierarchical database often can't be used to relate to structures in the real world.

➤ **Network database-management system**—This type of database was developed to be more flexible than the hierarchical database. The network database model is considered a lattice structure because each record can have multiple parent and child records.

➤ **Relational database-management system**—This form of database is considered a collection of tables that are linked by their primary keys. Many organizations use software based on the relational database design. Most relational databases use SQL as their query language.

➤ **Object-oriented database-management system**—This type of database is relatively new and was designed to overcome some of the limitations of large relational databases. Object-oriented databases don't use a high-level language such as SQL. These databases support modeling and the creation of data as objects.

Inference is a key security issue when dealing with databases. Inference is possible when authorized individuals can deduce information from accessing and reviewing authorized information. As an example, Mike knows that Clement is working on a secret project and that the governmental agency he works for is looking for steganography experts. Therefore, Mike infers that this is the project Clement is working on.

Transaction Processing

Transaction management is a big concern because locking mechanisms are needed to ensure that only one user at a time can alter data and that transactions are valid and complete. Programmers involved in database management talk about the ACID test when discussing whether a database-management system has been properly designed to handle transactions.

➤ **Atomicity**—Results of a transaction are either all or nothing.

➤ **Consistency**—Transactions are processed only if they meet system-defined integrity constraints.

➤ **Isolation**—The results of a transaction are invisible to all other transactions until the original transaction is complete.

➤ **Durability**—Once complete, the results of the transaction are permanent.

Database Terms

If you are not familiar with the world of databases, you might not be familiar with some other terms. These are listed here:

➤ **Aggregation**—The process of combining several low-sensitivity items, with the result being that these items produce a higher-sensitivity data item.

➤ **Attribute**—A component of a database, such as a column.

➤ **Field**—The smallest unit of data within a database.

➤ **Foreign key**—An attribute in one table whose value matches the primary key in another table.

➤ **Granularity**—Term that refers to the control one has over the view someone has of the database. Highly granular databases have the capability to restrict certain fields or rows from unauthorized individuals.

➤ **Relation**—Data that is represented by a collection of tables.

➤ **Tuple**—Represents a relationship among a set of values. In an RDBMS, it is synonymous with *record*.

➤ **Schema**—The structure of the entire database. It defines how it is structured.

➤ **Primary key**—Uniquely identifies each row and assists with indexing the table.

➤ **View**—Addresses what the end user can see and access.

Data Warehousing

A data warehouse is a database that contains data from many different databases. These warehouses have been combined, integrated, and structured so that they can be used to provide trend analysis and make business decisions. Data warehousing is used to get a strategic view.

Data Mining

Data mining is the process of analyzing data to find and understand patterns and relationships about the data. The result of data mining is metadata, or data about data. The patterns discovered in this data can help companies understand their competitors and understand usage patterns of their customers to carry out targeted marketing. Data mining is used to get a tactical view. As an example, a store might discover that digital camera buyers also purchase blank CDs, so by moving blank CDs to the camera department, they experience higher sales.

Knowledge Management

Knowledge management seeks to make use of all the knowledge of the organization. It attempts to tie together databases, document management, business processes, and information systems. It is used to interpret the data derived from these systems and automate the knowledge extraction. This knowledge-discovery process takes the form of data mining, in which patterns are discovered through artificial intelligence techniques. These are the three main approaches to knowledge extraction:

➤ **Classification approach**—Used for pattern discovery and in situations when large databases must be reduced to only a few individual records

➤ **Probabilistic approach**—Used in planning and control systems, and in applications that involve uncertainty

➤ **Statistical approach**—Used to construct rules and generalize patterns in the data

Exam Prep Questions

1. Which of the following types of computer viruses is considered one of the original forms of transmission and was most prevalent when floppies were shared?

   ❑ A. Macro virus
   ❑ B. Master boot record virus
   ❑ C. File infector virus
   ❑ D. VBS virus

2. QuickE Mart has just realized that by placing the baby food in their stores close to the aspirin, sales of both products will increase. These results were discovered after analyzing the buying habits of their customers. How did they arrive at this conclusion?

   ❑ A. Metadata
   ❑ B. Data mining
   ❑ C. Data warehousing
   ❑ D. Transaction processing

3. Which of the following tools can be used for change detection?

   ❑ A. DES
   ❑ B. Checksums
   ❑ C. MD5sum
   ❑ D. Parity bits

4. Bob has noticed that when he inputs too much data into his new Internet application, it momentarily locks up the computer and then halts the program. Which of the following best describes this situation?

   ❑ A. Fail safe
   ❑ B. Buffer overflow
   ❑ C. Fail open
   ❑ D. Fail soft

5. Which of the following types of database is considered a lattice structure, with each record having multiple parent and child records?

   ❑ A. Hierarchical database-management system
   ❑ B. Network database-management system
   ❑ C. Object-oriented database-management system
   ❑ D. Relational database-management system

6. What database function has the capability to restrict certain fields or rows from unauthorized individuals?

   ❑ A. Low granularity
   ❑ B. High resolution
   ❑ C. High granularity
   ❑ D. Low resolution

7. Which of the following is a DDoS tool?
   - ❑ A. LAND
   - ❑ B. Smurf
   - ❑ C. TFN
   - ❑ D. Fraggle

8. OmniTec's new programmer has left several entry points in its new e-commerce shopping cart program for testing and development. Which of the following terms best describes what the programmer has done?
   - ❑ A. Back door
   - ❑ B. Security flaw
   - ❑ C. SQL injection
   - ❑ D. Trapdoor

9. Generation 2 programming languages are considered what?
   - ❑ A. Assembly
   - ❑ B. Machine
   - ❑ C. High level
   - ❑ D. Natural

10. Which of the following is considered middleware?
   - ❑ A. Atomicity
   - ❑ B. OLE
   - ❑ C. CORBA
   - ❑ D. Object-oriented programming

Answers to Exam Prep Questions

1. Answer: B. The master boot record virus is considered the oldest form of virus attack. It functions by attacking the master boot record of floppy disks or the hard drive. The macro virus (answer A) and file infector (answer C) are both incorrect because they are newer techniques. Answer D, VBS virus, is considered a form of macro virus and is therefore also incorrect.

2. Answer: B. Data mining is the process of analyzing data to find and understand patterns and relationships between the data. Answer A is incorrect because the result of data mining is metadata. Answer C is incorrect because data warehousing is a database that contains data from many different databases. Answer D is incorrect because transaction processing addresses the way in which transaction data is protected and secured.

3. Answer: C. One of the ways in which malicious code can be detected is through the use of change-detection software. This software has the capability to detect changes to system and configuration files. Popular programs that perform this function include Tripwire and MD5sum. Answer A is incorrect because DES is an asymmetric algorithm. Answers B and D are incorrect because both checksums and parity bits can be easily changed and, therefore, do not protect the software from change.

4. Answer: D. A fail soft occurs when a detected failure terminates the application while the system continues to function. Answers A and C are incorrect because a fail-safe terminates the program and disables the system, and a fail open is the worst of events because it allows attackers to bypass security controls and easily compromise the system. Answer B is incorrect because although a buffer overflow could be the root cause of the problem, the question asks why the application is halting in the manner described.

5. Answer: B. Network database-management systems are designed for flexibility. The network database model is considered a lattice structure because each record can have multiple parent and child records. Answer A is incorrect because hierarchical database-management systems are structured like a tree. Each record can have only one owner; because of this restriction, hierarchical database often can't be used to relate to structures in the real world. Answer D is incorrect because relational database-management systems are considered a collection of tables that are linked by their primary keys. Answer C is incorrect because object-oriented database-management systems are not latticed based and don't use a high-level languages such as SQL.

6. Answer: C. Granularity refers to the control one has over the view someone has of the database. Highly granular databases have the

capability to restrict certain fields or rows from unauthorized individuals. Answer A is incorrect because low granularity gives the database manager little control. Answers B and D are incorrect because high resolution and low resolution do not apply to the question.

7. Answer: C. TFN is a DDoS tool; DDoS attacks are similar to DoS attacks, in that the goal of the attack is to disrupt service. The difference between DoS and DDoS is that DDoS is more powerful. It uses a large number of previous compromised systems to direct a coordinate attack against the target. LAND, Smurf, and Fraggle are all DoS attack tools.

8. Answer: D. A trapdoor is used by programmers as a secret entry point into a program. Programmers find these useful during application development; however, they should be removed before the code is finalized. All other answers are incorrect. There is a security flaw (answer B), but that answer is not specific enough. Back doors (answer A) are malicious in nature, and SQL injection (answer C) is targeted against databases.

9. Answer: A. Programming languages are structured as follows: Generation 1 is machine language, Generation 2 is assembly language, Generation 3 is high-level language, Generation 4 is very high-level language, and Generation 5 is natural language.

10. Answer: C. Common Object Request Broker Architecture (CORBA) is vendor-independent middleware. Its purpose is to tie together different vendor products so they can seamlessly work together over distributed networks. Answer B is incorrect because Object Linking and Embedding (OLE) is a proprietary system developed by Microsoft that allows applications to transfer and share information. Answer A is incorrect because atomicity deals with the validity of database transactions. Answer D is incorrect because object-oriented programming is a modular form of programming.

Need to Know More?

www.jebcl.com/riskdo/riskdo.htm—Risk assessment do's and don'ts

www.zdnet.com.au/insight/0,39023731,20281524,00.htm—Six steps to change management

http://computing-dictionary.thefreedictionary.com/object-oriented%20 programming—Object-oriented programming

www.linuxsecurity.com/content/view/119087/49/—Buffer overflows

http://lockdowncorp.com/trojandemo.html—How Trojan horse programs work

www.garykessler.net/library/ddos.html—The history of DDoS attacks

www.governmentsecurity.org/articles/SQLInjectionModesofAttackDefenceand WhyItMatters.php—SQL injection and database manipulation

www.omg.org/gettingstarted/corbafaq.htm—CORBA FAQ

www.cultural.com/web/security/compusec.glossary.html—Common security terms

8

Operations Security

. . . .

Terms you'll need to understand:

✓ Phreakers
✓ Denial of service
✓ Least privilege
✓ Penetration testing
✓ War driving
✓ Traffic analysis

Techniques you'll need to master:

✓ Identifying attack methodologies
✓ Understanding backup and recovery
✓ Implementing operational security
✓ Auditing and monitoring

Introduction

The operations security domain addresses the day-to-day activities that are needed to keep things running and operating securely. This domain introduces you to concepts that apply to daily activities such as how to respond to attacks, how to ensure good administrative management and control, how to handle violations, and how to establish a threshold to determine what a notable violation is. Violations to operational security aren't always malicious—things break and accidents happen. Therefore, operational security must also be prepared to deal with these occurrences.

Students preparing for the ISC² Certified Information Systems Security Professional exam and those reviewing the operational security domain must know what resources should be protected, the principles of good practice, methods to restrict access, the potential abuse of access, what are considered appropriate controls, and how to respond to attacks.

Hack Attacks

It is unfortunate but true that more organizations are subjected to hack attacks. A 2003 survey indicated that as many as 75% of companies polled cited employees as a likely source of hacking attacks. The same survey found that it cost those companies more than $120 million to recover from the activities of the malicious insiders. These numbers should start to drive home the importance of good operational controls. It is much cheaper to be proactive and build in the good controls than it is to be reactive and figure out how you are going to respond.

Who are the people you have to worry about? Well, generally, they can be divided into two groups:

➤ **Insiders**—These are the individuals who either currently work for the organization or have been fired or quit. These insiders could be disgruntled employees.

➤ **Outsiders**—This group of individuals has never worked for you, and you are probably lucky they haven't. Overall, outsiders can be segregated into several subgroups:

  ➤ **Script kiddies**—These individuals cause harm with scripts, tools, and rootkits written by other, more skilled individuals. Often they don't understand how the exploit that they are using works.

  ➤ **Corporate spies**—These individuals work for rival firms. Their goal is to steal your proprietary information.

➤ **Government spies**—Much like corporate spies, these individuals seek ways to advance their country. Your data might be the target.

➤ **Elite hackers**—Although they're not driven by corporate greed or the desire to advance their country, these individuals might have many different motives. Maybe they are looking for ways to proclaim their advanced hacking skills, or they might be at odds with a stand or position your organization has made.

So which group represents the biggest threat? You might have already guessed that it is insiders. Criminologists describe criminals as those who possess three items: means, motive, and opportunity. This is known as the *crime triangle*, shown in Figure 8.1. Insiders typically have the means and the opportunity to commit a crime. All they lack is a motive. Outsiders, on the other hand, are not trusted with access, and being outside the organization's structure could present them with little opportunity to launch an attack. Individuals must possess all three items shown in the crime triangle to successfully commit a crime.

Figure 8.1 Crime triangle.

Common Attack Methodologies

Hack attacks typically target one or more items that are tied to the security triad: confidentiality, integrity, or availability. Whereas confidentiality and integrity attacks actually give the attacker access to your data, availability attacks do not. Availability attacks usually result in denial of service (DoS).

DoS Attacks in Real Life

In February 2000, websites including Yahoo! and eBay were shut down due to persistent DoS attacks. Although the attack didn't give the attacker access to these networks, it caused a loss of service to the organizations. In 2001, a Canadian court sentenced a youth nicknamed Mafiaboy to 8 months in jail as a result of these attacks.

Hackers target a variety of devices, but their modus operandi remains fairly constant. Their methodology of attack generally proceeds as follows (see Figure 8.2):

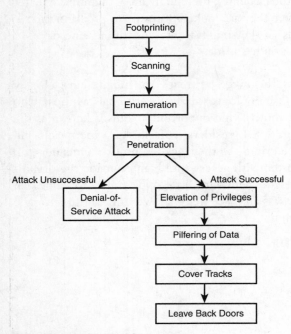

Figure 8.2 Attack methodology.

1. **Footprint**—The attackers identify potential targets, looking for information in such places as the organization's website, public databases, Google groups, and Edgar financial records.

2. **Scan**—This moves beyond passive information gathering. During this step of the assault, the attackers use a variety of tools to scan for open ports and processes.

3. **Enumerate**—Somewhat similar to scanning, this step involves obtaining more detailed information about target devices. Poorly protected shares and weak passwords are two items that are probed for at this step of the assault.

4. **Penetrate**—What makes this step different than the previous one is that the hacker already has actually attacked your network.

5. **Escalate**—Many times, the initial amount of access gained by an attacker is not root or administrator. Under these circumstances, the hacker attempts to escalate privilege.

6. **Cover tracks**—Once in control of the system, most hackers seek to destroy evidence of their activities. Most likely, they will attempt to plant tools and rootkits on the compromised system to further extend their stay.

Phreakers and Their Targets

Long before modern-day hacking existed, phreakers were practicing their trade. *Phreaking* is the art of hacking phone systems. Now, although this might sound like a rather complicated affair, back in the early 1970s, John Draper discovered how to make free phone calls by using a Capt. Crunch Whistle. The 2600Hz tone it produces is the same as what's required for bypassing the normal billing process.

Today phreakers can still pose a threat to operational security by hacking into PBX systems. Many times, these individuals sell off time on the victim's phone network. These charges are usually discovered after 30 to 60 days, but this window of opportunity allows the phreakers to run up thousands of dollars in phone charges. Other modern-day phreakers hack caller ID or target VoIP phone systems for DoS attacks.

Operational Security

By following the common practices laid out in this section, organizations can go a long way toward ensuring good day-to-day security. Because we have identified employees as one group of people who can affect operational security, the following items should be performed before an individual is ever hired. You should validate the job candidate's claims of education and skills, and perform a background check, if needed. You then should hire the individual under a probationary period, specify clearly whether the job candidate has to obtain special qualifications or security clearances for the job, and have him or her sign a noncompete agreement, a nondisclosure agreement, and possibly even a nonsolicitation agreement. These are all steps that should be done before making someone part of the organization's staff. Other operational security controls that can be put in place after someone is hired include instituting a new hire orientation, separation of duties, job rotation, least privilege, mandatory vacations, audit controls, and effective termination practices. Each of these are discussed next.

New-Hire Orientation

One great way to make sure your employees know what is expected of them is to perform a new-hire orientation. The goal of this training is to teach your employees established security policies and procedures. The training also informs employees of acceptable use policies (AUPs). Organizations are much better off having each employee actively participate in the security of the organization than having only a few IT security officers.

Other things can be done to keep employees focused on security. Some organizations hand out pens, note pads, or other items that outline a few of the organization's security policies. You might hold a semiannual policy review so that employees can review current policies and receive a signed copy that they have agreed to. Another idea is to send out periodic security-awareness emails or newsletters that reinforce the practices of good security.

Separation of Duties

This term is used to describe the process of dividing duties so that more than one person is required to complete a task. This concept closely ties to the principle of least privilege. As an example, some banks divide the safe combination numbers between two employees. Each employee has three of the six numbers needed to unlock the safe. Without some form of collusion, there is no way one person can obtain access to the safe's contents.

Job Rotation

Although it's always nice to have cross-trained employees, job rotation is about more than redundancy and backup. Its primary benefit is that it allows organizations to more easily identify fraudulent activities. For example, if John is stealing money from the company and Steve is rotated into that position, they will need a pretty deep friendship to keep Steve from telling the boss that John is a thief.

Least Privilege

Least privilege is another important concept that can go a long way toward achieving the security goals of an organization. Least privilege means that individuals have just enough resources to accomplish their required tasks.

As an example, imagine that your company has just added computer terminals to several of the conference rooms. These have been placed where meeting attendees, consultants, and sales representatives can access product information. Although these computers allow limited Internet access, all other activities are blocked. Services such as network browsing, email, File

Transfer Protocol (FTP), and Domain Name Service (DNS) are not available. This reduces the opportunity for resource misuse.

Over time, least privilege can result in authorization creep, in which employees move from job to job and keep picking up more rights and access. The rights and access they no longer need should be removed.

 Least privilege is not a concept strictly for individuals. In fact, it is extremely important when looking at privileged applications. All applications and processes should run with the minimum amount of privilege, to avoid further exploitation in case of compromise. A great example of this was IIS. It used to operate with system permission, this was way too much privilege for a web server. This has been corrected since Windows 2003.

Mandatory Vacations

Even though everyone thinks it's great that Bob hasn't taken a vacation in 10 years, the fact that the accountant is always at work might be a problem. Bob might not have taken a vacation because he is performing fraudulent activities. By remaining on the job, he is able and available to provide cover for his scheme. Fraudulent activities are much easier to uncover when employees are required to take their vacations. A week provides plenty of time for illicit activities to be discovered.

Termination

Termination sometimes is necessary, but many surveys show that it is one of the most disliked tasks managers are required to do. To protect the organization, managers should use standardized termination procedures. This structured process helps ensure that everyone is treated equally and that employees don't have the opportunity to destroy or damage company property. Some prudent steps to incorporate into this procedure include these:

1. Disabling computer access at the time of notification
2. Monitoring the employee while he or she packs belongings
3. Ensuring that at no time the employee is left alone after the termination process
4. Verifying that the employee returns company identification and any company property, including access tokens and laptops
5. Escorting the employee from the building

Auditing and Monitoring

Operation procedures should also include auditing and monitoring. Auditing and monitoring are tied to *accountability*. These items are tied together because if you don't have accountability for specific users, you cannot perform an effective audit. True security relies on the ability to verify that individual users perform specific actions. Without the capability to hold individuals accountable, organizations can't enforce security policies. Some of the primary ways accountability is established is by auditing user activity, analyzing traffic patterns, scanning for intrusions, and monitoring the movement of individuals throughout the organization's premises.

Make sure you know the difference between audit and accountability for the exam. Audit controls are detective controls, are utilized after the fact, and are usually implemented to detect fraud or other illegal activities. Accountability is the ability to track specific actions, transactions, changes, and resource usage to a specific user within the system. This is accomplished, in part, by having unique identification for each user and strong authentication mechanisms.

Auditing

Auditing produces audit trails. These trails can be used to re-create events and verify whether security policies were violated. The biggest disadvantage of the audit process is that it is detective in nature and that audit trails are usually examined after an event. Some might think of audit trails only as something that corresponds to logical access, but auditing can also be applied to physical access. Auditing tools can be used to monitor who entered the facility and what time certain areas were accessed.

Auditing Tools

The security professional has plenty of available tools that can help isolate the activities of individual users. Windows Event Viewer, Auditpol, and Elsave are all tools used to view and work with audit logs.

Many organizations monitor network traffic to look for suspicious activity and anomalies. Some monitoring tools enable administrators just to examine packet headers, whereas others can completely re-create network traffic. Snort and TCPdump are two such tools. Regardless of the tools used to capture and analyze this traffic, administrators need to make sure that policies are in place detailing how such activities will be handled. Items such as warning banners and AUPs go a long way in making sure that users are adequately informed of what to expect when using company resources.

A *warning banner* is the verbiage that the user sees at the point of entry into a system. Its purpose is to set the right expectations for users accessing those systems. It also aids in prosecuting those who violate the AUPs. A sample AUP is shown here:

WARNING: Unauthorized access to this system is forbidden and will be prosecuted by law. By accessing this system, you agree that your actions may be monitored if unauthorized use is suspected.

Clipping Levels

Have you ever tried to log in to your workplace 300 times at 4 a.m.? Most people have not, and that's where clipping levels come in. Clipping levels are a way to allow users to make an occasional mistake. A clipping level is a threshold for normal mistakes a user may commit before investigation or notification begins.

An understanding of the term *clipping level* is essential for mastery of the CISSP exam. A clipping level establishes a baseline violation count to ignore normal user errors.

The clipping level allows the user to make an occasional mistake, but if the established level is exceeded, violations are recorded or some type of response occurs. Look no further than your domain controller to see a good example of how clipping levels work. As a domain administrator, you might allow users to attempt to log in three times with an incorrect password. If the user can't get it right on the third try, the account is locked and he or she is forced to call an administrator for help. If an administrator or help-desk personnel is contacted to reset a password, some second type of authentication should be used to protect against a social-engineering attack. Social engineering is discussed in more detail in Chapter 3, "Security-Management Practices."

To prevent social-engineering attacks, individuals who call to have their password reset should be required to provide additional authentication, such as date of birth, PIN, or passphrase.

Intrusion Detection

Intrusion-detection systems detect inappropriate, incorrect, or anomalous activity. These devices work by matching the signatures of known attacks or by detecting deviations of normal behavior. Organizations that decide to implement IDS systems must determine not only what type to deploy, but also where to deploy the IDS. IDS systems can be deployed as follows:

➤ **Network**—These devices attach to the LAN and sniff for traffic that has been flagged to be anomalous.

➤ **Host**—This form of IDS resides upon the host device and examines only the traffic going to or coming from the host computer.

IDS systems don't prevent attacks, but they give administrators the capability to detect these events, determine their source, and decide how to respond.

Keystroke Monitoring

Keystroke monitoring is the process of recording the keystrokes entered by a computer user. Keystroke-monitoring tools can be software or hardware based. These tools enable the administrator to capture all user activity. Many of these tools even take snapshots of the computer screen and email these screen captures to a predetermined email account.

Keystroke Logging and the Law

For the administrator, it's important to note that the U.S. Department of Justice has noted that administrators should protect themselves by giving notice to users if keystroke monitoring has been implemented. This notification can be by means of company policy or warning banner. Administrators who fail to implement these operational policies that specify how keystroke monitoring is to be used could be subject to criminal and civil liabilities.

Facility Access Control

No monitoring plan is complete without implementing controls that monitor physical access. Some common facility access controls include these:

➤ Watching CCTV to monitor who enters or leaves the facility

➤ Installing card readers or biometric sensors on server room doors to maintain a log of who accesses this area

➤ Mounting alarm sensors on doors and windows to detect possible security breaches

➤ Using mantraps and gates to control traffic and log entry to secured areas

Categories of Control

You can increase operational security and protect an organization's assets in many ways. To a large degree, operational security is about control. There are six broad categories of controls:

➤ **Preventive controls**—Mechanisms and tools designed to prevent actions that increase risk or violate security policies. Physical barriers such as fences and locks are examples of a preventive control.

➤ **Detective controls**—Processes, tools, or methods used to identify and react to security violations. Administrative actions such as auditing are examples of a detective control.

➤ **Corrective controls**—Applications, programs, or practices used to react to an adverse event and to reduce or eliminate risks associated with the event. A technical solution such an IDS or IPS system that can respond to an adverse event is an example of a corrective control.

➤ **Recovery controls**—Practices, processes, or mechanisms to restore the operating state to normal after an attack or system failure. Technical solutions such as RAID and tape backup are examples of recovery controls.

➤ **Deterrent controls**—Systems, tools, and procedures used to discourage violations. An administrative policy stating that those who place unauthorized modems or wireless devices on the network could be fired is an example of a deterrent control.

➤ **Directive controls**—Procedures and documents used to preclude or mandate actions to reduce risk. An administrative policy stating that all employee candidates must have their educational and employment history background verified is an example of a directive control.

If you are wondering how to keep up with all these controls, it might help to consider that all the individual items discussed can be categorized as either an administrative, technical, or physical control.

Controls are separated into three main types: administrative, technical, and physical. Expect test questions to quiz your knowledge of this and the various categories discussed.

Fax Control

Fax machines can present some security problems if they are being used to transmit sensitive information. These vulnerabilities reside throughout the faxing process and include the following:

1. When the user feeds the document into the fax machine for transmission, wrongdoers have the opportunity to intercept and decode the information while in transit.

2. When the document arrives at its destination, it is typically printed and deposited into a fax tray. Anyone can retrieve the document and review its contents.

3. Many fax machine use ribbons. Anyone with access to the trash can retrieve the ribbons and use them as virtual carbon copies of the original documents.

Fax systems can be secured by one or more of the following techniques:

➤ Fax servers, which can send and receive faxes and then hold the fax in electronic memory. At the recipient's request, the fax can be forwarded to the recipient's email account or can be printed.

➤ Fax encryption, another technique that gives fax machines the capability to encrypt communications. Fax encryption requires both the transmitting and receiving devices to support a common protocol.

➤ Fax activity logs, which implement activity logs and exception reports, to monitor for anomalies.

 Although fax servers have solved many security problems, they have their own challenges. Many use large hard drives where companies store a large amount of commonly used administrative documents and forms. Others allow ftp access to the print queue, where someone can grab files. These issues must be addressed before effective security can be achieved.

Ethical Hacking

Ethical hacking is the process of testing the network infrastructure by employing ethical hackers to perform penetration tests. Ethical hackers perform the same activities as malicious hackers, but they do so with the approval of the organization and without causing damage. The goal is to test the network in much the same fashion as a malicious hacker would. Because of the global nature of the Internet and the increased emphasis on networking, these types of activates have gained increased prominence in the last several years.

Penetration Testing

Penetration testing is the process of evaluating the organization's security measures. These tests can be performed in a number of ways, including internal testing, external testing, whitebox testing (you know the infrastructure), and blackbox testing (you don't know the infrastructure). After the test methodology is determined, the penetration test team is responsible for determining the weaknesses, technical flaws, and vulnerabilities. When these tests are complete, the results are delivered in a comprehensive report to management.

Several good documents detail the ways in which to conduct penetration testing. One is NIST-800-42, which even includes recommendations for tools intended for self-evaluation. NIST divides penetration testing into four primary stages:

➤ **Planning**—As the old saying goes, success is 90% preparation and 10% perspiration. What's the point? Good planning is the key to success. Know where you are going, what your goals are, what the time frame is, and what the limits and boundaries are.

➤ **Discovery**—This stage consists of two distinct phases:

➤ **Passive**—During this stage, information is gathered in a very covert manner. Examples of passive information gathering include surfing the organization's website to mine valuable information, and reviewing job openings to gain a better understanding of the technologies and equipment used by the organization.

➤ **Active**—This phase of the test is split between network scanning and host scanning. As individual networks are enumerated, they are further probed to discover all hosts, determine their open ports, and attempt to pinpoint their OS. Nmap is a popular scanning program.

➤ **Attack**—At this point, the ethical hacker attempts to gain access, escalate privilege, browse the system, and, finally, expand influence.

➤ **Reporting**—This is the final step listed, but it is not least in importance. Reporting and documentation should be conducted throughout each step of the process. This documentation should be used to compile the final report. The report should serve as the basis for corrective action. Corrective action can range from nothing more than enforcing existing policies to closing unneeded ports and adding patches and service packs.

Contingency Planning, Backup, and Recovery

Things will go wrong; it is just a matter of when. Therefore, understanding how to react to and recover from errors and failures is an important part of operational security. Good operational security practices require security planners to perform contingency planning. Contingency planning requires that you develop plans and procedures to implement when things go wrong. This is covered in detail in Chapter 9, "Business-Continuity Planning," but it should be mentioned here because it is closely tied to operations security. Contingency planning should occur after you've identified operational risks and performed a risk analysis to determine the extent of the impact of the possible adverse events.

Successful recovery also means that systems have been put in place to prepare for these unfortunate events. Redundant Array of Inexpensive Disks (RAID) is one critical piece. RAID can be used for fault tolerance and for performance improvements. Another important part of contingency planning, backup, and recovery is some type of data-backup system. All hard drives and data storage systems fail. It's not a matter of if, but when. RAID and backup are discussed in the following sections.

RAID

As discussed earlier, RAID can be used to provide performance improvements and fault tolerance. RAID provides the following:

➤ Capacity benefits

➤ Performance improvements

➤ Fault tolerance

Although there are many types of RAID, the eight most common are discussed in Table 8.1. It is worth mentioning that RAID Level 0 is for performance only, not for redundancy reasons. The most expensive of these to implement is RAID Level 1 because all the data on disk A is mirrored to disk B. Mirroring also has another disadvantage: If data on disk A is corrupted, data on disk B will also become corrupted.

Table 8.1	RAID Levels and Services	
Level	**Title**	**Description**
Level 0	Striped Disk without Fault Tolerance	Provides data striping but no fault tolerance. If one drive fails, all data in the array is lost.
Level 1	Mirroring and Duplexing	Provides disk mirroring. Level 1 provides twice the read transaction rate of single disks and the same write transaction rate as single disks.
Level 2	Error-Correcting	Stripes data at the bit level rather than the block level. This is rarely used.
Level 3	Bit-Interleaved Parity	Offers byte-level striping with a dedicated parity disk.
Level 4	Dedicated Parity Drive	Provides block-level striping. This is a widely used implementation. If a data disk fails, the parity data is used to create a replacement disk.
Level 5	Block Interleaved Distributed Parity	Provides data striping at the byte level, good performance, and good fault tolerance. It is also one of the most popular.
Level 6	Independent Data Disks with Double Parity	Provides block-level striping with parity across all disks.
Level 10	A Stripe of Mirrors	Creates mirrors and a RAID 0 stripe. This is not one of the original RAID levels.

Backups

Three types of backup methods exist: full, incremental, and differential. The method your organization chooses depends on several factors:

➤ How much data needs to be backed up?

➤ How often should the backup occur?

➤ Where will the backups be stored?

➤ How much time do you have to perform the backup each day?

Each method has benefits and drawbacks. Full backups take the longest time but back up all files and data. So, even though it might seem best to do a full backup every day, it might not be possible because time and expense might prohibit it.

Two basic methods can be used to back up data: automated and on-demand. Automated backups are scheduled to occur at a predetermined time. On-demand backups can be scheduled at any time.

Full Backups

During a full backup, all data is backed up; no files are skipped or bypassed, you simply designate which server to back up. A full backup takes the longest to perform and the least time to restore because only one set of tapes is required.

Differential Backups

Using differential backup, a full backup is done typically once a week, and a daily differential backup is done only to those files that have changed since the last full backup. If you need to restore, you need the last full backup and the most recent differential backup. This method takes less time each day (as compared to a full backup) but longer to restore.

Differential and incremental backups make use of something called the archive bit. This small bit of binary magic makes these different types of backup possible. A full backup clears the archive bit for each file that is saved. Then if anyone makes changes to a previously saved file, the archive bit is toggled on. During a differential backup, all the files that have the archive bit on are saved; because more files will likely be accessed during the week, the differential backup time will increase each night until another full backup is performed.

Incremental Backups

With this backup strategy, a full backup is scheduled for once a week, and only files that have changed since the previous incremental backup are backed up each day. This is the fastest backup option, yet it takes the longest to restore.

Incremental backups are unlike differential backups. When files are being saved, the archive bit is reset; therefore, incremental backups back up only changes that were made since the last incremental backup.

Tape-Rotation Schemes

Tapes and other media used for backup will eventually fail. It is important to periodically test backup media to verify its functionality. The most common tape-rotation scheme is known as the Grandfather-Father-Son (GFS) method. This scheme performs a full backup once a week, known as the Father. The daily backups, which can be differential or incremental, are known as the Son. The last full backup of the month is retained for a year and is known as the Grandfather.

Exam Prep Questions

1. Which of the following groups presents the largest threat to your organization?
   - ❑ A. Insiders
   - ❑ B. Corporate spies
   - ❑ C. Government spies
   - ❑ D. Script kiddies

2. Which of the following is *not* a security or operational reason to use mandatory vacations?
   - ❑ A. It allows the organization the opportunity to audit employee work.
   - ❑ B. It ensures that the employee is well rested.
   - ❑ C. It keeps one person from easily being able to carry out covert activities.
   - ❑ D. It ensures that employees will know that illicit activities could be uncovered.

3. What type of control is an audit trail?
   - ❑ A. Application
   - ❑ B. Administrative
   - ❑ C. Preventative
   - ❑ D. Detective

4. Which of the following is *not* a benefit of RAID?
   - ❑ A. Capacity benefits
   - ❑ B. Increased recovery time
   - ❑ C. Performance improvements
   - ❑ D. Fault tolerance

5. Separation of duties is related to which of the following?
   - ❑ A. Dual controls
   - ❑ B. Principle of least privilege
   - ❑ C. Job rotation
   - ❑ D. Principle of privilege

6. Phreakers target which of the following resources?
   - ❑ A. Mainframes
   - ❑ B. Networks
   - ❑ C. PBX systems
   - ❑ D. Wireless networks

7. Ethical hackers are different than hackers in which of the following ways?
   - ❑ A. They have permission to destroy a network.
   - ❑ B. Their goal is to do no harm.
   - ❑ C. They cannot be held liable for any damage.
   - ❑ D. They cannot be prosecuted or jailed.

8. What is it called when employees move from job to job and keep obtaining more rights and access with each new job?

❑ A. Principle of least privilege

❑ B. Project creep

❑ C. Principle of increased privilege

❑ D. Authorization creep

9. Which RAID type provides data striping but no redundancy?

❑ A. RAID 0

❑ B. RAID 1

❑ C. RAID 3

❑ D. RAID 4

10. Which of the following is the fastest backup option but takes the longest to restore?

❑ A. Incremental

❑ B. Differential

❑ C. Full

❑ D. Grandfathered

Answers to Exam Prep Questions

1. Answer: A. Insiders represent the biggest threat to the organization because they possess two of the three things needed to attempt malicious activity: means and opportunity. Answers B, C, and D are incorrect because although outsiders might have a motive, they typically lack the means or opportunity to attack your organization.

2. Answer: B. Mandatory vacations are not primarily for employee benefit, but to better secure the organization's assets. Answers A, C, and D are incorrect. As answer A states, this gives the organization the opportunity to audit employee work. In answer C, it keeps one person from easily being able to carry out covert activities. In answer D, it ensures that employees will know that illicit activities could be uncovered. Each is a valid reason to use mandatory vacations.

3. Answer: D. Audit trails are considered a detective type of control. Answers A, B, and C are incorrect because audit trails are not an application, administrative, or preventive control.

4. Answer: B. RAID provides capacity benefits, performance improvements, and fault tolerance; therefore, answers A, C, and D are incorrect. Although RAID might reduce recovery time, it certainly won't increase it.

5. Answer: B. Separation of duties is closely tied to the principle of least privilege. Separation of duties is the process of dividing duties so that more than one person is required to complete a task, and each person has only the minimum resources needed to complete the task. Answer A is incorrect because dual controls are implemented to require more than one person to complete an important task. Answer C is incorrect because job rotation is used to prevent collusion. Answer D is incorrect because the principle of privilege would have an adverse affect from what is required.

6. Answer: C. Phreakers target phone and voice systems. Answer A is incorrect because mainframes are typically not a target of phreakers. Answer B is incorrect because networks might be a target of hackers, but phreakers target phone systems. Answer D is incorrect because wireless networks are targeted by war drivers or hackers, not phreakers.

7. Answer: B. Ethical hackers use the same methods as crackers and black-hat hackers, but they report the problems they find instead of taking advantage of them. Ethical hacking has other names, such as penetration testing, intrusion testing, and red-teaming. Ethical hackers do not typically have permission to destroy a network, can be held responsible if they exceed the limits of their contracts, and can be jailed or prosecuted if they break laws or exceed their legal privilege. Answer A is incorrect because ethical hackers do not have permission to destroy

networks. Answer C is incorrect because ethical hackers can be held liable. Answer D is incorrect because ethical hackers can be jailed if they break the law or exceed the terms of their contract.

8. Answer: D. Authorization creep occurs when employees move from job to job and keep picking up more rights and access. Rights and privileges should be terminated if users no longer need them to perform their job. Answer A is incorrect because the principle of least privilege addresses the broad idea of providing only what is needed for a task. Answer B is incorrect because the term *project creep* defines a project that continues to grow beyond its original scope. Answer C is incorrect because the principle of increased privilege could be used to describe the fact that a user is picking up added rights, but this is not the correct term.

9. Answer: A. RAID 0 provides data striping but no redundancy. Answers B, C, and D are incorrect because RAID 1 provides disk mirroring, RAID 3 provides byte-level striping with a dedicated parity disk, and RAID 4 is considered a dedicated parity drive.

10. Answer: A. Incremental backup is the fastest backup option yet takes the longest to restore. Answers B, C, and D are incorrect: A grandfathered backup is not a valid answer, a differential backup takes less time each day but longer to restore, and a full backup takes the longest to perform and the longest to restore.

Need to Know More?

www.penetration-testing.com/#4/—Penetration testing methodologies

www.isecom.org/osstmm/—The Open Source Security Testing Methodology Manual

www.police.txstate.edu/Presentations/internal.ppt/—Employee controls

http://keystroke-loggers.staticusers.net/laws.shtml/—Keystroke-monitoring ethics and laws

www.disasterplan.com//—Contingency-management plans

Business Continuity Planning

Terms you'll need to understand:

✓ Disaster recovery plan
✓ Business continuity plan
✓ Hot site
✓ Warm site
✓ Cold site
✓ Contingencies
✓ Maximum tolerable downtime
✓ Remote journaling
✓ Electronic vaulting
✓ Disk shadowing

Techniques you'll need to master:

✓ The process and development of contingency plans
✓ Business impact analysis processes and procedures
✓ Backup procedures and alternatives
✓ BCP testing strategies
✓ Recovery strategies

Introduction

Much of the material you have read in this book has dealt with the ways in which security incidents can be prevented. The business continuity plan (BCP) and disaster-recovery plan (DRP) domains address what to do and how to respond when things go wrong. This chapter discusses how to preserve business operations in the face of major disruptions. The BCP is about assessing risk and determining how the business would respond should these risks occur. Some of the steps of the BCP process include project management and planning, business impact analysis (BIA), continuity planning design and development, and BCP testing and training. The DRP is a subset of your BCP plan; it is about the planning and restoration actions the business would undertake if a disastrous event occurred.

To pass the business continuity planning domain of the ISC² Certified Information Systems Security Professional (CISSP) exam, you will need to know the steps that make up the BCP process. You will also need to know the differences between BCP and DRP. Attention to understanding ways in which the BCP can be tested, including tabletop, full interruptions, checklists, and functional tests, is also required.

The Risks of Poor Business Planning

Natural disasters such as earthquakes, floods, and fires often come at the least expected time. Others, such as hurricanes and tornados, are increasing in severity and destruction. Many reports and studies have found that only about 50% of businesses have comprehensive business continuity plans in place. Disasters can come in many shapes and forms. To those foolish enough not to be prepared, it could mean the death of the business. Organizations must plan for these types of disasters:

➤ **Natural**—Earthquakes, storms, fires, floods, hurricanes, tornados, and tidal waves

➤ **System/technical**—Outages, malicious code, worms, and hackers

➤ **Supply systems**—Electrical power problems, equipment outages, utility problems, and water shortages

➤ **Human-made/political**—Disgruntled employees, riots, vandalism, theft, crime, protesters, and political unrest

Each of these can cause aninterruption in operations. The length of time that services could be interrupted are defined as follows:

➤ **Minor**—Operations are disrupted for several hours to less than a day.

➤ **Intermediate**—An event of this stature can cause operations to be disrupted for a day or longer. The organization might need a secondary site to continue operations.

➤ **Major**—This type of event is a true catastrophe. In this type of disaster, the entire facility would be destroyed. A long-term solution would require building a new facility.

Business Continuity Management

Business Continuity Management is about more than just developing a plan for recovery in case of an outage. It takes a long, hard look at the way in which the organization does business. The goal is not to just reduce outage time, but also to find better ways to manage its products and services. The Business Continuity Institute (www.thebci.org), a professional body for business continuity management, defines business community management in the following terms:

> Business Continuity Management is a holistic management process that identifies potential impacts that threaten an organization and provides a framework for building resilience and the capability for an effective response that safeguards the interests of its key stakeholders, reputation, brand, and value creating activities.

Business Continuity Plan (BCP)

The BCP is developed to prevent interruptions to normal business. If these events cannot be prevented, the goal of the plan is to minimize the outage. The other goal of the plan is to reduce the potential costs that such disruptions might cost an organization. Therefore, the business continuity plan should also be designed to help minimize the cost associated with the disruptive event and mitigate the risk associated with it. The BCP process as defined by the ISC^2 has the following five steps:

1. Project management and initiation

2. Business impact analysis

3. Recovery strategy

4. Plan design and development

5. Testing, maintenance, awareness, and training

Each of these is discussed in the following sections.

Project Management and Initiation

Before the BCP process can begin, you need to make your case to management. You have to establish the need for the BCP. One way to start is to perform a risk analysis to identify and document potential outages to critical systems. The results should be presented to management so they understand the potential risk. That's a good time to remind them that, ultimately, they are responsible. Customers, shareholders, stockholders, or anyone else could bring a civil suit against senior management if they feel they have not practiced due care. If you don't get management's support, you will not have funds to successfully complete the project, and it will be marginally successful, if at all.

With management on board, you can start to develop a plan of action. This management plan should include the following:

➤ **Scope of the project**—A properly defined scope is a tremendous help in ensuring that an effective BCP plan is devised. At this point in the process, the decision to do only a partial recovery or a full recovery would be made. In larger organizations, office politics can pull the project in directions that it might not need to be going. Another problem is project creep, which occurs when more items are added to the plan that were not part of original project plan. This can delay completion of the project or cause it to run over budget.

➤ **Appointment of a project planner**—The project planner is a key role because this person drives the process. The project planner must ensure that all elements of the plan are properly addressed and that a sufficient level of research, planning, and analysis has been performed before the plan begins. This individual must also have enough creditability with senior management to influence them when the time comes to present the results and recommendations.

➤ **Determination of who will be on the team**—Team members should have representatives from senior management, the legal staff, recovery team leaders, the information security department, various business units, networking, and physical security. You want to make sure that the individuals who would be responsible for executing the plan are involved in the development process.

➤ **Finalize the project plan**—This step is similar to traditional project plan phases. The team leader and the team must finalize issues such as needed resources (personnel, financial), time schedules, budget estimates, and critical success factors. Scheduling meetings and BCP completion dates are two critical items that must be addressed at this point.

➤ **Determine the data-collection method**—Different tools can be used to gather the data. Strohl Systems BIA Professional and SunGard's Paragon software can automate much of the BCP process. If you choose to use these tools, be sure to add time into your schedule. A learning curve is involved anytime individuals are introduced to software they are not familiar with.

Business Impact Analysis (BIA)

The BIA is the second step of the process. Its role is to describe what impact a disaster would have on critical business functions. The BIA is an important step in the process because it looks at the threats to these functions and the costs of a potential outage. As an example, the BIA might uncover the fact that DoS attacks that result in 2 hours of downtime of the company's VoIP phone system will result in $28,000 in lost revenue, whereas an 8-hour outage to the web server might cost the company only $1,000 in lost revenue. These types of numbers will help the organization determine what needs to be done to ensure the survival of the company. The eight steps in the BIA process are as follows:

1. Select individuals to interview.

2. Determine the methods to be used for gathering information.

3. Develop a customized questionnaire to gather specific monetary and operational impact information. This should include questions that inquire about both quantitative and qualitative losses. The goal is to use this data to help determine how the loss of any one function.

4. Analyze the compiled data.

5. Determine the time-critical business processes and functions.

6. Determine maximum tolerable downtimes for each process and function.

7. Prioritize the critical business process or function based on its maximum tolerable downtime (MTD).

8. Document the findings and report your recommendations to management.

MTD is a measurement of the longest time that an organization can survive without a specific business function. MTD estimates include critical (minutes to hours), urgent (24 hours or less), important (up to 72 hours), average (up to 7 days), and nonessential (these services can experience outages up to 30 days).

The impact or loss that an organization faces because of lost service or data can be felt in many ways. These are generally measured by one of the following:

➤ **Allowable business interruption**—What is the maximum tolerable downtime (MTD) the organization can survive without that function or service?

➤ **Financial and operational considerations**—What will this outage cost? Will there be a loss of revenue or operational capital, or will we be held personally liable? Cost can be immediate or delayed. Other potential costs include any losses incurred because of failure in meeting the SLA requirements of customers.

➤ **Regulatory requirements**—What violations of law or regulations could this cause? Is there a legal penalty?

➤ **Organizational reputation**—Will this affect our competitive advantage, market share, or reputation?

The BIA builds the groundwork for determining how resources should be appropriated for recovery-planning efforts.

A vulnerability assessment is often part of a BIA. Although the assessment is somewhat similar to the risk-assessment process discussed in Chapter 3, "Security-Management Practices," this one focuses on providing information that is used just for the business continuity plan.

Recovery Strategy

Recovery strategies are the predefined actions that management has approved to be followed in case normal operations are interrupted. Operations can be interrupted in several different ways:

➤ **Data interruptions**—The focus here is on recovering the data. Solutions to data interruptions include backups, offsite storage, and remote journaling.

➤ **Operational interruptions**—The interruption is caused by the loss of some type of equipment. Solutions to this type of interruption include hot sites, redundant equipment, Redundant Array of Inexpensive Disks (RAID), and Backup Power Supplies (BPS).

➤ **Facility and supply interruptions**—Causes of these interruptions can include fire, loss of inventory, transportation problems, Heating Ventilation and Air Conditioner (HVAC) problems, and telecommunications.

➤ **Business interruptions**—These interruptions can be caused by loss of personnel, strikes, critical equipment, supplies, and office space.

To evaluate the losses that could occur from any of these interruptions and determine the best recovery strategy, follow these steps:

1. Document all costs for each possible alternative.

2. Obtain cost estimates for any outside services that might be needed.

3. Develop written agreements with the chosen vendor for such services.

4. Evaluate what resumption strategies are possible in case there is a complete loss of the facility.

5. Document your findings and report your chosen recovery strategies to management for feedback and approval.

Plan Design and Development

In this phase, the team prepares and documents a detailed plan for recovery of critical business systems. The plan should be a guide for implementation. The plan should include information on both long-term and short-term goals and objectives:

1. Identify critical functions and priorities for restoration.

2. Identify support systems that are needed by critical functions.

3. Estimate potential disasters and calculate the minimum resources needed to recover from the catastrophe.

4. Select recovery strategies and determine what vital personnel, systems, and equipment will be needed to accomplish the recovery.

5. Determine who will manage the restoration and testing process.

6. Calculate what type of funding and fiscal management is needed to accomplish these goals.

The plan should also detail how the organization will interface with external groups, such as customers, shareholders, the media, the community, and region and state emergency services groups. The final step of the phase is to combine this information into the BCP plan and interface it with the organization's other emergency plans.

Testing, Maintenance, Awareness, and Training

This final phase of the process is for testing and maintaining the BCP. Training and awareness programs are also developed at this point. Testing the disaster-recovery plan is critical. Without performing a test, there is no way to know whether the plan will work. Testing helps make theoretical plans reality. As a CISSP candidate, you should be aware of the five different types of BCP testing:

➤ **Checklist**—Although this is not considered a replacement for a real test, it is a good start. A checklist test is performed by sending copies of the plan to different department managers and business unit managers for review. Each person the plan is sent to can review it to make sure nothing was overlooked.

➤ **Tabletop**—A tabletop test is performed by having the members of the emergency management team and business unit managers meet in a conference to discuss the plan. The plan then is "walked through" line by line. This gives all attendees a chance to see how an actual emergency would be handled and to discover dependencies. By reviewing the plan in this way, some errors or problems should become apparent.

 The primary advantage of the tabletop testing method is to discover dependencies between different departments.

➤ **Walkthrough**—This is an actual simulation of the real thing. This drill involves members of the response team acting in the same way as if there had been an actual emergency. This test proceeds to the point of recovery or to relocation of the alternative site. The primary purpose of this test is to verify that members of the response team can perform the required duties.

➤ **Functional**—A functional test is similar to a walkthrough but actually starts operations at the alternative site. Operations of the new and old sites can be run in parallel.

➤ **Full interruption**—This plan is the most detailed, time-consuming, and thorough. A full interruption test mimics a real disaster, and all steps are performed to startup backup operations. It involves all the individuals who would be involved in a real emergency, including internal and external organizations.

The CISSP exam will require you to know the differences of each BCP test type. You should also note the advantages and disadvantages of each.

When the testing process is complete, a few additional items still need to be done. The organization must put controls in place to maintain the current level of business continuity and disaster recovery. This is best accomplished by implementing change-management procedures. If changes are required to the approved plans, you will then have a documented, structured way to accomplish this. A centralized command and control structure eases this burden. Controls also should be built into the procedures to allow for periodic retesting. Life is not static, and neither should be the organization's BCP plans. The individuals responsible for specific parts of the BCP process are listed in Table 9.1.

Table 9.1 BCP Process Responsibilities	
Person or Department	**Responsibility**
Senior management	Project initiation, ultimate responsibility, overall approval and support
Midmanagement or business unit managers	Identification and prioritization of critical systems
BCP committee and team members	Planning, day-to-day management, implementation and testing of the plan
Functional business units	Plan implementation, incorporation, and testing

Senior management is ultimately responsible for the BCP. This includes project initiation, overall approval, and support.

Awareness and Training

The goal of awareness and training is to make sure all employees know what to do in case of an emergency. If employees are untrained, they might simply stop what they're doing and run for the door anytime there's an emergency. Even worse, they might not leave when an alarm has sounded and they have been instructed to leave because of possible danger. Therefore, the organization should design and develop training programs to make sure each employee knows what to do and how to do it. Employees assigned to specific tasks should be trained to carry out needed procedures. Plan for cross-training of teams, if possible, so those team members are familiar with a variety of recovery roles and responsibilities.

The number one priority of any BCP or DRP plan is to protect the safety of employees.

Disaster Recovery Planning (DRP)

Although BCP deals with what is needed to keep the organization running and what functions are most critical, the DRP's purpose is to get a damaged organization restarted where critical business functions can resume. Because the DRP is more closely related to IT issues, this portion of the chapter also introduces such topics as alternative sites, reciprocal agreements, backups, and electronic vaulting.

Individuals involved in disaster recovery must deal with many things, but when called to action, their activities center on assessing the damage, restoring operations, and determining whether an alternate location will be needed until repairs can be made. These items can be broadly grouped into salvage and recovery. Both activities are discussed here:

➤ **Salvage**—Restoring functionality to damaged systems, units, or the facility. This includes the following steps:

1. A damage assessment to determine the extent of the damage

2. A salvage operation to recover any repairable equipment

3. Repair and cleaning to eliminate any damage to the facility and restore equipment to a fully functional state

4. Restoration of the facility so that it is fully restored, stocked, and ready for business

➤ **Recovery**—Focused on the responsibilities needed to get an alternate site up and running. This site will be used to stand in for the original site until operations can be restored there.

Physical security is always of great importance after a disaster. Steps such as guards, temporary fencing, and barriers should be deployed to prevent looting and vandalism.

Alternative Sites and Hardware Backup

When disaster strikes your organization and your DRP team reports that the data center is unusable, that is not the time to start discussions on alternate sites. This discussion should have occurred long ago. Many options are available, from a dedicated offsite facility, to agreements with other organizations for shared space, to the option of building a prefab building and leaving it empty as a type of cold backup site. The following sections look at some of these options.

Reciprocal Agreement

This frequently discussed option requires two organizations to pledge assistance to one another in case of disaster. This would be carried out by sharing space, computer facilities, and technology resources. On paper, this appears to be a cost-effective approach, but it does have its drawbacks. The parties to this agreement must place their trust in the other organization to their aid in case of disaster. However, the nonvictim might be hesitant to follow through if such a disaster did occur. There is also the issue of confidentiality because the damaged organization is placed in a vulnerable position and must trust the other party with confidential information. Finally, if the parties of the agreement are near each other, there is always the danger that disaster could strike both parties, thereby, rendering the agreement useless.

The biggest drawback to reciprocal agreements is that they are hard to enforce and that many times incompatibilities in company cultures, hardware, or other, are not discovered until after a disaster strikes.

Hot, Warm, and Cold Sites

Because data centers are expensive and critical to the continuation of business, the organization might decide to have a dedicated to use a hot, warm, cold, or mobile site.

➤ **Cold site**—This is basically an empty room with only rudimentary electrical, power, and computing capability. It might have a raised floor and some racks, but it is nowhere near ready for use. It might take several weeks to a month to get the site operational.

➤ **Warm site**—Somewhat of an improvement over a cold site, this facility has data equipment and cables, and is partially configured. It could be made operational in anywhere from a few hours to a few days.

➤ **Hot site**—This facility is ready to go. It is fully configured and is equipped with the same system as the production network. Although it is capable of taking over operations at a moment's notice, it is the most expensive option discussed.

Mobile sites are a nonmainstream alternative to traditional recovery options. Mobile sites typically consist of fully contained tractor-trailer rigs that come with all the needed facilities of a data center. They can be quickly moved to any needed site.

Multiple Data Centers

Another option or the organization is to maintain multiple data centers. Each of these sites is capable of handling all operations if another fails. Although there is an increased cost, it gives the company fault tolerance by maintaining multiple redundant sites. If the redundant sites are geographically dispersed, the possibility of more than one being damaged is low. The organization also does not have to depend on a third party or wait for a hot/warm/cold/mobile site to become operational.

Service Bureaus

Organizations might opt to contract their offsite needs to a service bureau. The advantage of this option is that the responsibility of this service is placed on someone else. The disadvantage is the cost and possible problems with resource contention if a large-scale emergency occurs.

Other Alternatives

Some other alternatives for backup and redundancy have not been discussed yet. Some organizations use these by themselves or in combination with other services:

➤ **Database shadowing**—Databases are a high-value asset for most organizations. File-based incremental backups can read only entire database tables and are considered too slow. A database shadowing system uses two physical disks to write the data to. It creates good redundancy by duplicating the database sets to mirrored servers. Therefore, this is an excellent way to provide fault tolerance and redundancy.

➤ **Electronic vaulting**—Electronic vaulting makes a copy of backup data to a backup location. This is a batch-process operation that functions to keep a copy of all current records, transactions, or files at an offsite location.

➤ **Remote journaling**—Remote journaling is similar to electronic vaulting, except that information is processed in parallel. By performing live data transfers, it allows the alternate site to be fully synchronized and ready to go at all times. It provides a very high level of fault tolerance.

Software Backups

Equipment is not much good without the software to run on it. Part of a good disaster-recovery plan should consist of ways to back up and restore software. This backup can be stored either on- or offsite. The decision to store offsite is usually made as a type of insurance policy in case the primary site is damaged or destroyed. Software can be vulnerable even when good backup policies are followed because sometimes software vendors go out of business or no longer support needed applications. In these instances, *escrow agreements* can help.

> Escrow agreements are one possible software-protection mechanism. Escrow agreements allow an organization to obtain access to the source code of business-critical software if the software vendor goes bankrupt or otherwise fails to perform as required.

Backup Types

If you are using tape as your backup solution, you must decide what form of tape backup you perform. You have the choice of a faster backup, a longer restore, or more tapes used.

➤ **Full**—A full backup backs up all files, regardless of whether they have been modified. It removes the archive bit.

➤ **Incremental**—An incremental backup backs up only those files that have been modified since the previous backup of any sort. Incremental backups are performed after an initial full backup. Each night, the incremental backup copies any files that changed during the previous day. Because the incremental backup clears the archive bit, each night's backup operation can be completed quickly; however, a restoration will require all incremental backup tapes plus the last full backup.

➤ **Differential**—A differential backup backs up all files that have been modified since the last full backup. It does not remove the archive bit. Differential backups take longer to perform than incremental backups but can be restored quicker than incremental backups. Restoring from a differential backup means that only two restores will be required: the full backup and the last differential backup.

> Questions regarding different backup types can be quite tricky. Make sure you clearly know the difference before the exam.

Tape-Rotation Strategies

It's important to remember that you will want to periodically test your backup tapes. These tapes will be of little use if you find during a disaster that they have malfunctioned and no longer work. Tape-rotation strategies can range from simple to complex.

➤ **Simple**—A simple tape-rotation scheme uses one tape for every day of the week and then repeats the next week. One tape can be for Monday, one for Tuesday, and so on. You add a set of new tapes each month and then archive the monthly sets. After a predetermined number of months, you put the oldest tapes back into use.

➤ **Grandfather-father-son**—This scheme (GFS) includes four tapes for weekly backups, one tape for monthly backups, and four tapes for daily backups (assuming you are using a 5-day work week). It is called grandfather-father-son because the scheme establishes a kind of hierarchy. Grandfathers are the one monthly backup, fathers are the four weekly backups, and sons are the four daily backups.

➤ **Tower of Hanoi**—This tape-rotation scheme is named after a mathematical puzzle. It involves using five sets of tapes, each set labeled A through E. Set A is used every other day; set B is used on the first non-A backup day and is used every 4th day; set C is used on the first non-A or non-B backup day and is used every 8th day; set D is used on the first non-A, non-B, or non-C day and is used every 16th day; and set E alternates with set D.

Exam Prep Questions

1. The most important aspect of disaster recovery is
   - ❏ A. A complete damage assessment
   - ❏ B. Control of critical assets
   - ❏ C. Restoration of business functions
   - ❏ D. Protection of individual life

2. Which of the following groups is responsible for project initiation?
   - ❏ A. Functional business units
   - ❏ B. Senior management
   - ❏ C. BCP team members
   - ❏ D. Midmanagement

3. This team is focused on the responsibilities needed to get an alternate site up and running.
   - ❏ A. Salvage team
   - ❏ B. BCP management team
   - ❏ C. IT management
   - ❏ D. Recovery team

4. Which of the following is considered a disadvantage of a mutual aid agreement?
   - ❏ A. Low cost
   - ❏ B. Reliability
   - ❏ C. Documentation
   - ❏ D. Testing

5. Which of the following uses batch processing?
   - ❏ A. Remote journaling
   - ❏ B. Hierarchical storage management
   - ❏ C. Electronic vaulting
   - ❏ D. Static management

6. Which of the following is not considered a real BCP test?
   - ❏ A. Functional
   - ❏ B. Tabletop
   - ❏ C. Walkthrough
   - ❏ D. Checklist

7. A software escrow agreement
   - ❏ A. Provides the vendor with additional assurances that the software will be used per licensing agreements
   - ❏ B. Specifies how much a vendor can charge for updates
   - ❏ C. Gives the company access to the source code under certain conditions
   - ❏ D. Provides the vendor access to the organization's code if there are questions of compatibility

8. Which of the following will a business impact analysis *not* provide?
   - ❏ A. Determining the maximum outage time before the company is permanently crippled
   - ❏ B. Detailing how training and awareness will be performed and how the plan will be updated
   - ❏ C. Establishing the need for BCP
   - ❏ D. Selecting recovery strategies

9. Which tape-backup method is the fastest to perform but takes the longest to restore?
   - ❏ A. Full
   - ❏ B. Structured
   - ❏ C. Differential
   - ❏ D. Incremental

10. This tape-rotation scheme involves using five sets of tapes, with each set labeled A through E.
    - ❏ A. Tower of Hanoi
    - ❏ B. Son-father-grandfather
    - ❏ C. Complex
    - ❏ D. Grandfather-father-son

Answers to Exam Prep Questions

1. Answer: D. The protection of individual life is the number one priority of security management. While answer A is important as a damage assessment needs to be made, the most important item is the protection of individual life. Answer B is incorrect because even though the control of critical assets is important the number on aspect of disaster recovery should be the protection of life. Answer C is incorrect as the protection of life should be your number one concern.

2. Answer: B. Although the other groups listed have responsibilities in the BCP process, senior management is responsible for project initiation, overall approval, and support, and is ultimately responsible if someone is to be held liable. Answer A is incorrect because the functional business units are responsible for implementation, incorporation, and testing. Answer C is incorrect because the BCP team members are responsible for planning, day-to-day management, and implementation and testing of the plan. Answer D is incorrect because midmanagement is responsible for the identification and prioritization of critical systems.

3. Answer: D. An important part of the disaster-recovery process is the recovery team because it is focused on the responsibilities needed to get an alternate site up and running. Answer A is incorrect because the salvage team is responsible for assessing the damage and determining what can be recovered after a disastrous has occurred. Answer B is incorrect because the management team consists of the individuals who are in charge of the plan overall. Answer C is incorrect because IT management is responsible for day-to-day operations.

4. Answer: B. The parties to this agreement must place their trust in the other organization to come to their aid in the event of a disaster. However, the nonvictim might be hesitant to follow through if such a disaster occurred. None of the other answers represents a disadvantage because this is a low-cost alternative, it can be documented, and some tests to verify that it would work can be performed.

5. Answer: C. Electronic vaulting makes a copy of backup data to a backup location. This is a batch process operation that functions to keep a copy of all current records, transactions, or files at an offsite location. Remote journaling is similar to electronic vaulting, except that information is processed in parallel, so answer A is incorrect. Hierarchical storage management provides continuous online backup functionality, so answer B is incorrect. Static management is a distracter and is not a valid choice, so answer D is incorrect.

6. Answer: D. A checklist test is performed by sending copies of the plan to different department managers and business unit managers for review. Each person the plan is sent to can review it to make sure nothing was overlooked or should be removed. All of the other answers listed are considered real tests, so answers A, B, and C are incorrect.

7. Answer: C. A software escrow agreement allows an organization to obtain access to the source code of business critical software if the software vendor goes bankrupt or otherwise fails to perform as required. Answer A is incorrect because an escrow agreement does not provide the vendor with additional assurances that the software will be used per licensing agreements. Answer B is incorrect because an escrow agreement does not specify how much a vendor can charge for updates. Answer D is incorrect as escrow agreement does not address compatibility issues; it grants access to the source code only under certain conditions.

8. Answer: A. A BIA is a process used to help business units understand the impact of a disruptive event. Part of that process is determining the maximum outage time before the company is permanently crippled. The other answers are part of the BCP process but are not specifically part of the BIA portion, so answers B, C, and D are incorrect.

9. Answer: D. Incremental backups take less time to perform but longer to restore. Answer A is incorrect because a full backup backs up everything and, therefore, takes the longest. Answer B is incorrect because the term *structured* addresses how a backup is carried out, not the method used. Answer C is incorrect because a differential backup does not reset the archive bit; it takes increasingly longer each night but would require a shorter period to restore because only two restores would be needed: the last full and the last differential.

10. Answer: A. This tape-rotation scheme is named after a mathematical puzzle. It involves using five sets of tapes, with each set labeled A through E. Set A is used every other day. Set B is used on the first non-A backup day and is used every 4th day. Set C is used on the first non-A or non-B backup day and is used every 8th day. Set D is used on the first non-A, non-B, or non-C day and is used every 16th day. Set E alternates with set D. Answer B is incorrect because Son-father-grandfather is a distracter. Answer C is incorrect as complex does not refer to a specific backup type. Answer D is incorrect as Grandfather-father-son includes four tapes for weekly backups, one tape for monthly backups, and four tapes for daily backups and does not match the description described in the question.

Need to Know More?

http://thebci.org/—Business Continuity Institute

www.exabyte.com/support/online/documentation/whitepapers/basicbackup.pdf—Tape-backup strategies

www.crime-research.org/library/Richard.html—Vulnerability assessment information

www.professorbainbridge.com/2003/11/substantive_due.html—Information on due care and due diligence

www.disaster-resource.com/articles/electric_vault_rapid_lindeman.shtml—Electronic vaulting

www.ncasia.com/ViewArt.cfm?Artid=15255&catid=4&subcat=43—Recovery strategies

10

Law, Investigations, and Ethics

Terms you'll need to understand:

✓ Data diddling
✓ Spoofing
✓ Social engineering
✓ United Nations Commission on International Trade Law (UNCITRAL)
✓ The European Union (EU)
✓ The World Trade Organization (WTO)
✓ International Organization on Computer Evidence (IOCE)
✓ Categories of law
✓ RFC 1087
✓ ISC² Code of Ethics

Techniques you'll need to master:

✓ Understanding incident response
✓ Describing the chain of custody
✓ Implementing forensic procedures

Introduction

Crime has been around as long as man has inhabited Earth. Technology and computers have brought us many advances and also have changed the ways crimes are committed. Computers are usually found to be a component of modern crime. Problems such as identity theft, phishing schemes, and war driving were unheard of 25 years ago.

The Law, Investigations, and Ethics domain addresses computer crime, laws, regulations, and investigation techniques. Test candidates are expected to know not only whether a crime has been committed, but also the laws that apply to the crime, the ethical issues, and the code of conduct that all Certified Information Systems Security Professionals (CISSP) should abide by. CISSP candidates must be prepared to deal with these issues, understand major legal systems, have a general understanding of forensic procedures, and be familiar with the ISC² Code of Ethics. These are the topics that are discussed in this chapter.

Computer Crimes

Some reports show that computers are used in as many as 80% of all crimes. Either a computer is used as a tool to commit the crime, a computer or network is the victim of a crime, or the computer is used in planning, tracking, and controlling the crime. So, although more computers are involved in the criminal process, it's commonly thought that only one-tenth or so of all the crimes committed against and using computer systems are detected.

How could this be true? It is difficult to develop accurate numbers regarding the detection and reporting of computer crime. Many crimes go undetected, and others that are detected are never reported to law-enforcement agencies or the general public. Some companies are worried about a possible negative image; others are afraid that it might make them appear vulnerable. Another big issue with computer crime is determining who has jurisdiction. If a user in country A hacks a computer in country B to attack a company in country C, who has the right or ability to prosecute the crime? The United States has proposed legislation that will claim jurisdiction over any criminal activity that travels through a U.S.-controlled portion of the Internet, regardless of starting or destination country.

Software Piracy

The unauthorized copying and sharing of software is considered software piracy, which is illegal. Don't think that the copy of that computer game you gave a friend is hurting anyone? Software piracy is big business. The International

Intellectual Property Alliance (IPPA) says that major U.S. copyright industries claimed in 1996 alone a loss of more than $2.8 billion domestically due to piracy. Internationally, the losses were more than $18 billion.

Major software companies are fighting back and have formed the Software Protection Association, which is one of the primary bodies that actively fights to enforce licensing agreements. Microsoft and others are also actively fighting to protect their property rights. The Business Software Alliance and The Federation Against Software Theft are both international groups targeting software piracy.

Terrorism

It would be hard to include a section such as this and not talk about terrorist attacks. These individuals are definitely in a category of their own. Their attacks typically target innocent civilians. Although not all terrorists directly target networked devices, known as *cyberterrorism*, most use computers in preparing their deeds. Attacks can also be carried out remotely, which means they are harder to detect and deter. In the end, no one knows exactly how terrorists will use the Internet in their next attack or exploit, but they likely will use computer systems in some way.

Pornography

Although some debate might arise on the legality of adult porn, child pornography is illegal in the United States and most other countries. Child porn is not specifically a computer crime, but the Internet allows it to be distributed, so this falls under a computer crime activity. The individuals who deal in child porn are pedophiles and are directly tied to violent crime.

Child pornography is just part of the problem. Some reports have indicated that more than 200,000 individuals in the United States are hopelessly addicted to Internet porn. If that statistic doesn't capture your attention, this should: The same sources also found that about 70% of Internet porn traffic occurs between 9 a.m. and 5 p.m. This raises the question of acceptable use policies (AUPs). U.S. law requires companies to provide a safe workplace where employees are free from sexual harassment and offensive behavior. Therefore, companies that fail to enforce AUPs could find themselves in legal hot water.

Common Attacks

Computers can be attacked in many different ways. A determined hacker can target your company for a low-tech social-engineering attack or attempt a very advanced technique such as a cross-site scripting attack. Depending on what their motives are, they can do a huge amount of damage if they are successful.

Keystroke Logging

Keystroke logging is an attack that is accomplished with software or hardware devices. These devices can record everything a person types, including usernames, passwords, and account information. The hardware version of these devices is usually installed while users are away from their desks. Hardware keystroke loggers are completely undetectable except for their physical presence. Even then, they can be overlooked because they resemble a balum or extension. How many people do you know who pay close attention to the plugs on the back of their computer? Who even looks back there?

The software version of this device is basically a shim that sits between the operating system and the keyboard. Most of these software programs are very simple, but some are more complex and can even email the logged keystrokes back to a preconfigured address. What they all have in common is that they operate in stealth mode and can be a serious threat to confidentiality.

 Before you attempt any type of keystroke monitoring, be sure to check with your organization's legal department. Most states and federal law require that each user using the computer be notified of such activities. Otherwise, you could be breaking some laws.

Wiretapping

Closely related to keystroke logging, *wiretapping* is used to eavesdrop on voice calls. A variety of tools is available for attackers to accomplish this—even scanners that no longer support cordless phone sniffing can be hacked or rewired to add such functionality. Wiretapping is illegal in the United States without a court order. Another related type of passive attack is the practice of sniffing. Sniffing operates on the same principle as wiretapping but is performed on data lines. The danger of both wiretapping and sniffing is that they are hard to detect.

 A *traffic-analysis attack* is a form of sniffing attack in which the data is encoded. By observing the victim's activities and analyzing traffic patterns, the attacker might be able to make certain assumptions. For example, if an attacker observes one financially strong company sending large amounts of communication to a financially weak company, the attacker might infer that they are discussing a merger.

Spoofing Attacks

Spoofing attacks take advantage of the fact that an attacker is changing his identity to avoid capture or to trick someone into believing he is someone else. Some examples are described here:

➤ **IP spoofing**—The intruder puts a wrong IP address in the source IP address field of the packets he sends out. It's a common practice when DoS tools are used to help the attacker mask his identity.

➤ **DNS spoofing**—This trusting protocol can be spoofed to point victims to the wrong domain. These attacks are possible because the client takes the domain name and queries the IP address. The returned IP address is trusted. If an attacker can control this mapping, he can establish the validity of any system under a given logical address.

➤ **ARP spoofing**—Normally, ARP works to resolve known IP addresses to unknown physical addresses. This information is used to address the Ethernet frame. After the two-step ARP process takes place, the results are stored in a cache for a short period of time. The ARP cache contains hardware-to-IP mapping information. The information maintained in the ARP cache can be corrupted if a hacker sends a bogus ARP response with his hardware address and an assumed IP address of a trusted host. Packets from the target are now routed to your hardware address. The target believes that your machine is the trusted host.

 ARP spoofing is considered a local area network (LAN) attack because hardware addresses do not pass through routers.

➤ **Hijacking**—This more advanced spoof attack works by subverting the TCP connection between a client and a server. If the attacker learns the initial sequence numbers and can get between the client and the server, he can use this information to hijack the already-established connection. At this point, the attacker has a valid connection to the victim's network and is authenticated with the victim's credentials.

Manipulation Attacks

Manipulation attacks can use different methods, but they have the same goal: manipulating data to steal money, embezzle funds, or change values. Some common forms of these attacks include the following:

➤ **Shopping cart attacks**—Hackers compromise shopping carts by tampering with the forms used to pass dollar values to e-commerce servers. This allows the attackers to get huge discounts on goods and services. This is possible if the victims use the GET method for their forms or if they use hidden input tags in the order forms. Hackers save these pages to their hard drive, alter the price listed in the URL or the hidden tag, and then submit the order to the victim's site for processing.

➤ **Salami attacks**—This form of attack works by systematically whittling away assets in accounts or other records with financial value. The small amounts are deducted from balances regularly and routinely, and might not be noticed, allowing the attacker to amass large amounts of funds.

➤ **Data diddling**—This type of attack occurs when the attacker enters a system or captures network traffic and makes changes to selected files or packets. He doesn't delete the files—he merely edits and corrupts the data in some fashion. This attack can do a lot of damage but might not be quick or easy to uncover.

Social Engineering

Social engineering predates the computer era. *Social engineering* is much like an old-fashioned con game, in that the attacker uses the art of manipulation to trick a victim into providing private information or improper access. P. T. Barnum once said, "There's a sucker born every minute"— unfortunately, he was right.

One common social-engineering attack has targeted e-Bay, Hotmail, PayPal, and Citibank users. The attacker sends an official-sounding email asking users to verify their Internet password via return mail. When they do so, their passwords are sent to the attacker, who can then access the accounts at will. Another common social-engineering hack is to call an organization's help desk and pretend to be a high-ranking officer. The lowly help desk employee can often be bullied or scared into giving out a password or other important information.

The best defense against social engineering is to educate your users and staff to never give out passwords and user IDs over the phone, via email, or to anyone who isn't positively verified as being who they say the are. Training can go a long way toward teaching employees how to spot these scams.

Dumpster Diving

Plenty of valuable information can be stolen the low-tech way. One popular technique is to retrieve passwords and other information by *dumpster diving* and looking for scraps of paper used to write down important numbers and then thrown in the trash. Although this is not typically illegal, it is considered an unethical practice.

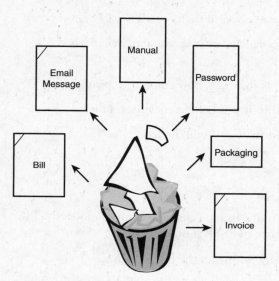

Figure 10.1 Dumpster diving.

 Dumpster diving might not be considered illegal, but it is considered unethical.

Ethics

This section reviews some of the ethical standards and codes that a CISSP should be aware of. Ethics are a set of principles of right conduct. Ethical standards are sometimes different than legal standards: Laws define what we *must* do, whereas ethics define what we *should* do. CISSPs should uphold high ethical standards and promote these ethical standards in others. Some of the ways CISSPs can help promote proper ethical behavior include making sure that organizations have guides to computer ethics, ensuring that ethical issues are included in employee handbooks, promoting computer ethics training, and helping to develop ethical policies on issues such as email and other privacy-related topics. With that being said, you must also remember that not everyone will always act ethically.

Some of the reasons you might hear include the following common ethical fallacies:

➤ **Computer game**—If they don't protect it, it's fair game to attack.

➤ **Law-abiding citizen**—It's not physical theft, so it's not illegal.

➤ **Shatterproof**—If I don't do damage or it can be repaired, what's the problem?

➤ **Candy-from-a-baby**—If it is that easy, how could it be wrong?

➤ **Hackers**—If I learn from this, it will benefit society and me.

➤ **Free information**—All information should be free.

ISC² Code of Ethics

It's a requirement for CISSP candidates to subscribe to and support the ISC² Code of Ethics, which states that a CISSP should

➤ Protect society, the commonwealth, and the infrastructure

➤ Act honorably, honestly, justly, responsibly, and legally

➤ Provide diligent and competent service to principals

➤ Advance and protect the profession

Exam candidates must read the full Code of Ethics because the exam always includes one or two questions related to the code. It is located at www.isc2.org/cgi/content.cgi?category=12.

Computer Ethics Institute

The Computer Ethics Institute is a group that focuses specifically on ethics in the technology industry. Its website, www.cosr.org, lists the following Ten Commandments of Computer Ethics:

1. Thou shalt not use a computer to harm other people.

2. Thou shalt not interfere with other people's computer work.

3. Thou shalt not snoop around in other people's computer files.

4. Thou shalt not use a computer to steal.

5. Thou shalt not use a computer to bear false witness.

6. Thou shalt not copy or use proprietary software for which you have not paid.

7. Thou shalt not use other people's computer resources without authorization or proper compensation.

8. Thou shalt not appropriate other people's intellectual output.

9. Thou shalt think about the social consequences of the program you are writing or the system you are designing.

10. Thou shalt always use a computer in ways that ensure consideration and respect for your fellow humans.

 Exam candidates are advised to read the Ten Commandments of Computer Ethics and be able to differentiate it from the ISC² Code of Ethics.

Internet Activities Board

RFC 1087 was published by the Internet Activities Board (IAB) in January 1987. Its goal is to characterize unethical and unacceptable behavior. It states that the following activities are unethical:

➤ Seeking to gain unauthorized access to the resources of the Internet

➤ Disrupting the intended use of the Internet

➤ Wasting resources (people, capacity, computer) through such actions

➤ Destroying the integrity of computer-based information

➤ Compromising the privacy of users

 Print and review RFC 1087 before you attempt the CISSP exam. It is available at www.faqs.org/rfcs/rfc1087.html.

International Property Laws

Although the laws discussed in the following list are specific to the United States, intellectual property is agreed upon and enforced worldwide by various organizations, including the United Nations Commission on International

Trade Law (UNCITRAL), the European Union (EU), and the World Trade Organization (WTO).

➤ **Trade secret**—A *trade secret* is a confidential design, practice, or method that must be proprietary or business related. For a trade secret to remain valid, the owner must take certain security precautions.

➤ **Copyright**—A *copyright* is a legal device that provides the creator of a work of authorship the right to control how the work is used and protects that person's expression on a specific subject. This includes the reproduction rights, distribution rights, right to create, and right to public display.

➤ **Trademark**—A *trademark* is a symbol, word, name, sound, or thing that identifies the origin of a product or service in a particular trade. The ISC² logo is an example of a trademarked logo. The term *service mark* is sometimes used to distinguish a trademark that applies to a service rather than to a product.

➤ **Patent**—A *patent* grants the owner a legally enforceable right to exclude others from practicing or using the invention's design for a defined period of time.

Privacy Laws

Privacy laws are of interest to many individuals because technology has made it much easier for large amounts of data to be accumulated about them. Commercial databases contain tremendous amounts of data that can be used to infringe on people's sense of privacy and anonymity. The misuse of these databases can lead to targeted advertising and disclosure of personal preferences that some individuals believe is intrusive. Privacy is increasingly being recognized as a fundamental right in many countries. The EU has been on the forefront in developing laws that protect individual privacy. EU privacy guidelines enacted in 1998 state the following:

➤ Data is to be used only for the purposes for which it was collected and within a reasonable time.

➤ If requested, individuals are entitled to receive a report on data about them.

➤ An individual's personal data cannot be disclosed to third parties unless authorized by statute or consent of the individual.

➤ Persons have a right to make corrections to their personal data.

➤ Transmission to locations where equivalent personal data protection cannot be assured is prohibited.

Other Notable Laws

Although the exam does not cover country-specific laws, security professionals should be aware of the laws that pertain to them. Therefore, the following laws are mentioned briefly:

➤ **Computer Fraud and Abuse Act of 1986**—Amended in 1996 to including hacking. Deals with computers used by the federal government.

➤ **Federal Sentencing Guidelines of 1991**—Provides guidelines to judges so that sentences are handed down in a more uniform manner.

➤ **Economic Espionage Act of 1996**—Defines strict penalties for those accused of espionage.

➤ **U.S. Child Pornography Prevention Act of 1996**—Enacted to combat and reduce the use of computer technology to produce and distribute pornography.

➤ **U.S. Health Insurance Portability and Accountability Act**—Establishes privacy and security regulations for the health-care industry.

➤ **U.S. Patriot Act of 2001**—Strengthens computer crime laws and has been the subject of some controversy.

Parameters of Investigation

Security incidents can come in many forms. It could be an honest mistake by an employee who thought he was helping, or it could be the result of an intentional attack. Whatever the motive or reason, the response should always be the same. Security breaches should be investigated in a structured, methodical manner. Most companies would not operate a business without training their employees how to respond to fires, but many companies do not build good incident-response and investigation procedures.

Computer Crime Investigation

Investigating computer crime is a complex and involved one made up of these steps:

1. Plan and prepare by means of procedures, policies, and training.

2. Secure and isolate the scene, to prevent contamination.

3. Record the scene by taking photographs and recording data in an investigator's notebook.

4. Interview suspects and witnesses.

5. Systematically search for other physical evidence.

6. Collect or seize the suspected system or media.

7. Package and transport evidence.

8. Submit evidence to the lab for analysis.

Incident-Response Procedures

Good incident-response procedures give the organization an effective and efficient means of dealing with the situation in a manner that reduces the potential impact. These procedures should also provide management with sufficient information to decide on an appropriate course of action. By having these procedures in place, the organization can maintain or restore business continuity, defend against future attacks, and deter attacks by prosecuting violators.

The primary goal of incident response is to contain the damage, find out what happened, and prevent it from reoccurring. This list identifies the basic steps of incident response:

1. **Identify**—Detect the event. Is it a real event or simply a false positive? A range of mechanisms is used here, including IDS, firewalls, audits, logging, and employee observations.

2. **Coordinate**—This is where preplanning kicks in, with the use of predeveloped procedures. The incident-response plan should detail what action is to be taken by whom. Your incident-response team will need to have had the required level of training to properly handle the response.

3. **Mitigate**—The damage must be contained, and the next course of action must be determined.

4. **Investigate**—What happened? When the investigation is complete, a report, either formal or informal, must be prepared. This is needed to evaluate any necessary changes to the incident response policies.

5. **Educate**—At this final step, all those involved must review what happened and why. Most important is determining what changes must be put in place to prevent future problems. Learning from what happened is the only way to prevent it from happening again.

Incident-Response Team

Incident-response team members need to have diverse skill sets. Internal teams should include representation from various departments:

➤ Information security

➤ Legal

➤ Human resources

➤ Public relations

➤ Physical security

➤ Network and system administration

➤ Internal auditors

Forensics

Computer forensics is a clear, well-defined methodology used to preserve, identify, recover, and document computer or electronic data. Although the computer forensics field is relatively new to the corporate sector, law enforcement has been practicing this science since the mid-1980s. Growth in this field is directly related to the ever-growing popularity of electronics.

Computers are one of the most targeted items of examination, but they are not the only devices subject to forensic analysis. Cellphones, PDAs, pagers, digital cameras, and just about any electronic device also can be analyzed. Attempted hacking attacks and allegations of employee computer misuse have added to the organization's need to examine and analyze electronic devices. Mishandling concerns can cost companies millions. Companies must handle each in a legal and defensible manner. Because electronic information can be easily changed, a forensic examination usually follows these three steps:

1. **Acquire**—This is usually performed by means of a bit-level copy. A *bit-level copy* is an exact duplicate of the original data, allowing the examiner to scrutinize the copy while leaving the original copy intact.

2. **Authenticate**—This process requires an investigator to show that the data is unchanged and has not been tampered with. Authentication can be accomplished through the use of checksums and hashes such as MD5 and SHA.

 Message digests such as MD5 and SHA are used to ensure the integrity of files and data, and to ensure that no changes have occurred.

3. **Analyze**—The investigator must be careful to examine the data and ensure that his actions are documented. The investigator usually

recovers evidence by examining drive slack space, file slack space, hidden files, swap data, Internet cache, and other locations, such as the recycle bin. Copies of the original disks, drive, or data are usually examined to protect the original evidence.

How Forensics Was Used to Catch the Creator of the Melissa Virus

When the Melissa virus was released, it quickly slowed the Internet. By disguising itself as email from friends or colleagues, it spread quickly and took down networks. As the manhunt intensified to find the creator, computer forensics was put to the test. David Smith was tracked down and apprehended in about one week.

Many were surprised by how quickly the FBI found the perpetrator. Much of this success was linked to the FBI's ability to use software to sniff newsgroups to determine where the virus was originally posted and then by examining and tracking a globally unique identifier (GUID). A GUID is a unique number embedded in a Word file that shows which computer the file was created on. David Smith received a $5,000 fine and 20 months in prison. The Melissa virus is believed to have caused more than $80 million in damages.

Handling Evidence

The handling of evidence is of special importance to the forensic investigator. This is addressed through the *chain of custody*, a process that helps protect the integrity and reliability of the evidence by providing an evidence log that shows every access to evidence, from collection to appearance in court. A complete chain of custody report also includes any procedures or activities that were performed on the evidence.

A primary image is the original image. It should be held in storage and kept unchanged. The working image is the one used for analysis purposes.

Trace Evidence

Locard's Exchange Principle states that whenever two objects come into contact, a transfer of material will occur. The resulting trace evidence left behind during this transfer can be used to associate objects, individuals, or locations to a crime. Simply stated, no matter how hard someone tries, some trace evidence always remains. Although criminals can make recovery harder by deleting files and caches, some trace evidence always remains.

Drive Wiping

Drive wiping is the process of overwriting all addressable locations on the disk. The Department of Defense (DoD) drive-wiping standard #5220-22M states, "All addressable locations must be overwritten with a character, its complement, then a random character and verify." By making several passes over the media, an organization can further decrease the possibility of data recovery. Organizations worried about proper disposal of used media then get clean, unrecoverable media. In the hands of the criminal, drive wiping offers the chance to destroy evidence.

Standardization of Forensic Procedures

In March 1998, the International Organization on Computer Evidence (IOCE) was appointed to draw international principles for the procedures relating to digital evidence. The goal was to harmonize methods and practices among nations and guarantee the capability to use digital evidence collected by one state in the courts of another state. The IOCE (www.ioec.org) has established the following six principles to govern these activities:

➤ When dealing with digital evidence, all generally accepted forensic and procedural principles must be applied.

➤ Upon seizing digital evidence, actions taken should not change that evidence.

➤ When it is necessary for a person to access original digital evidence, that person should be trained for the purpose.

➤ All activity relating to the seizure, access, storage, or transfer of digital evidence must be fully documented, preserved, and available for review.

➤ An individual is responsible for all actions taken with respect to digital evidence while the digital evidence is in his possession.

➤ Any agency that is responsible for seizing, accessing, storing, or transferring digital evidence is responsible for compliance with these principles.

Major Legal Systems

Legal systems vary throughout the world in the rights of the accused, the role of the judge, the nature of evidence, and other essential legal concepts. These can be handled quite differently:

➤ **Civil (code) law**—Also known as Napoleonic law. This law evolved in Europe and is based on a comprehensive system of written rules of law.

➤ **Common law**—This form of law was developed in England and is present in the United States, Canada, United Kingdom, Australia, and New Zealand. It is based on the rule of reasonable doubt and that you are innocent until proven guilty.

➤ **Customary law**—Usually found to be combined with another legal system, it is based on the concept of what is customary and considered normal conduct.

➤ **Muslim law**—The Muslim legal system is an autonomous legal system based on religious tenants and references items found in the Qur'an.

➤ **Civil law**—In civil law, there is no prison time. Victims are compensated by means of financial awards of punitive, compensatory, or statutory damages.

➤ **Criminal law**—Criminal law exists to punish someone who violates the government's laws. Punishment can include financial penalties, imprisonment, or both.

➤ **Administrative law**—Administrative law establishes standards of performance and conduct expected by governmental agencies from industries, organizations, officials, and officers. Individuals and organizations that violate these laws can be punished by financial penalties and/or imprisonment. It is typically applied to industries such as health care, financial, industrial, and pharmaceutical.

Evidence Types

The gathering, control, storage, and preservation of evidence are extremely critical in any legal investigation. Evidence can be computer generated, oral, or written. Because computer evidence is easily altered, special care must be taken when handling it. Different types of evidence have different levels of validity in court. For evidence to be accepted in court, it must meet certain standards:

➤ Relevant

➤ Legally permissible

➤ Reliable

➤ Identifiable

➤ Properly preserved and documented

There are also various types of evidence, different ways in which the evidence can be gathered, and legal and illegal ways in which those who break the law can be prosecuted:

➤ **Best evidence**—Best evidence is considered the most reliable form of evidence. Original documents are an example of best evidence.

➤ **Secondary evidence**—Although not as reliable or as strong as best evidence, secondary evidence can still be used in court. A copy of evidence and an oral description of its contents are examples of secondary evidence.

➤ **Hearsay evidence**—Hearsay is generally not admissible in court because it is considered secondhand information. Some computer-generated records and other business records fall under this category.

➤ **Direct evidence**—This form of evidence either proves or disproves a specific act through oral testimony. It is based on information gathered through the witness's five senses.

➤ **Enticement and entrapment**—Enticement is the legal activity of luring an individual to perform a questionable activity. Using a honeypot to observe and monitor individuals attempting to hack your network could be seen as an act of enticement. Entrapment occurs when individuals illegally induce or trick a person into committing a crime that he had not previously considered.

Trial

Basically two types of trials occur: one heard by a judge and the other heard by a jury. Most jury panels are composed of ordinary citizens from the court's surrounding geographical area. Computer crimes are difficult to prosecute in court because the advancement of technology is fast, whereas change in the legal system is slow. Trials also require a prosecutor with experience in computer crime. Even when cases are successful, computer criminals sometimes receive lighter sentences because this is considered a white-collar crime.

Negligence is the failure to meet the required standards in protecting information.

Exam Prep Questions

1. IP spoofing is commonly used for which of the following types of attacks?
   - ❏ A. Salami
   - ❏ B. Keystroke logging
   - ❏ C. DoS
   - ❏ D. Data diddling

2. Which of the following best describes session hijacking?
   - ❏ A. Session hijacking works by first subverting the DNS process. If this is successful, an attacker can use an already established TCP connection.
   - ❏ B. Session hijacking subverts the UDP protocol. It allows an attacker to use an already established connection.
   - ❏ C. Session hijacking targets the TCP connection between a client and a server. If the attacker learns the initial sequence, he might be able to hijack a connection.
   - ❏ D. Session hijacking works by first subverting the DNS process. If this is successful, an attacker can use an already established UDP connection.

3. Several of your company's employees have been hit with email scams over the last several weeks. One of these attacks successfully tricked an employee into revealing his username and password. Management has asked you to look for possible solutions to these attacks. Which of the following represents the best answer?
   - ❏ A. Implement a new, more robust password policy that requires complex passwords
   - ❏ B. Start a training and awareness program
   - ❏ C. Increase the organization's email-filtering ability
   - ❏ D. Develop a policy that restricts email to official use only

4. In part, the ISC² Code of Ethics states
   - ❏ A. Thou shalt not use a computer to harm other people.
   - ❏ B. Compromising the privacy of users is unethical.
   - ❏ C. All information should be free.
   - ❏ D. Act honorably, honestly, justly, responsibly, and legally.

5. Which of the following is a legal device that gives the creator of a work of authorship the right to control how the work is used?
   - ❏ A. Patent
   - ❏ B. Trademark
   - ❏ C. Copyright
   - ❏ D. Trade secret

6. Locard's Exchange Principle states
   - ❑ A. The chain of custody should never be broken.
   - ❑ B. There is always some trace evidence.
   - ❑ C. Three things are required for a crime: means, motive, and opportunity.
   - ❑ D. Checksums should be used to authenticate evidence.

7. Which of the following international organizations was established to standardize the handling of forensic evidence?
   - ❑ A. The International Organization on Forensic Analysis
   - ❑ B. The EU Policy Council of Criminal Evidence
   - ❑ C. The United Nations Organization on Computer Evidence
   - ❑ D. The International Organization on Computer Evidence

8. For evidence to be used in court, it must *not* be which of the following?
   - ❑ A. Relevant
   - ❑ B. Properly preserved
   - ❑ C. Identifiable
   - ❑ D. Justifiable

9. Hearsay evidence
   - ❑ A. Can be used in civil cases
   - ❑ B. Is not admissible in court
   - ❑ C. Is considered third-hand information
   - ❑ D. Can be used to verify what has been presented through best evidence

10. In France, the legal system is based upon
    - ❑ A. Civil law
    - ❑ B. Common law
    - ❑ C. Administrative law
    - ❑ D. Customary law

Answers to Exam Prep Questions

1. Answer: C. IP spoofing is a common practice when DoS tools are used to help the attacker mask his identity. Salami attacks, data diddling, and keystroke logging do not typically spoof IP addresses, so answers A, B, and D are incorrect.

2. Answer: C. This more advanced spoof attack works by subverting the TCP connection between a client and a server. If successful, the attacker has a valid connection to the victim's network and is authenticated with his credentials. This attack is very hard to do with modern operating systems but is trivial with older operating systems. Answer A is incorrect because session hijacking does not involve DNS; it functions by manipulating the TCP sequence number. Answer B is incorrect because session hijacking does not use the UDP protocol. UND is used for stateless connections. Answer D is incorrect because, again, session hijacking is not based on DNS and UDP. These two technologies are unrelated to TCP sequence numbers.

3. Answer: B. The best defense against social engineering is to educate your users and staff. Training can go a long way toward teaching employees how to spot these scams. Although the other answers are not bad ideas, they will not prevent social engineering, so answers A, C, and D are incorrect.

4. Answer: D. It's a requirement for CISSP candidates to subscribe to the ISC² Code of Ethics, which, in part, states, "Act honorably, honestly, justly, responsibly, and legally." All other answers are incorrect.

5. Answer: C. A copyright is a legal device that gives the creator of a work of authorship the right to control how the work is used. All other answers are incorrect: A patent (answer A) grants the owner a legally enforceable right to exclude others from practicing or using the inventions design for a defined period of time. A trademark (answer B) is a symbol, word, name, sound, or thing that identifies the origin of a product or service in a particular trade. A trade secret (answer D) is a process, formula, or other knowledge that is unique to a manufacturer that gives it an advantage over competitors.

6. Answer: B. Locard's Exchange Principle states that whenever two objects come into contact, a transfer of material will occur. Answers A, C, and D are incorrect because they do not properly answer the question.

7. Answer: D. The International Organization on Computer Evidence (IOCE) was appointed to draw up international principles for the procedures relating to digital evidence. The goal was to harmonize methods and practices among nations and guarantee the capability to use digital evidence collected by one state in the courts of another state. Answer A is incorrect because the International Organization on Forensic Analysis is not the correct name of the forensic organization requested. Answer B is

incorrect because the EU Policy Council of Criminal Evidence is not the international organization that was established to standardize the handling of forensic evidence. Answer C is incorrect because, again, the United Nations Organization on Computer Evidence is not the name of the proper world body.

8. Answer: D. For evidence to be accepted in court, it must meet certain standards: It must be relevant (answer A), legally permissible, reliable, identifiable (answer C), and properly preserved (answer B) and documented. Because the question asked which is *not* applicable, the only possible answer is D, justifiable.

9. Answer: B. Hearsay is generally not admissible in court because it is considered secondhand information. Answer A is incorrect because hearsay evidence cannot be used in civil cases. Answer C is incorrect because hearsay evidence is considered secondhand information. Answer D is incorrect because hearsay evidence cannot be used to verify what has been presented through best evidence.

10. Answer: A. Civil law, also known as Napoleonic law, evolved in Europe and is based on a comprehensive system of written rules of law. It is the rule of law in France. Answer B is incorrect because common law is the rule of law in England, not France. Answer C is incorrect because administrative law addresses regulations typically placed on industries and organizations. Answer D is incorrect because customary law is usually found to be combined with another legal system and is not the basis of law in France.

Need to Know More?

www.faqs.org/rfcs/rfc1087.html—RFC 1087

www.cert.org/—Computer Emergency Response Team

www.cybercrime.gov/—DOJ site on cybercrime

www.2600.com/—The Hacker Quarterly

www.defcon.org/—Underground Hacking Event

https://www.isc2.org/cgi-bin/content.cgi?category=12—ISC² Code of Ethics

www.ioec.org—Forensic procedure information

http://europa.eu.int/comm/internal_market/privacy/index_en.htm—EU privacy laws

www.idtheftcenter.org/index.shtml—Identity theft information

Cryptography

Terms you'll need to understand:

✓ Symmetric algorithms
✓ Asymmetric algorithms
✓ Message digests
✓ Public key infrastructure (PKI)
✓ Steganography
✓ IPSec
✓ Link encryption
✓ End-to-end encryption

Techniques you'll need to master:

✓ Identifying cryptographic attacks
✓ Enumerating advantages and disadvantages of cryptographic systems
✓ Understanding the structure of public key infrastructure
✓ Understanding the components of IPSec
✓ Determining the differences between block and stream ciphers

Introduction

Cryptography is the science and study of secret writing. It is concerned with the ways in which information can be encoded to prevent disclosure. It is tied closely to two of the three basic pillars of security: integrity and confidentiality. Cryptography offers its users the capability to protect the confidentiality of information through eavesdropping or other interception techniques. Cryptography protects integrity by ensuring that only the individuals who have been authenticated and authorized can access and view the data. Cryptography provides integrity services by detecting the modification to, addition to, or deletion of data while in transit or in storage.

The CISSP candidate is expected to know basic information about cryptographic systems, such as symmetric algorithms, asymmetric algorithms, public key infrastructure, message digests, key management techniques, and alternatives to traditional cryptography, such as steganography.

Cryptographic Basics

Before you start to sweat the thought of learning cryptography for the CISSP exam, it's good to know that you won't need to learn the interworkings of these systems; no advanced math degree is required. The exam expects you to know only a basic understanding of the systems and their strengths and weaknesses. Following are some common terms used in this chapter:

➤ **Algorithm**—A set of rules or ordered steps used to encrypt and decrypt data.

➤ **Cryptographic key**—A key is a piece of information that controls how the cryptographic algorithm functions. It can be used to control the transformation of plain text to cipher text, or cipher text to plain text. As an example, the Caesar cipher uses a key that moves forward three characters to encrypt and back by three characters to decrypt.

➤ **Encryption**—Transforming data into an unreadable format. As an example, using Caesar's cipher to encrypt the word *cat* would result in *fdw*. Encryption here has moved each character forward by three letters.

➤ **Cryptanalysis**—The act of obtaining plain text from cipher text without a cryptographic key. It is used by governments, the military, enterprises, and malicious hackers to find weaknesses and crack cryptographic systems.

➤ **Digital signature**—A hash value that has been encrypted with the private key of the sender. It is used for authentication and integrity.

➤ **Plain text**—Clear text that is readable.

➤ **Cipher text**—Data that is scrambled and unreadable.

When plain text is converted into cipher text, the transformation can be accomplished in basically two ways:

➤ **Block ciphers**—Function by dividing the message into blocks for processing

➤ **Stream ciphers**—Function by dividing the message into bits for processing

Symmetric and asymmetric cryptography are the two basic types. Symmetric cryptography uses a single shared key. Asymmetric cryptography uses two keys, one public and one private. Both of these concepts are discussed in more detail later in the chapter. At this point, it is important to understand that, for both symmetric and asymmetric cryptography, data is encrypted by using a key. The key is fed into the encryption algorithm to tell the algorithm what mathematical functions, permutation, substitution, or binary math to perform.

The key size goes a long way in determining the strength of the cryptosystem. As an example, imagine that you're contemplating buying a combination lock for your prized baseball card collection. One lock has three digits, while the other has four, as shown in Figure 11.1.

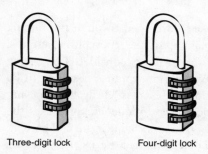

Three-digit lock   Four-digit lock

Figure 11.1   Key size and strength.

Maybe you don't think that just a one-digit increase can make much of a difference. Well, for the three-digit lock, there's a total of 1,000 possible combinations, but the four-digit lock has a total of 10,000 possible combinations. As you can see, the more possible keys or combinations there are, the longer it will take an attacker to guess the right key or combination needed to gain access to your most prized collection. Although key size is important, though, it's also important that the key remain secret. You could buy a seven-digit combination lock, but it would do you little good if everyone knew the combination was your phone number.

Depending on how cryptography is used, it can provide three main items to help ensure security:

➤ Confidentiality

➤ Integrity

➤ Nonrepudiation

History of Encryption

Encryption dates back through the ages. Ancient Hebrews used a basic cryptographic system called ATBASH that worked by replacing each letter used with another letter the same distance away from the end of the alphabet; *A* was sent as a *Z*, and *B* was sent as a *Y*.

The Spartans also had their own form of encryption, called scytale. This system functioned by wrapping a strip of papyrus around a rod of fixed diameter on which a message was written. The recipient used a rod of the same diameter on which he wrapped the paper to read the message. If anyone intercepted the paper, it appeared as a meaningless letter.

The Caesar cipher used the alphabet but swapped one letter for another by incrementing by three characters. In this system, Caesar wrote *D* instead of *A* and *E* instead of *B*.

More complicated substitution ciphers were developed through the middle ages as individuals became better at breaking simple encryption systems. In the ninth century, Abu al-Kindi published what is considered to be the first paper that discusses how to break cryptographic systems, titled "A Manuscript on Deciphering Cryptographic Messages." It deals with using frequency analysis to break cryptographic codes. Frequency analysis is the study of how frequent letters or groups of letters appear in cipher text. Uncovered patterns can aid individuals in determining patterns and breaking the cipher text.

 All three encryption techniques discussed are considered substitution ciphers, which operate by replacing bits, bytes, or characters with alternate bits, bytes, or characters. Substitution ciphers are vulnerable to frequency analysis and are no longer used.

Around the beginning of the twentieth century, mechanical devices such as the German Enigma machine, which used a series of internal rotors to perform the encryption, and the Japanese Purple Machine were developed to counter the weaknesses of substitution ciphers. Today, in the United States the

National Security Agency (NSA) is responsible for coding and code breaking. It helped lead the implementation of the Data Encryption Standard (DES).

 Modern cryptographic systems no longer use substitution and transposition. Today block ciphers and stream ciphers are used. A block cipher, such as DES, operates on fixed-length groups of bits. A stream cipher inputs and encrypts one digit at a time.

Symmetric Encryption

In *symmetric encryption*, a single shared secret key is used for encryption and decryption, as shown in Figure 11.2. These dual-use keys can be used to lock and unlock data. Symmetric encryption is the oldest form of encryption. Systems such as scytale and Caesar's cipher are examples of symmetric encryption. Symmetric encryption provides confidentiality by keeping individuals who do not have the key from knowing the true contents of the message.

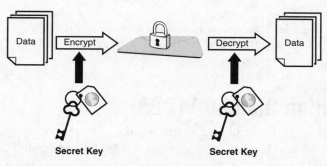

Figure 11.2 Symmetric encryption.

For symmetric encryption systems to be effective, there must be a secure method in which to transfer keys; therein lies the weakness of symmetric encryption. Movement of the secret key from one party to another must typically be done in some type of out-of-band method. If email is to be secured, it does little good to send the key via unsecured email because anyone could intercept the email and thereby compromise the security of the encrypted information. Because of this, an out-of-band key exchange must be used. Common out-of-band methods include in-person delivery and snail mail.

Symmetric encryption also suffers from scalability issues. For example, if you need to communicate details about this book to 10 people in a secure manner, the total keys needed would be calculated as follows: N (N − 1) / 2 or [10 (10 − 1) / 2 = 45 keys]. Therefore, key management becomes the second big issue when dealing with symmetric encryption.

You might be thinking that I have offered you nothing but bad news about symmetric encryption, but it does have features that make it an excellent choice for securing data and providing confidentiality. Symmetric encryption is fast. It can encrypt and decrypt very quickly. It also is considered strong. Symmetric encryption is very hard to break if a large key is used. Symmetric algorithms include these:

➤ **DES**—Data Encryption Standard was once the most common symmetric algorithm used. It has now been officially retired by NIST.

➤ **Blowfish**—This is a general-purpose symmetric algorithm intended as a replacement for the DES replaced by AES and Twofish.

➤ **Rijndael**—This is a block cipher adopted as the Advanced Encryption Standard (AES) by the U.S. government to replace DES.

➤ **RC4**—Rivest Cipher 4 is a stream-based cipher. Stream ciphers treat the data as a stream of bits.

➤ **RC5**—Rivest Cipher 5 is a block-based cipher. RC5 processes data in blocks of 32, 64, or 128 bits.

➤ **SAFER**—Secure and Fast Encryption Routine is a block-based cipher that processes data in blocks of 64 and 128 bits.

Data Encryption Standard (DES)

DES grew out of an early 1970s project that was originally developed by IBM. IBM and the National Institute of Standards and Technology (NIST) modified IBM's original encryption standard, known as Lucifer, to use a 56-bit key. The revised standard was endorsed by the NSA. The DES standard was published in 1977 and was released by the American National Standards Institute (ANSI) in 1981.

DES is a symmetric encryption standard that is based on a 64-bit block. DES processes 64 bits of plain text at a time to output 64-bit blocks of cipher text. DES uses a 56-bit key and has four modes of operation: Electronic Codebook (ECB) mode, Cipher Block Chaining (CBC) mode, Cipher Feedback (CFB) mode, and Output Feedback (OFB) mode.

All four modes use the 56-bit key. Although the standard reports the key to be 64 bits, 8 bits are actually used for parity; their purpose is to ensure the integrity of the remaining 56 bits. Therefore, for all practical purposes, the key is really only 56 bits long. Each 64-bit plain-text block is separated into two 32-bit blocks and then processed by the 56-bit key. The plain text is processed by the key through 16 rounds of transpositions and substitutions.

Electronic Codebook (ECB) Mode

ECB is the native encryption mode of DES. Although it produces the highest throughput, it is also the easiest form of DES encryption to break. If used with large amounts of data, it can be easily attacked because the same plain text encrypted with the same key will always produce the same cipher text. This is why it is best used on small amounts of data, such as the encryption of PIN numbers at ATM machines.

Cipher Block Chaining (CBC) Mode

The CBC mode of DES is widely used and is similar to ECB. CBC processes 64-bit blocks of data but inserts some of the cipher text created from the previous block into the next one. This process is called XORing, and it makes the cipher text more secure and less susceptible to cracking. CBC is aptly named because data from one block is used in the next; therefore, the blocks are chained together. As they are chained, any error in one block can be propagated to others. This can make it impossible to decrypt that block and the following blocks as well.

Cipher Feedback (CFB) Mode

CFB is a stream cipher that can be used to encrypt individual characters. Although it is a stream cipher, it is similar to OFB, in that previously generated cipher text is added to subsequent streams. Because the cipher text is streamed together, errors and corruption can propagate through the encryption process.

Output Feedback (OFB) Mode

OFB is also a stream cipher. Unlike CFB, OFB uses plain text to feed back into stream of cipher text. Transmission errors do not propagate throughout the encryption process. An initialization vector is used to create the seed value for the first encrypted block. DES XORs the plain text with a seed value to be applied with subsequent data.

 Although DES remained secure for many years, the Electronic Frontier Foundation (EFF) was able to crack DES in 1998 in about 23 hours. Now that DES has been officially retired, it is recommended that Triple-DES (3DES) be used to ensure security. Triple-DES is scheduled to be replaced by the Advanced Encryption Standard (AES).

Triple-DES (3DES)

Before discussing Triple-DES, some of you must be wondering what happened to Double-DES. Although Double-DES has a 112-bit key, it is no more secure than DES; it requires the same work factor to crack as that of DES.

To extend the usefulness of the DES encryption standard, Triple-DES is now being used. Triple-DES can use two or three keys to encrypt data, depending on how it is implemented. Although it is much more secure, it is up to three times as slow as 56-bit DES:

➤ DES EEE2 uses two keys. The first key is reused during the third round of encryption. The encryption process is performed three times (encrypt, encrypt, encrypt).

➤ DES EDE2 uses two keys. Again, the first key is reused during the third round of encryption. Unlike DES EEE2, DES EDE2 encrypts, decrypts, and then encrypts.

➤ DES EEE3 uses three keys and performs the encryption process three times.

➤ DES EDE3 uses three keys but operates by encrypting, decrypting, and then encrypting the data.

Advanced Encryption Standard (AES)

All good things must end, and that is what NIST decided in 2002 when Rijindael replaced DES and became the new U.S. standard for encrypting sensitive but unclassified data. Rijindael can be implemented in one of three key sizes, including 128, 192, and 256 bits. It is considered a fast, simple, robust encryption mechanism.

International Data Encryption Algorithm (IDEA)

This 64-bit block cipher uses a 128-bit key. Although it has been patented by a Swiss company, it is freely available for noncommercial use. It is considered a secure encryption standard, and there have been no known attacks against it. It operates in four distinct modes, similar to DES. At one time, it was thought that IDEA would replace DES, but patent fees prevented that from happening.

Other Symmetric Algorithms

Other symmetric algorithms include these:

➤ **Blowfish**—This is a 64-bit block cipher that can support key lengths up to 448 bits.

➤ **Twofish**—A finalist in the AES selection process, Twofish operates on 128-bit blocks and can support a key length up to 256 bits.

➤ **RC5**—RC5, or Rivest Cipher 5, is a fast block cipher. It is different than other symmetric algorithms, in that it supports a variable block size, a variable key size, and a variable number of rounds. Allowable choices for the block size are 32, 64, and 128 bits. The number of rounds can range from 0 to 255, and the key can range up to 2040 bits.

➤ **Skipjack**—Skipjack and the clipper chip are both government-devised methods for commercial encryption. Skipjack faces opposition because the government would maintain a portion of the information required to reconstruct a Skipjack key, so that legal authorities could decrypt communications between the affected parties when approved by a warrant or approval of the court.

Be sure to take the time to review the various encryption types, block sizes, and key lengths; you can expect to see these items on the exam.

Asymmetric Encryption

Asymmetric encryption or public key cryptography is unlike symmetric encryption, in that it uses two unique keys, as shown in Figure 11.3. One key is used to encrypt the data, and the other is used to decrypt it. One of the greatest things about asymmetric encryption is that it overcomes one of the big barriers of symmetric encryption: key distribution.

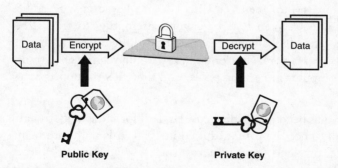

Figure 11.3 Asymmetric encryption.

Here's how asymmetric encryptions: Imagine that you want to send a client a message. You use your client's public key to encrypt the message. When your client receives the message, he uses his private key to decrypt it. The important concepts here are that if the message is encrypted with the public key, only the matching private key will decrypt it. The private key is generally kept secret, whereas the public key can be given to anyone. If properly designed, it should not be possible for someone to easily deduce the private key of a pair if that person has only the public key.

Public key cryptography is made possible by the use of one-way functions. A one-way function, or trap door, is a math operation that is easy to compute in one direction, yet next to impossible to compute in the other. Depending on what type of asymmetric encryption used, this difficulty is based on either the discrete logarithm problem or the factoring of a large number into the prime number used. As an example, it you are given two large prime numbers, it is easy to multiply them. However, if you are given only their product, it difficult or impossible to find the factors with today's processing power.

The trap door function allows someone with the public key to reconstruct the private key if he knows the trap door value. Therefore, anyone who knows the trap door can perform the function easily in both directions, but anyone lacking the trap door can perform the function only in one direction. The forward direction is used for encryption and signature verification, and the inverse or backward direction is used for decryption and signature generation. We have people like Dr. W. Diffie and Dr. M. E. Hellman to thank for helping develop public key encryption; they released the first key-exchange protocol in 1976.

RSA

RSA was developed in 1977 by Ron Rivest, Adi Shamir, and Len Adleman at MIT. The name is based on their initials. Although RSA is much slower than symmetric encryption cryptosystems, it offers secure key exchange and is considered very secure. Cryptanalysts or anyone attempting to crack RSA would be left with a difficult challenge because of the difficulty of factoring a large integer into its two factors. Cracking the key would require an extraordinary amount of computer processing power and time. RSA supports a key size up to 2040 bits.

The RSA algorithm has become the de facto standard for industrial-strength encryption, especially since the patent expired in 2000. It is built into many protocols, software products, and systems such as Microsoft Internet Explorer and Firefox.

Diffie-Hellman

Diffie-Hellman was the first public key-exchange algorithms. It was developed for key exchange, not for data encryption of digital signatures. The Diffie-Hellman protocol allows two users to exchange a secret key over an insecure medium without any prior secrets. It's vulnerable to man-in-the-middle attacks because the key exchange does not authenticate the participants. To alleviate this vulnerability, digital signatures should be used. Diffie-Hellman is used in conjunction with several authentication methods, including the Internet Key Exchange (IKE) component of IPSec.

El Gamal

El Gamal is an extension of the Diffie-Hellman key exchange. It can be used for digital signatures, key exchange, and encryption. El Gamal consists of three discrete components, including a key generator, an encryption algorithm, and a decryption algorithm. It was released in 1985, and its security rests in part on the difficulty of solving the discrete logarithm problems.

Elliptical Curve Cryptosystem (ECC)

Although it is not as fast as the previous mentioned systems, it is considered more secure because elliptic curve systems are harder to crack than those based on discrete log problems. ECC is being implemented in smaller, less powerful devices, such as cellphones and handheld devices.

Merkle-Hellman Knapsack

This asymmetric algorithm is based on fixed weights. Although this system was popular for a while, it has fallen from favor because it was broken in 1982.

Before attempting the exam, it is prudent that you know what categories each of the asymmetric algorithms discussed fits into. The following shows how each functions:

➤ Functions by using a discreet logarithm in a finite field
  ➤ Diffie-Hellman
  ➤ El Gamal
  ➤ Elliptical Curve Cryptosystem
➤ Functions by the product of large prime numbers
  ➤ RSA
➤ Functions by means of fixed weights
  ➤ Merkle-Hellman Knapsack

Integrity and Authentication

As mentioned previously, one of the things cryptography offers its users is the capability to verify integrity and authentication. Integrity ensures that the information remains unchanged and is in its true original form.

Authentication provides the capability to ensure that messages were sent from those you believed sent them and that the message is sent to its intended recipient.

Message Digests

Message digests are produced by using one-way hashing functions. They are not intended to be used to reproduce the data. The purpose of a digest is to verify the integrity of data and messages. A well-designed message digest examines every bit of the data while it is being condensed, and even a slight change to the data will result in a large change in the message hash.

MD Series

All of the MD algorithms were developed by Ron Rivest. These have progressed through the years as technology has advanced. The original was MD2, which was optimized for 8-bit computers and is somewhat outdated. It has also fallen out of favor because MD2 has been found to suffer from collisions. MD4 was the next to be developed. The message is processed in 512-bit blocks, and a 64-bit binary representation of the original length of the message is added to the message. As with MD2, MD4 was found to be subject to possible attacks. That's why MD5 was developed: It could be considered an MD4 with additional safety mechanisms. MD5 processes a variable-size input and produces a fixed 128-bit output. As with MD4, it processes the data in blocks of 512 bits. MD5 has also been broken.

Collisions occur when two message digests produce the same hash value. This is undesirable because it can mask the fact that someone might have changed the contents of a file or message.

SHA-1

SHA-1 is a secure hashing algorithm (SHA) that is similar to MD5. It is considered the successor to MD5 and produces a 160-bit message digest. SHA-1 processes messages in 512-bit blocks and adds padding, if needed, to get the data to add up to the right number of bits. SHA-1 has only 111-bit effectiveness. SHA-1 is part of a family of SHA algorithms, including SHA-0, SHA-1, and SHA-2. SHA-0 is no longer considered secure, and SHA-1 is also now considered vulnerable to attacks. Safe replacements are SHA-256 and SHA-512.

HAVAL

HAVAL is another one-way hashing algorithm that is similar to MD5. Unlike MD5, HAVAL is not tied to a fixed message-digest value. HAVAL-3-128 makes three passes and produces a 128-bit fingerprint, and HAVAL-4-256 makes four passes and produces a 256-bit fingerprint length.

HMAC

The Hashed Message Authentication Code (HMAC) was designed to be immune to the multicollision attack. This functionality was added by including a shared secret key. In simple terms, HMAC functions by using a hashing algorithm such as MD5 or SHA-1 and altering the initial state by adding a password. Even if someone can intercept and modify the data, it's of little use if that person does not possess the secret key. There is no easy way for the person to re-create the hashed value without it.

Digital Signatures

Digital signatures are based on public key cryptography and are used to verify the authenticity and integrity of a message. Digital signatures are created by passing a message's contents through a hashing algorithm. The hashed value is encrypted with the sender's private key. Upon receiving the message, the recipient decrypts the encrypted sum and then recalculates the expected message hash. These values should match to ensure the validity of the message and prove that it was sent by the party believed to have sent it because only that party has access to the private key.

Message Authentication Code (MAC)

A Message Authentication Code (MAC) is similar to a digital signature, except that it uses symmetric encryption. MACs are created and verified with the same secret (symmetric) key. Four types of MACs exist: unconditionally secure, hash function–based, stream cipher–based, and block cipher–based.

Digital Signature Algorithm (DSA)

Things are much easier when we have standards, and that is what the Digital Signature Algorithm (DSA) was designed for. The DSA standards were proposed by NIST in 1991 to standardize Digital Signature Standards (DSS). The DSA digital signature algorithm involves key generation, signature generation, and signature verification. It uses SHA-1 in conjunction with public key encryption to create a 160-bit hash. Signing speeds are equivalent to RSA signing, but signature verification is much slower. The DSA digital signature is a pair of large numbers represented as binary digits.

Steganography

Steganography is the art of secret writing that dates back to the time of ancient Greece. The goal of steganography is to hide information by embedding it in other messages. Computer graphics such as bitmaps are commonly used. Steganography works by altering the least significant bit of each byte of information. To the viewer of the image, the picture remains the same, but in reality, information has been hidden in it. The hidden information can be plain text, cipher text, or even other images.

Special tools are required to use steganography, and it can be used for legitimate and illegal purposes. Artists might consider using it to watermark or fingerprint their digital art. This would allow them to prove that they are the creator, if the need arose. Hackers, terrorists, and others could also use steganography to move information from one location to another without detection. *USA Today* reported after 9/11, governmental agencies believed that Al Qaeda operatives had used steganography to hide illicit communications.

Public Key Infrastructure (PKI)

Dealing with brick-and-mortar businesses gives us plenty of opportunity to develop trust with a vendor. We can see the store, talk to the employees, and get a good look at how they do business. Internet transactions are far less transparent. We can't see who we are dealing with, don't know what type of operation they really run, and might not be sure we can trust them. The public key infrastructure (PKI) was made to address these concerns and bring trust, integrity, and security to electronic transactions.

PKI is a framework that consists of hardware, software, and policies that exists to manage, create, store, and distribute keys and digital certificates. The components of this framework include the following:

➤ The Certificate Authority (CA)

➤ The Registration Authority (RA)

➤ The Certificate Revocation List (CRL)

➤ Digital certificates

➤ A certificate distribution system

Certificate Authority (CA)

The best analogy of a CA is that of the Department of Motor Vehicles (DMV). This is the state entity that is responsible for issuing a driver's license, the gold standard for physical identification. If you cash a check, go to a night club, or catch a plane, your driver's license will be the one document universally accepted at all these locations to prove your identity. CAs are like DMVs: They vouch for your identity in a digital world. VeriSign, Thawte, and Entrust are some of the companies that perform CA services.

Now, a CA doesn't have to be an external third party; many companies decide to tackle these responsibilities by themselves. Regardless of who performs the services, the following steps must be performed:

1. The CA verifies the request for certificate with the help of the RA.

2. The individual's identification is validated.

3. A certificate is created by the CA, which verifies that the person matches the public key that is being offered.

Registration Authority (RA)

The RA is like a middle man: It's positioned between the client and the CA. Although the RA cannot generate a certificate, it can accept requests, verify a person's identity, and pass along the information to the CA for certificate generation.

RAs play a key role when certificate services are expanded to cover large geographic areas. One central CA can delegate its responsibilities to regional RAs, such as having one RA in the United States, Canada, Mexico, and Brazil.

 Expect to see exam questions that deal with the workings of PKI. It's important to understand that the RA cannot issue certificates.

Certificate Revocation List (CRL)

Just as with a drivers licenses, digital certificates might not always remain valid. Individuals might leave the company, information might change, or someone's private key might become compromised. For these reasons, the CRL must be maintained.

The CRL is maintained by the CA, which signs the list to maintain its accuracy. Whenever problems are reported with digital certificates, they are considered invalid and the CA has the serial number added to the CRL. Anyone requesting a digital certificate can check the CRL to verify the certificate's integrity.

Digital Certificates

Digital certificates are at the heart of the PKI system. The digital certificate serves two roles. First, it ensures the integrity of the public key and makes sure that the key remains unchanged and in a valid form. Second, it validates that the public key is tied to the stated owner and that all associated information is true and correct. The information needed to accomplish these goals is added into the digital certificate. Digital certificates are formatted to the X.509 standard. The most current version of X.509 is version 3. One of the key developments in version 3 was the addition of extensions. Version 3 includes the flexibility to support other topologies, such as bridges and meshes. It can operate as a web of trust, much like PGP. An X.509 certificate includes the following elements:

➤ Version

➤ Serial number

➤ Algorithm ID

➤ Issuer

➤ Validity

   ➤ Not Before (a specified date)

   ➤ Not After (a specified date)

➤ Subject

➤ Subject public key information

   ➤ Public key algorithm

   ➤ Subject public key

➤ Issuer-unique identifier (optional)

➤ Subject-unique identifier (optional)

➤ Extensions (optional)

The Client's Role in PKI

Now, it might seem that, up to this point, all the work falls on the shoulders of the CAs, this is not entirely true. Clients are responsible for requesting digital certificates and for maintaining the security of their private key. Loss or compromise of the private key would mean that communications would no longer be secure. Loss of the private key would be devastating. If you are dealing with credit card numbers or other pieces of user identity, this type of loss of security could lead to identity theft.

Protecting the private key is an important issue because it's easier for an attacker to target the key than to try to crack the certificate service. Organizations should concern themselves with seven key management issues:

➤ Generation

➤ Distribution

➤ Installation

➤ Storage

➤ Key change

➤ Key control

➤ Key disposal

Cryptographic Services

Did you ever really consider that security is like a cake? Well, it is: It is best in layers. Just like your favorite cake, cryptography can be layered to help build a true defense in depth. Many types of cryptographic solutions can be applied, from the application layer all the way down to the data frame.

Secure Email

Standard email uses the Simple Mail Transfer Protocol (SMTP), port 25, to accept messages from clients; and Post Office Protocol (POP3) version 3 and port 110 to retrieve email from server-based inboxes. Sending an email is much like sending a postcard through the postal service: Anyone along the way can easily read the note you wrote to your mom while visiting Niagara Falls. Fortunately, several digital services enable you to seal the mail in an envelope.

Pretty Good Privacy (PGP)

PGP was developed in 1991 by Phil Zimmermann to provide privacy and authentication. Over time, it evolved into an open standard known as OpenPGP. PGP is unlike PKI, in that there is no CA. PGP builds a web of trust, which is developed as users sign and issue their own keys. Users must determine what level of trust they are willing to place in other parties. The goal of PGP was for it to become the "everyman's encryption." No longer would encryption be available only to companies and corporations. Popular programs such as Hushmail and Veridis are based on PGP.

Other Email Security Applications

Secure email solutions are important because email is one of the most widely used Internet applications. Several other applications are available to help secure email:

➤ **Secure Multipurpose Internet Mail Extensions (S/MIME)**—S/MIME adds two valuable components to standard email: digital signatures and public key encryption. S/MIME supports X.509 digital certificates and RSA encryption.

➤ **Privacy Enhanced Mail (PEM)**—PEM is an older standard that has not been widely implemented but that was a developed to provide authentication and confidentiality. PEM public key management is hierarchical. PEM uses MD2/MD5 and RSA for integrity and authentication.

➤ **Message Security Protocol (MSP)**—MSP is the military's answer to PEM. Because it was developed by the NSA, it has not been opened to public scrutiny. It is part of the DoD's Defense Messaging System and provides authentication, integrity, and nonrepudiation.

Secure TCP/IP Protocols

Securing email is just one of the CISSP's goals. Other cryptographic solutions are available to increase security at all the layers of the TCP/IP stack. Because security wasn't one of the driving forces when the TCP/IP protocols were developed, these solutions can go a long way toward protecting the security of the organization.

Application-Layer Cryptographic Solutions

The following application-layer protocols can be used to add confidentiality, integrity, or nonrepudiation:

➤ **Secure Shell (SSH)**—SSH is an Internet application that provides secure remote access. It is considered a replacement for FTP, Telnet, and the Berkley "r" utilities. SSH defaults to port 22. SSH version 1 has been found to contain vulnerabilities, so it is advisable to use SSH V2 or above.

➤ **Secure Hypertext Transfer Protocol (S-HTTP)**—S-HTTP is a superset of HTTP that was developed to provide secure communication with a web server. S-HTTP is a connectionless protocol that is designed to send individual messages securely.

➤ **Secure Electronic Transaction (SET)**—Visa and MasterCard wanted to alleviate fears of using credit cards over the Internet, so they developed SET. This specification uses a combination of digital certificates and digital signatures among the buyer, merchant, and the bank so that privacy and confidentiality are ensured.

Transport- and Internet-Layer Cryptographic Solutions

The transport and Internet layers of the TCP/IP stack can also be used to add cryptographic solutions to data communications. Some common examples follow:

➤ **Secure Sockets Layer (SSL)**—SSL was developed by Netscape for transmitting private documents over the Internet. Unlike S-HTTP, SSL is application independent. SSL is its cryptographic independence. The protocol itself is merely a framework for communicating certificates, encrypted keys, and data.

➤ **Transport Layer Security (TLS)**—TLS encrypts the communication between a host and a client. TLS consists of two layers, including the TLS Record Protocol and the TLS Handshake Protocol. Although it is not interoperable, it is protocol independent.

IPSec

Internet Protocol Security (IPSec) is an end-to-end security technology that allows two devices to communicate securely. IPSec was developed to address the shortcomings of IPv4. Although it is an add-on for IPv4, it is built into IPv6. IPSec can be used to encrypt just the data or the data and the header.

➤ **Encapsulated secure payload (ESP)**—ESP provides confidentiality by encrypting the data packet. The encrypted data is hidden from prying eyes, so its confidentiality is ensured.

➤ **Authentication header (AH)**—The AH provides integrity and authentication. The AH uses a hashing algorithm and symmetric key to calculate a message authentication code. This message-authentication code is known as the integrity check value (ICV). When the AH is received, an ICV value is calculated and checked against the received value to verify integrity.

➤ **Security Association (SA)**—For AH and ESP to work, there must be some information exchanged to set up the secure session. This job is the responsibility of the SA. The SA is a one-way connection between the two parties. If both AH and ESP are used, a total of four connections are required. SAs use a symmetric key to encrypt communication. The Diffie-Hellman algorithm is used to generate this shared key.

▶ **IPSec Internet Key Exchange (IKE)**—The SA must have a procedure to exchange key information between clients. The Internet Key Exchange (IKE) is the default standard for exchanging symmetric keys. IKE is considered a hybrid protocol because it combines the functions of two other protocols: the Internet Association and Key Management Protocol (ISAKMP) and the OAKLEY protocol.

▶ **The Internet Association and Key Management Protocol (ISAKMP)**—This subset of IKE sets up the framework of what can be negotiated during the handshake process. This could include items such as algorithms types and key sizes.

▶ **OAKLEY Protocol**—This portion of the IKE is responsible for carrying out the negotiations.

▶ **Transport and tunnel modes**—AH and ESP can work in one of two modes: transport mode or tunnel mode. Transport mode encrypts the data that is sent between peers. Tunnel mode encapsulates the entire packet and adds a new IPv4 header. Tunnel mode is designed to be used by VPNs.

Lower-Layer Cryptographic Solutions

Physical-layer cryptographic solutions include these:

▶ **Password Authentication Protocol (PAP)**—PAP is used for authentication but is not secure because the username and password are transmitted in clear text.

▶ **Challenge Handshake Authentication Protocol (CHAP)**—CHAP is more secure than PAP because of the method used to validate the username and password. CHAP sends the client a random value that is used only once. Both the client and the server know the predefined secret password. The client uses the random value and the secret password, and calculates a one-way hash. The hash value is sent to the server. The server compares this value to one that it has calculated separately using the stored secret password and the same random value that was sent to the client. If the values match, the client is authenticated.

▶ **Point-to-Point Tunneling Protocol (PPTP)**—PPTP was developed by a group of vendors. It consists of two components: the transport that maintains the virtual connection, and the encryption, which ensures confidentiality. It can operate at a 40-bit or 128-bit encryption setting. PPTP uses TCP port 1723.

Moving the Data

As the various protocols have shown, there are many ways to encrypt and secure data. One final decision that must be considered is how information is to be moved between clients. You could decide to choose a method that simply encrypts the data payload (end-to-end encryption), or one that encrypts everything (link state encryption), including the data and the header:

➤ End-to-end encryption encrypts the message and the data packet. Header information, IP addresses, and routing data are left in clear text. Although this means that an individual can intercept packets and learn the source and target destination, the data itself is secure. The advantage of this type of encryption is speed. No time or processing power is needed to decode address information. The disadvantage is that even with the data encrypted, an attacker might be able to make an inference attack.

➤ Link encryption encrypts all the data sent from a specific communication device. This includes the headers, addresses, and routing information. Its primary strength is that it provides added protection against sniffers and eavesdropping. Its disadvantage is that all intermediate devices must have the necessary keys, software, and algorithms to encrypt and decrypt the encrypted packets at each hop along the trip. This adds complexity, consumes time, and requires additional processing power.

Cryptographic Attacks

Attacks on cryptographic systems are nothing new. Whenever someone has information to hide, there is usually someone who would like to reveal it. William Frederick Friedman is considered one of the best cryptologists of all time. He helped break the encryption scheme used by the Japanese Purple Machine. Many of his inventions and cryptographic systems were never patented because they were considered so significant that the release of any information about them might aid an enemy. Following are some common attacks that an enemy might use to attack a cryptographic system:

➤ **Known plain-text attack**—This attack requires the attacker to have the plain text and cipher text of one or more messages.

➤ **Cipher text–only attack**—This attack requires the attacker to obtain several encrypted messages that have been encrypted using the same encryption algorithm. The attacker does not have the associated plain text; he attempts to crack the code by looking for patterns and using statistical analysis.

➤ **The birthday attack**—The birthday attack gets its name from the birthday paradox, which states that for a given number of individuals, two or more will share the same birthday. This same logic is applied to calculate collisions in hash functions. Digital signatures can be susceptible to birthday attacks if the output of the hash function is not large enough to avoid collisions.

➤ **Man-in-the middle attack**—This attack is carried out when attackers place themselves between two users. Whenever the attackers can place themselves in the communications path, the possibility exists that they can intercept and modify communications.

➤ **Chosen cipher text**—The chosen cipher text attack is carried out when the attacker can decrypt portions of the cipher-text message. The decrypted portion of the message can then be used to discover the key.

➤ **Chosen plain text**—The chosen plain text attack is carried out when a attacker can have the plain text messages encrypted and can then analyze the cipher text output of the event.

➤ **Replay attack**—This form of attack occurs when the attacker can intercept cryptographic keys and reuse them later to either encrypt or decrypt messages the attacker should not have access to.

Exam Prep Questions

1. This attack requires the attacker to obtain several encrypted messages that have been encrypted using the same encryption algorithm.
   - ❑ A. Known plain-text attack
   - ❑ B. Cipher-text attack
   - ❑ C. Clear-text attack
   - ❑ D. Replay attack

2. Which of the following best describes obtaining plain text from cipher text without a key?
   - ❑ A. Frequency analysis
   - ❑ B. Cryptanalysis
   - ❑ C. Decryption
   - ❑ D. Cracking

3. This attack occurs when the attacker can intercept session keys and reuse them at a later date.
   - ❑ A. Known plain-text attack
   - ❑ B. Cipher-text attack
   - ❑ C. Man-in-the-middle attack
   - ❑ D. Replay attack

4. Which of the following is a disadvantage of symmetric encryption?
   - ❑ A. Key size
   - ❑ B. Speed
   - ❑ C. Key management
   - ❑ D. Key strength

5. Which of the following is *not* an example of a symmetric algorithm?
   - ❑ A. DES
   - ❑ B. RC5
   - ❑ C. AES
   - ❑ D. RSA

6. Which of the following forms of DES is considered the most vulnerable to attack?
   - ❑ A. CBC
   - ❑ B. ECB
   - ❑ C. CFB
   - ❑ D. OFB

7. DES uses which of the following for a key size?

   ❑ A. 56 bit
   ❑ B. 64 bit
   ❑ C. 96 bit
   ❑ D. 128 bit

8. What implementation of Triple-DES uses the same key for the first and third iterations?

   ❑ A. DES-EEE3
   ❑ B. HAVAL
   ❑ C. DES-EEE2
   ❑ D. DES-X

9. Which of the following algorithms is used for key distribution, not encryption or digital signatures?

   ❑ A. El Gamal
   ❑ B. HAVAL
   ❑ C. Diffie-Hellman
   ❑ D. ECC

10. What hashing algorithm produces a 160-bit output?

   ❑ A. MD2
   ❑ B. MD4
   ❑ C. SHA-1
   ❑ D. El Gamal

Answers to Exam Prep Questions

1. Answer: B. A cipher-text attack requires the attacker to obtain several encrypted messages that have been encrypted using the same encryption algorithm. Answer A is incorrect because a known plain-text attack requires the attacker to have the plain text and cipher text of one or more messages. Answer C is incorrect because there would be no reason to perform an attack if the information was already in clear text. Answer D is incorrect because a reply attack occurs when the attacker can intercept session keys and reuse them at a later date.

2. Answer: B. Cryptanalysis is the act of obtaining plain text from cipher text without a key. Cryptanalysis is the study of breaking encryption systems. Although it can mean obtaining the plain text from the cipher text without a key, it can also mean that the cryptosystem was cracked because someone found a weakness in the cryptosytem's implementation. Such was the case with wired equivalent privacy (WEP). Answer A is incorrect because although the cryptanalyst can use frequency analysis to aid in cracking, it is not a valid answer. Answer C is incorrect because encryption is the act of unencrypting data. Answer D is incorrect because *cracking* is a term used to describe criminal hackers and the art of illegally accessing source code.

3. Answer: D. A reply attack occurs when the attacker can intercept session keys and reuse them at a later date. Answer A is incorrect because a known plain-text attack requires the attacker to have the plain text and cipher text of one or more messages. Answer B is incorrect because a cipher-text attack requires the attacker to obtain several encrypted messages that have been encrypted using the same encryption algorithm. Answer C is incorrect because a man-in-the middle attack is carried out when the attacker places himself between two users.

4. Answer: C. Key management is a primary disadvantage of symmetric encryption. Answers A, B, and D are incorrect because encryption speed, key size, and key strength are not disadvantages of symmetric encryption.

5. Answer: D. RSA is an asymmetric algorithm. Answers A, B, and C are incorrect because DES, RC5, and AES are examples of symmetric algorithms.

6. Answer: B. Electronic Code Book is susceptible to known plain-text attacks because the same clear text always produces the same cipher text. Answers A, C, and D are incorrect. Because CBC, CFB, and OFB all use some form of feedback, they do not suffer from this deficiency and are considered more secure.

7. Answer: A. Each 64-bit plain-text block is separated into two 32-bit blocks and then processed by the 56-bit key. Total key size is 64 bits, but 8 bits are used for parity, thereby making 64, 96, and 128 bits incorrect.

8. Answer: C. DES-EEE2 performs the first and third encryption passes using the same key. Answers A, B, and D are incorrect: DES-EEE3 uses three different keys for encryption. HAVAL is used for hashing; it is not used by DES. DES-X is a variant of DES, with only a 56-bit key size.

9. Answer: C. Diffie-Hellman is used for key distribution, not encryption or digital signatures. Answer A is incorrect because El Gamal is used for digital signatures, data encryption, and key exchange. Answer B is incorrect because HAVAL is used for hashing. Answer D is incorrect because ECC is used for digital signatures, data encryption, and key exchange.

10. Answer: C. SHA-1 produces a 160-bit message digest. Answers A, B, and D are incorrect because MD2 and MD4 both create a 128-bit message digest, and El Gamal is not a hashing algorithm.

Need to Know More?

http://cybercrimes.net/Cryptography/Articles/Hebert.html—History of cryptography

www.ietf.org/html.charters/pkix-charter.html—IETF PKI Working Group

www.ietf.org/rfc/rfc3280.txt—RFC 3280 information on PKI

http://docs.hp.com/en/J4255-90011/ch04.html—An overview of IPSec

www.wired.com/news/politics/0,1283,41658,00.html—Steganography in real life

http://www.itl.nist.gov/fipspubs/fip186.htm—Digital signature algorithm

www2.cddc.vt.edu/www.eff.org/pub/Privacy/Crypto/Crypto_misc/DESCracker/—Cracking DES

http://msdn.microsoft.com/library/default.asp?url=/library/en-us/vsent7/html/vxconWhatIsSecurability.asp—Hashing and security

www.abanet.org/scitech/ec/isc/dsg-tutorial.html—Digital signatures

Practice Exam 1

You will have 90 minutes to complete the exam, which consists of 60 questions. The score given will be either Pass or Fail, without numeric scoring provided. Care should be taken in reading each question, looking for details that would rule out any of the answers. Many times there will be two or more apparently correct answers, while only one correct answer is truly acceptable. In that case, choose the most correct answer. Leaving a question blank will count against you, so you are always better off taking your best guess. It's best to work through the entire test once, answering the questions that you can easily answer. On the second pass, work on the more difficult questions. Others you have already answered could help you answer the remaining questions.

Practice Exam Questions

1. What type of access control is typically used by organizations such as the DoD, the NSA, and the FBI?
   - ❏ A. Restricted access control
   - ❏ B. Discretionary access control
   - ❏ C. Mandatory access control
   - ❏ D. Role-based access control

2. Which of the following is *not* a form of single sign-on (SSO)?
   - ❏ A. NetSP
   - ❏ B. SESAME
   - ❏ C. Kerberos
   - ❏ D. RADIUS

3. What form of biometric system analyzes the features that exist in the colored tissue surrounding the pupil to validate access?

   ❑ A. Retina
   ❑ B. Cornea
   ❑ C. Iris
   ❑ D. Optic nerve

4. What is the most important item to consider when examining biometric systems?

   ❑ A. The crossover acceptance rate—the lower the number, the better the biometric system
   ❑ B. The crossover error rate—the higher the number, the better the biometric system
   ❑ C. The crossover acceptance rate—the lower the number, the better the biometric system
   ❑ D. The crossover error rate—the lower the number, the better the biometric system

5. What type of biometric error occurs when an unauthorized individual is granted access?

   ❑ A. Type I
   ❑ B. Type II
   ❑ C. Type III
   ❑ D. Type IV

6. What height of fence will deter only casual trespassers?

   ❑ A. 2–3 feet
   ❑ B. 3–4 feet
   ❑ C. 4–5 feet
   ❑ D. 5–7 feet

7. When discussing policies and procedures, who is strictly responsible for the protection of the company's assets and data?

   ❑ A. User
   ❑ B. Data owner
   ❑ C. Data custodian
   ❑ D. Security auditor

8. Which of the following is considered a flaw, loophole, oversight, or error that makes the organization susceptible to attack or damage?

   ❑ A. Risk
   ❑ B. Vulnerability
   ❑ C. Exposure
   ❑ D. Threat

9. Which of the following are the correct steps involved in determining the single loss expectancy?

   ❑ A. Single loss expectancy = Asset value · Exposure factor
   ❑ B. Single loss expectancy = Asset value × Exposure factor
   ❑ C. Single loss expectancy = Risk · Exposure factor
   ❑ D. Single loss expectancy = Vulnerability × Exposure factor

10. Estimating potential loss is an important task of CISSP-certified professionals. In order, which of the following are the steps used to perform a quantitative assessment?

   ❑ A. Estimate potential losses, perform a vulnerability assessment, and determine annual loss expectancy
   ❑ B. Estimate potential losses, conduct a threat analysis, and rank losses as high, medium, or low
   ❑ C. Assemble a team, prepare a matrix of critical systems and services, and rank losses as high, medium, or low
   ❑ D. Estimate potential losses, conduct a threat analysis, and determine annual loss expectancy

11. What is the Delphi Technique an example of?

   ❑ A. A BCP analysis technique
   ❑ B. A quantitative-assessment technique
   ❑ C. A DRP analysis technique
   ❑ D. A qualitative-assessment technique

12. What is the formula for total risk?

   ❑ A. (Threat − Countermeasure) / Asset value = Total risk
   ❑ B. (Threat − Countermeasure) × Asset value = Total risk
   ❑ C. Threat × Vulnerability × Asset value = Total risk
   ❑ D. Threat × Vulnerability / Asset value = Total risk

13. What method of dealing with risk occurs when individuals accept the potential cost and loss?

   ❑ A. Risk reduction
   ❑ B. Risk rejection
   ❑ C. Risk transference
   ❑ D. Risk acceptance

14. The security kernel is found at what protection ring level?

   ❑ A. Ring 0
   ❑ B. Ring 1
   ❑ C. Ring 2
   ❑ D. Ring 4

15. At what protection ring are applications found?

   ❑ A. Ring 1
   ❑ B. Ring 2
   ❑ C. Ring 3
   ❑ D. Ring 4

16. Which of the following are considered temporary storage units within the CPU?

   ❑ A. I/O buffer
   ❑ B. Registers
   ❑ C. Control circuit
   ❑ D. ALU

17. Confidentiality and integrity are important concepts when discussing security models. Which of the following was the first model developed to address the concerns of both confidentiality and integrity?

   ❑ A. Biba
   ❑ B. Clark-Wilson
   ❑ C. Brewer and Nash
   ❑ D. Clark-Phillips

18. Which of the following is considered the first security model to be based on confidentiality?

   ❑ A. Biba
   ❑ B. Bell-LaPadula
   ❑ C. Graham-Denning
   ❑ D. Clark-Wilson

19. What piece of documentation was developed to evaluate integrity and is also know as TNI?

   ❑ A. The Orange Book
   ❑ B. The Red Book
   ❑ C. Common Criteria
   ❑ D. CTCPEC

20. Which level of Orange Book protection is considered discretionary protection?

   ❑ A. D
   ❑ B. C
   ❑ C. B
   ❑ D. A

21. What is considered the smallest set of code that can be scheduled for processing?
    - ❑ A. Subroutine
    - ❑ B. Line
    - ❑ C. Process
    - ❑ D. Thread

22. Which of the following frequencies do cordless phones *not* use?
    - ❑ A. 850MHz
    - ❑ B. 900MHz
    - ❑ C. 2.4GHz
    - ❑ D. 5.8GHz

23. Which of the following wireless standards used frequency-hopping spread spectrum (FHSS) by default?
    - ❑ A. Bluetooth
    - ❑ B. 802.11a
    - ❑ C. 802.11b
    - ❑ D. 802.11g

24. Which of the following is the original technique used to digitize voice with 8 bits of sampling 8,000 times per second, which yields 64Kbps for one voice channel?
    - ❑ A. DAT
    - ❑ B. CDMA
    - ❑ C. PCM
    - ❑ D. GMS

25. How many DS0 channels are bundled to make a T1?
    - ❑ A. 18
    - ❑ B. 21
    - ❑ C. 24
    - ❑ D. 32

26. Which of the following protocols was developed in the mid-1970s for use in Systems Network Architecture (SNA) environments?
    - ❑ A. SDLC
    - ❑ B. ISDN
    - ❑ C. LAP-B
    - ❑ D. X.25

27. Which of the following best defines transaction persistence?

   ❑ A. Database transactions should be all or nothing to protect the integrity of the database.

   ❑ B. The database should be in a consistent state, and there should not be a risk of integrity problems.

   ❑ C. The database should be the same before and after a transaction has occurred.

   ❑ D. Databases should be available to multiple users at the same time without endangering the integrity of the data.

28. What is the capability to combine data from separate sources to gain information?

   ❑ A. Metadata

   ❑ B. Inference

   ❑ C. Aggregation

   ❑ D. Deadlocking

29. Joey considers himself a skillful hacker. He has devised a way to replace the existing autoexec.bat file between the time that the system boots and checks to see if there is an autoexec file yet before the system actually executes the autoexec.bat file. He believes that if he can perfect his attack, he can gain control of the system. What type of attack is described here?

   ❑ A. Synchronous attack

   ❑ B. TOC/TOU attack

   ❑ C. DCOM attack

   ❑ D. Smurf attack

30. Which of the following is evidence that is not based on personal knowledge but that was told to the witness?

   ❑ A. Best evidence

   ❑ B. Secondary evidence

   ❑ C. Conclusive evidence

   ❑ D. Hearsay evidence

31. Which of the following is considered the fastest mode of DES?

   ❑ A. ECB

   ❑ B. CBC

   ❑ C. CFB

   ❑ D. OFB

32. What mode of Triple DES uses three keys?

   ❑ A. DES E3

   ❑ B. DES-EEE3

   ❑ C. 3DES

   ❑ D. DES EDE2

33. Which asymmetric cryptosystem is used for digital signatures?
    - ❏ A. DES
    - ❏ B. SHA1
    - ❏ C. Diffie-Hellman
    - ❏ D. ECC

34. When developing the organization's contingency plan, which of the following should *not* be included in the process?
    - ❏ A. Damage-assessment team
    - ❏ B. Legal counsel
    - ❏ C. Salvage team
    - ❏ D. Tiger team

35. Which of the following is a valid form of attack against ARP?
    - ❏ A. Flooding
    - ❏ B. Corruption of the tree
    - ❏ C. Name server poisoning
    - ❏ D. Reverse lookups

36. Which of the following is considered the weakest form of authentication?
    - ❏ A. CHAP
    - ❏ B. EAP
    - ❏ C. MS-CHAP
    - ❏ D. PAP

37. Which of the following address ranges is *not* listed in RFC 1918?
    - ❏ A. 10.0.0.0 to 10.255.255.255
    - ❏ B. 172.16.0.0 to 172.31.255.255
    - ❏ C. 172.16.0.0 to 172.63.255.255
    - ❏ D. 192.168.0.0 to 192.168.255.255

38. Which of the following is *not* a reason why email should be encrypted?
    - ❏ A. Encryption is a time-consuming process.
    - ❏ B. Faking email is easy.
    - ❏ C. Sniffing email is easy.
    - ❏ D. Stealing email is not difficult.

39. Which of the following statements about instant messaging is incorrect?
    - ❏ A. No capability for scripting
    - ❏ B. Can bypass corporate firewalls
    - ❏ C. Lack of encryption
    - ❏ D. Insecure password management

40. ActiveX is used by which of the following technologies?
   - ❑ A. Java
   - ❑ B. CORBA
   - ❑ C. EJB
   - ❑ D. DCOM

41. Which of the following protocols is said to use "a web of trust"?
   - ❑ A. PKI
   - ❑ B. IGMP
   - ❑ C. PGP
   - ❑ D. PEM

42. Which of the following is considered the act of inducing a person to commit a crime in order to bring criminal charges against him?
   - ❑ A. Inducement
   - ❑ B. Entrapment
   - ❑ C. Honeypotting
   - ❑ D. Enticement

43. Which of the following terms describes the U.S. law enforcement agreements that are carried out with law enforcement agents in other nations to fight computer crime and terrorism?
   - ❑ A. G8
   - ❑ B. MLAT
   - ❑ C. SWAT
   - ❑ D. UN Resolution 1154

44. Which of the following is *not* one of the main BCP testing strategies?
   - ❑ A. Partial interruption
   - ❑ B. Structured walk-through
   - ❑ C. Parallel
   - ❑ D. Full interruption

45. When discussing the BCP, critical resources are usually divided into five primary categories. The categories are which of the following groups?
   - ❑ A. Business, administrative, user, technical, and data
   - ❑ B. Administrative, policy, user, technical, and data
   - ❑ C. Business, facility and supply, user, technical, and nontechnical
   - ❑ D. Business, facility and supply, user, technical, and data

46. Which of the following is *not* one of the three layers used by the Java interpreter?
   - ❑ A. Java language
   - ❑ B. Java script
   - ❑ C. Java libraries
   - ❑ D. Java interpreter

47. Which of the following protocols is used for router multicasting?

   ❑   A.   ICMP
   ❑   B.   RIP
   ❑   C.   224.0.0.1
   ❑   D.   IGMP

48. VoIP uses which of the following because network congestion can be such a critical problem?

   ❑   A.   Time-division multiplexing
   ❑   B.   TCP protocol
   ❑   C.   VLANs technology
   ❑   D.   Isochronous design

49. Which of the following is considered a network technology based on transferring data in cells or packets of a fixed size?

   ❑   A.   ATM
   ❑   B.   ISDN
   ❑   C.   SMDS
   ❑   D.   Frame Relay

50. WEP has been publicized as having vulnerabilities. Which of the following is *not* a reason why it is vulnerable?

   ❑   A.   Shared WEP keys among all clients
   ❑   B.   An RC4 engine not properly initialized
   ❑   C.   20-bit initialization vector
   ❑   D.   400-bit WEP keys

51. You are an advisory board member for a local nonprofit charity. The charity has been given a new server, and members plan to use it to connect their 24 client computers to the Internet for email access. Currently, none of these computers has antivirus software installed. Your research indicates that there is a 95% chance these systems will become infected after email is in use. A local vendor has offered to sell 25 copies of antivirus software to the nonprofit organization for $400. Even though the nonprofit's 10 paid employees make only about $9 an hour, there's a good chance that a virus could bring down the network for an entire day. They would like you to tell them what the ALE for this proposed change would be. How will you answer them?

   ❑   A. $423
   ❑   B. $950
   ❑   C. $720
   ❑   D. $684

52. A Common Criteria rating of structurally tested means the design meets what level of verification?

   ❑ A. EAL 1
   ❑ B. EAL 2
   ❑ C. EAL 4
   ❑ D. EAL 5

53. Which of the following is *not* a valid Red Book rating?

   ❑ A. A1
   ❑ B. B2
   ❑ C. C1
   ❑ D. C2

54. What Bell-LaPadula model rule states that someone at one security level cannot write information to a lower security level?

   ❑ A. Star * property
   ❑ B. Simple security rule
   ❑ C. Simple integrity property
   ❑ D. Strong star rule

55. You are an advisory board member for a nonprofit organization that has decided to go forward with a proposed Internet and email connectivity project. The CEO would like to know how much money, if any, will be saved through the purchase of antivirus software. Here are the projected details:

   24 computers connected to the Internet

   95% probability of virus infection

   10 paid employees who make $9 an hour

   A successful virus outage could bring down the network for an entire day

   25 copies of antivirus software will cost the nonprofit $399

   ❑ A. $218
   ❑ B. $285
   ❑ C. $380
   ❑ D. $490

56. Which of the following is considered the first line of defense against human behavior?

   ❑ A. Cryptography
   ❑ B. Physical security
   ❑ C. Business continuity planning
   ❑ D. Policies

57. HVAC should provide which of the following?
    ❑ A. HVAC should be a closed-loop system with negative pressurization.
    ❑ B. HVAC should be an open-loop system with positive pressurization.
    ❑ C. HVAC should be an open-loop system with negative pressurization.
    ❑ D. HVAC should be a closed-loop system with positive pressurization.

58. Which of the following types of fire detectors uses rate-of-rise sensors?
    ❑ A. Flame activated
    ❑ B. Heat activated
    ❑ C. Smoke activated
    ❑ D. Ion activated

59. A fire caused by electrical equipment is considered which class of fire?
    ❑ A. D
    ❑ B. C
    ❑ C. B
    ❑ D. A

60. Which of the following types of water sprinkler systems is known as a closed-head system?
    ❑ A. Deluge
    ❑ B. Dry pipe
    ❑ C. Preaction
    ❑ D. Wet pipe

Answers to Practice Exam 1

Answer Key

1. C	16. B	31. A	46. B
2. D	17. A	32. B	47. D
3. C	18. B	33. D	48. D
4. D	19. B	34. D	49. A
5. B	20. B	35. A	50. C
6. B	21. D	36. D	51. D
7. B	22. A	37. C	52. B
8. B	23. A	38. A	53. A
9. B	24. C	39. A	54. A
10. D	25. C	40. D	55. B
11. D	26. A	41. C	56. B
12. C	27. B	42. B	57. D
13. D	28. C	43. B	58. B
14. A	29. B	44. A	59. C
15. C	30. D	45. D	60. D

Answers to Practice Exam Questions

1. The correct answer is C. A mandatory access control (MAC) model is static and based on a predetermined list of access privileges. Therefore, in a MAC-based system, access is determined by the system rather than the user. Answer A is incorrect because there is no access-control model known as restricted access control. Answer B is incorrect because discretionary access control (DAC) leaves access control up to the owner's discretion. Answer D is incorrect because role-based access control models are used extensively by banks and other organizations that have very defined roles.

2. The correct answer is D. Remote Authentication and Dial-In User Service (RADIUS) is a UDP-based client/server protocol used for access control. Answers A, B, and C are all examples of SSO technologies.

3. The correct answer is C. Iris recognition functions by analyzing the features that exist in the colored tissue surrounding the pupil, to confirm a match. These systems can analyze more than 200 points for comparison. Answer A is incorrect because retina scanning analyzes the layer of blood vessels in the eye. Answer B is incorrect because there is no cornea scan. Answer D is incorrect because there is no optic nerve scan.

4. The correct answer is D. The crossover error rate is defined as a percentage in which a lower number indicates a better biometric system. It is the most important measurement when attempting to determine the accuracy of the system. Answer A is incorrect because there is no crossover acceptance rate. Answer B is incorrect because higher numbers are less accurate. Answer C is incorrect because, again, there is no crossover acceptance rate.

5. The correct answer is B. Type II errors occur when unauthorized individuals are granted access to resources and devices they should not have. Answer A is incorrect because Type I errors occur when legitimate users are improperly denied access. Answers C and D are incorrect because there are no Type III or Type IV errors.

6. The correct answer is B. A 3- to 4-foot fence will deter only casual trespassers. Answers A, C, and D do not correctly address the question: Fences that are 5–7 feet high are considered too difficult to climb, and fences that are 8 feet high should be used to prevent a determined intruder. Fences 2 to 3 feet high can be easily crossed and would not be considered a deterrent.

7. The correct answer is B. The data owner, who is typically a member of senior management, is responsible for protecting company assets and data. Answer A is incorrect because the user is the individual who uses the documentation. Answer C is incorrect because the data custodian is responsible for maintaining and protecting the company's assets and data. Answer D is incorrect because the auditor makes periodic reviews

of the documentation, verifies that it is complete, and ensures that users are following its guidelines.

8. The correct answer is B. A vulnerability is a flaw, loophole, oversight, or error that makes the organization susceptible to attack or damage. Answer A is incorrect because a risk is the potential harm that can arise from an event. Answer C is incorrect because exposure is the amount of damage that could result from the vulnerability. Answer D is incorrect because a threat is a natural or man-made event that could have some type of negative impact on the organization.

9. The correct answer is B. The correct formula to determine single loss expectancy is: Single loss expectancy = Asset value × Exposure factor. Answers A, C, and D are incorrect because they are not the correct formula. Items to consider when calculating the SLE include the physical destruction or theft of assets, the loss of data, the theft of information, and threats that might cause a delay in processing.

10. The correct answer is D. Quantitative assessment deals with numbers and dollar amounts. It attempts to assign a cost (monetary value) to the elements of risk assessment and to the assets and threats of a risk analysis. To complete the assessment, first estimate potential losses, then conduct a threat analysis, and finally determine annual loss expectancy. Answer A, B, and C do not detail the steps needed to perform a quantitative assessment.

11. The correct answer is D. The Delphi Technique is an example of a qualitative-assessment technique. It is not used for quantitative assessment, DRP, or BCP; therefore, answers A, B, and C are incorrect.

12. The correct answer is C. It properly defines the formula for total risk. Total risk is calculated by Threat × Vulnerability × Asset value. Answers A, B, and D are incorrect because they do not properly define the formula.

13. The correct answer is D. Risk acceptance means that the risk has been analyzed and the individuals responsible have decided that they will accept such risk. Answer A is incorrect because risk reduction occurs when a countermeasure is implemented to alter or reduce the risk. Answer B is incorrect because risk rejection means that the responsible party has decided to ignore the risk. Answer C is incorrect because risk transference transfers the risk to a third party.

14. The correct answer is A. Layer 0 is the most trusted level. The security kernel resides at this level, and protection rings support the security of the system. Answers B, C, and D are incorrect because the security kernel is not located at the respective rings.

15. The correct answer is C. Ring 3 contains applications. Rings of protection typically run from 0 to 3, with lower numbers representing more protected processes. Answers A, B, and D are incorrect because Ring 1 contains portions of the OS and Ring 2 contains I/O drivers, utilities, and low-level processes. Ring 4 does not exist.

16. The correct answer is B. Registers are considered the temporary storage units within the CPU. CPUs consist of registers, arithmetic/logic unit (ALU), and control circuitry. Answers A, C, and D are incorrect because the I/O buffers, control circuitry, and the ALU are not considered temporary storage units in the CPU.

17. The correct answer is A. The Biba model, which was published in 1977, was the first model developed to address the concerns of integrity. Answer B is incorrect because although the Clark-Wilson model is based on integrity, it was not the first model. Answer C is incorrect because the Brewer and Nash model is based on confidentiality. Answer D is incorrect because there is not a model named Clark-Phillips.

18. The correct answer is B. Bell-LaPadula was the first model to address the concerns of confidentiality. It was developed in the 1970s and was considered groundbreaking because it supported multilevel security. Answer A is incorrect because the Biba model is an integrity model. Answer C is incorrect because the Graham-Denning model was not the first model to be developed on integrity. Answer D is incorrect because the Clark-Wilson model is another example of an integrity model.

19. The correct answer is B. The Red Book was developed to evaluate integrity and availability. It is also know as Trusted Network Interpretation (TNI). Answer A is incorrect because the Orange Book addresses confidentiality. Answer C is incorrect because Common Criteria is a combined version of TCSEC, ITSEC, and the CTCPEC. Answer D is incorrect because the CTCPEC is the Canadian version of the Orange Book.

20. The correct answer is B. The Orange Book rates systems into one of four categories: Category A is verified protection, B is mandatory protection, C is discretionary protection, and D is minimal protection. Therefore, answers A, C, and D are incorrect.

21. The correct answer is D. Threads are the smallest sets of code a processor can schedule for processing. Answer A is incorrect because a subroutine is a sequence of code. Answer B is incorrect because a line of code is just that, a line of code; it is not the smallest set that is used for processing. Answer C is incorrect because a process is a task being run by a computer, and many tasks can run simultaneously.

22. The correct answer is A. Cordless phones do not use the 850MHz frequency. Analog cellphones use the 824–894MHz frequencies. Because the question asks what frequencies are not used, answers B, C, and D are incorrect because cordless phones and some other consumer electronics such as baby monitors use those three frequencies.

23. The correct answer is A. Bluetooth uses frequency-hopping spread spectrum (FHSS). FHSS functions by modulating the data with a narrowband carrier signal that "hops" in a random but predictable sequence from frequency to frequency. Bluetooth can be susceptible to war chipping and other forms of attack. Answer B is incorrect because

802.11a uses orthogonal frequency-division multiplexing. Answer C is incorrect because 802.11b uses direct sequence spread spectrum (DSSS) technology. Answer D is incorrect because 802.11g also uses orthogonal frequency-division multiplexing.

24. The correct answer is C. Pulse code modulation (PCM) is the original technique used to digitize voice with 8 bits of sampling 8,000 times per second, which yields 64Kbps for one voice channel. Answer A is incorrect because DAT is digital audio tape and is an analog voice-transmission method. Answers B and D are incorrect because CDMA and GMS are both methods for cellphone transmission.

25. The correct answer is C. Twenty-four DS0 lines are bundled to make one T1. A T1 line has a composite rate of 1.544Mb. Answers A, B, and D are incorrect because 18, 21, and 32 DS0 lines do not exist.

26. The correct answer is A. The Synchronous Data Link Control (SDLC) protocol was developed in the mid-1970s for use in Systems Network Architecture (SNA) environments. SDLC is unique, in that it was the first synchronous, link-layer, bit-oriented protocol. The ISO modified SDLC to create the High-Level Data Link Control (HDLC) protocol and release it as a standard. Answer B is incorrect because ISDN is an end-to-end telephone service that is digital in nature. Answer C is incorrect because Link Access Procedure–Balanced (LAP-B) is a subset of HDLC and is not used by SNA. Answer D is incorrect because X.25 is an efficient protocol that was developed in the 1970s for packet-switched networks.

27. The correct answer is B. Transaction persistence means that the state of the database security is the same after a transaction has occurred. In addition, there is no risk of integrity problems. Answer A is incorrect because it does not define transaction persistence. Answer C is wrong because transaction persistence does not state that the database should be the same before and after a transaction. Answer D is incorrect because even though databases should be available to multiple users at the same time without endangering the integrity of the data, that is not a definition of transaction persistence.

28. The correct answer is C. Aggregation is the capability to combine data from separate sources to gain information. Answer A is incorrect because metadata is data about data. Answer B is incorrect because inference attacks occur when authorized users infer information by analyzing the data they have access to. Answer D is incorrect because deadlocking is a database stalemate.

29. The correct answer is B. A TOC/TOU attack can occur when the contents of a file have changed between the time the system security functions checked the contents of the variables, and the time the variables are actually used or accessed. This is a form of asynchronous attack. Answer A is incorrect because the description describes an

asynchronous attack. Answer C is incorrect because the example does not describe a DCOM attack. Answer D is incorrect because although the network might be vulnerable to a Smurf attack, the subsequent lock would not change status of such an attack.

30. The correct answer is D. Hearsay evidence is not based on personal knowledge, but is information that was told to a witness from another person. It is inadmissible. Answer A is incorrect because best evidence is the preferred type of evidence. Answer B is incorrect because secondary evidence is admissible and is usually a copy of original evidence. Answer C is incorrect because conclusive evidence is also admissible.

31. The correct answer is A. Electronic Code Book is the fastest of all four of the listed modes of DES. Answer B is incorrect because Cipher Block Chaining (CBC) is not the fastest, but it is the most used mode of DES. Answer C is incorrect because Cipher Feedback (CFB) is not the fastest, but it can be used to emulate a stream cipher. Answer D is incorrect because Output Feedback (OFB) is not the fastest but is faster than CFB because it can pregenerate the key stream independent of the data.

32. The correct answer is B. DES-EEE3 is a form of Triple DES that performs three encryptions with three different keys. Answer A is incorrect because there is no mode of Triple DES known as DES E3. Answer C is incorrect because 3DES does not describe a mode of Triple DES. Answer D is incorrect because Triple DES EDE2 uses two keys, not three.

33. The correct answer is D. Elliptic curve cryptosystems (ECC) is an asymmetric cryptosystem that was created in the 1980s to create and store digital signatures in a small amount of memory. Answer A is incorrect because DES is a symmetric algorithm. Answer B is incorrect because SHA1 is a hashing algorithm. Answer C is incorrect because Diffie-Hellman is used for key exchange.

34. The correct answer is D. The tiger team's purpose is to penetrate security. Tiger teams are sometimes called red teams or penetration testers. Answers A, B, and C are incorrect because individuals from all those groups should be involved in the contingency-planning process.

35. The correct answer is A. Attacks can attack ARP by flooding the switch and other devices with bogus MAC addresses or by ARP poisoning. Answer B is incorrect because corruption of the tree is a type of attack that would target DNS; DNS has a treelike structure, and ARP does not. Answer C is incorrect because name server poisoning is another type of DNS attack. Answer D is incorrect because a reverse lookup is a term associated with DNS, not ARP.

36. The correct answer is D. Password Authentication Protocol (PAP) is the weakest form of authentication because it sends passwords in clear text. Answers A, B, and C are incorrect because all of these protocols are more secure than PAP. EAP is considered the most secure because,

unlike PAP and CHAP, it can be extended to use more advanced forms of authentication, such as digital certificates.

37. The correct answer is C. RFC 1918 specifies the addresses that are to be used for private address schemes. Addresses 172.16.0.0 to 172.63.255.255 are not part of the specified range; therefore, answer C is the correct choice. Answers A, B, and D are incorrect because RFC 1918 specifies 10.0.0.0 to 10.255.255.255, 172.16.0.0 to 172.31.255.255, and 192.168.0.0 to 192.168.255.255.

38. The correct answer is A. Encrypting email is not time consuming or hard. Email is one of the most popular Internet applications and deserves protection. Although answers B, C, and D are incorrect, they all outline potential vulnerabilities in standard email. Faking, sniffing, and stealing email are all relatively easy to do.

39. The correct answer is A. Instant messaging (IM) has the capability for scripting. This is one of the reasons it is dangerous for the organization. Answers B, C, and D do not properly answer the question because they are all reasons why IM is vulnerable. IM can bypass corporate firewalls, most versions lack encryption, and IM uses insecure password management.

40. The correct answer is D. The Distributed Object Component Model (DCOM) allows applications to be divided into pieces and objects to be run remotely over the network. Potential vulnerabilities exist because of the way ActiveX is integrated with DCOM. Answer A is incorrect because Java is not used by ActiveX. Answer B is incorrect because CORBA is a set of standards that addresses the need for interoperability between hardware and software. Answer C is incorrect because Enterprise Java Bean (EJB) is designed for enterprise networks.

41. The correct answer is C. Pretty Good Privacy (PGP) uses a weblike model because there are no Certificate Authorities; there are only end users. Anyone who uses PGP must determine whom they trust: Without a Certificate Authority, there is no centralized or governing agency to control and validate other users. Answer A is incorrect because PKI does not use a web of trust. Answer B is incorrect because IGMP is used for multicast router group management. Answer D is incorrect because Privacy Enhanced Email (PEM) is an email-security protocol.

42. The correct answer is B. Entrapment is considered the act of inducing a person to commit a crime in order to bring criminal charges against him or her. Although entrapment might be seen as illegal behavior, enticement usually is not. Answer A is incorrect because inducement is the act of bringing about the desired result. Answer C is incorrect because a honeypot is a trap set to detect or slow attempts at unauthorized use of information systems. Answer D is incorrect because enticement is the act of influencing by exciting hope or desire.

43. The correct answer is B. Mutual Legal Assistance Treaties (MLAT) are agreements that U.S. law-enforcement agencies have with law-enforcement agencies in other nations to fight computer crime and terrorism. MLATs are relatively recent developments that were created to improve the effectiveness of judicial assistance and to regularize and facilitate cooperation. Answer A is incorrect because the G8 is a group of economically advanced nations that have agreed to work together. Answer C is incorrect because SWAT is a term used for Special Weapons and Tactics police teams. Answer D is incorrect because UN resolution 1154 deals with weapons inspections in Iraq.

44. The correct answer is A. The five main types of BCP testing strategies include checklist, structured walk-through, simulation, parallel, and full interruption. Therefore, answers B, C, and D are incorrect because the question asked which is not a valid type. Answer A describes a partial interruption, which is not one of the five valid types.

45. The correct answer is D. Business, facility and supply, user, technical, and data are the five primary categories. Answers A, B, and C are incorrect because they do not describe the five categories.

46. The correct answer is B. The Java script is used by the Java interpreter and is not one of the three layers. Answers A, C, and D do not successfully answer the question, but they do comprise the three layers used by the Java interpreter. These include the Java language, which interprets code downloaded from a website; Java libraries, which prevent undesired access to resources and help implement a security policy; and the Java interpreter, which converts the code into native machine code.

47. The correct answer is D. Internet Group Management Protocol (IGMP) is used by hosts to report multicast group memberships to neighboring multicast routers. Security problems exist with IGMP because anyone can start a multicast group or join an existing one. Answer A is incorrect because IGMP is used for logical errors and diagnostics. Answer B is incorrect because the Routing Information Protocol (RIP) is a broadcast-based routing protocol. Answer C is incorrect because although 224.0.0.1 is a multicast address, it is not a protocol used for multicast management.

48. The correct answer is D. VoIP is very time sensitive and, as such, should be based on an isochronous design. This means that the entire system must be engineered to deliver output with exactly the same timing as the input. Firewire is another example of a device that contains an isochronous interface. Answer A is incorrect because VoIP does not use time-division multiplexing. Answer B is incorrect because VoIP uses UDP, not TCP. Answer C is incorrect because VLANs are not used for timing and delay problems, but are used to separate the VoIP from general traffic to make it more secure from sniffing.

49. The correct answer is A. ATM creates a fixed channel, or route, between two points whenever data transfer begins, and packages the data into 53-byte fixed-length cells. ATM can be used in LANS, WANS, and MANS. It supports high-bandwidth data needs. Answer B is incorrect because ISDN provides a completely end-to-end digital connection. Answer C is incorrect because Switched Multimegabit Data Service (SMDS) is a low-market-share service that is used to interconnect LANS. Answer D is incorrect because Frame Relay does not package data into 53-byte fixed-length cells.

50. The correct answer is C. The IV vector was 24 bites, not 20. Answers A, B, and D are incorrect, but each answer does detail some of the vulnerabilities of WEP. For example, WEP uses a single shared key among all clients, which means that you are authenticating groups, not devices or single users. Also, RC4 is the correct encryption type, but WEP does not properly initialize it. This means that the first part of the key stream is predictable. Finally, a 24-bit IV vector is too short, and a 40-bit key is vulnerable to attack.

51. The correct answer is D. The formula for the annual loss expectancy is this:

    ALE = ARO × SLE, or .95 × 720 = $684

    Annual rate of occurrence is 95%, or .95

    Single loss expectance is ($9 per hour × 8 hours) × 10 employees = $720

    Therefore, the nonprofit could expect to lose $684 by not using antivirus software.

52. The correct answer is B. An evaluation that is carried out and meets an evaluation assurance level (EAL) 2 specifies that the design has been structurally tested. Answers A, C, and D are incorrect because EAL 1 = functionally tested; EAL 4 = methodically designed, tested, and reviewed; and EAL 5 = semiformally designed and tested.

53. The correct answer is A. The Red Book lists the following ratings: B2 Good, C2 Fair, C1 Minimum, and None. Therefore, answers B, C, and D are incorrect because the question asks what is not a valid rating.

54. The correct answer is A. The star * property rule states that someone at one security level cannot write information to a lower security level. Answer B is incorrect because the simple security rule states that someone cannot read information at a higher security level. Answer C is incorrect because the simple integrity property deals with the Biba model, not Bell-LaPadula. Answer D is incorrect because it states that read and write privileges are valid only at the level at which the user resides.

55. The correct answer is B. Annual loss expectancy is calculated this way:

    ALE = ARO × SLE, or .95 × 720 = $684

    The annual savings is the ALE minus the cost of the deterrent, or $684 − $399 = $285. Therefore, answers A, C, and D are incorrect.

56. The correct answer is B. Physical security is considered the first line of defense against human behavior. Items such as gates, guards, locks, and cameras can be used for physical defense. Answer A is incorrect because cryptography is best used to protect the integrity and confidentiality of data. Answer C is incorrect because business continuity planning should be used to prevent critical outages. Answer D is incorrect because policies are an administrative control.

57. The correct answer is D. HVAC should be a closed-loop system with positive pressurization. Closed loop means that the air inside the building is filtered and continually reused. Positive pressurization should be used to ensure that inside air is pushed out. This is a big safety feature in case the building catches on fire. Answers A, B, and C are incorrect because they do not contain both closed-loop systems and positive pressurization.

58. The correct answer is B. Heat-activated sensors can be either rate-of-rise or fixed-temperature sensors. Answer A is incorrect because flame-activated sensors respond to the infrared energy that emanates from a fire. Answer C is incorrect because smoke-activated sensors use a photoelectric device. Answer D is incorrect because there is no category of fire detector known as ion activated.

59. The correct answer is B. Electrical fires are considered Class C fires. All other answers are incorrect because Class A fires consist of wood and paper products, Class B fires consist of liquids such as petroleum, and Class D fires result from combustible metals.

60. The correct answer is D. A wet-pipe system is also known as a closed-head system because water is in the pipe ready to be released and is held back only by the closed head. All other answers are incorrect because deluge systems release a large amount of water in a very short period of time, dry-pipe systems hold back the water by means of a valve, and preaction systems release water into the pipe only when a specified temperature triggers its release.

Practice Exam 2

You will have 90 minutes to complete the exam, which consists of 60 questions. The score given will be either Pass or Fail, without numeric scoring provided. Care should be taken in reading each question, looking for details that would rule out any of the answers. Many times there will be two or more apparently correct answers, while only one correct answer is truly acceptable. In that case, choose the most correct answer. Leaving a question blank will count against you, so you are always better off taking your best guess. It's best to work through the entire test once, answering the questions that you can easily answer. On the second pass, work on the more difficult questions. Others you have already answered could help you answer the remaining questions.

Practice Exam Questions

1. Which of the following types of fire detectors works by means of a photoelectric sensor?
   - ❏ A. Flame activated
   - ❏ B. Heat activated
   - ❏ C. Pressure activated
   - ❏ D. Smoke activated

2. A fire caused by combustible metals would be considered which class of fire?
   - ❏ A. A
   - ❏ B. B
   - ❏ C. C
   - ❏ D. D

3. Which of the following types of water sprinkler systems works by leaving the sprinkler head open and filling the pipe only when a fire has been detected?

☐ A. Deluge

☐ B. Dry pipe

☐ C. Preaction

☐ D. Wet pipe

4. Which of the following types of card keys contains rows of copper?

☐ A. Magnetic strip

☐ B. Electronic circuit

☐ C. Magnetic stripe

☐ D. Active electronic

5. Tony's company manufactures proprietary cellphone-tracking devices. Now that employees will be issued laptops, Tony is concerned about the loss of confidential information if an employee's laptop is stolen. Which of the following represents the best defensive method?

☐ A. Use integrity programs such as MD5 and SHA to verify the validity of installed programs

☐ B. Place labels on the laptops offering a reward for stolen or missing units

☐ C. Issue laptop users locking cables to secure the units and prevent their theft

☐ D. Encrypt the hard drives

6. Under what conditions can halon be expected to degrade into toxic compounds?

☐ A. At temperatures greater than 500°F

☐ B. At temperatures greater than 900°F and concentrations greater than 10%

☐ C. At temperatures greater than 900°F

☐ D. At temperatures greater than 500°F and concentrations greater than 7%

7. According to NIST perimeter lighting standards, critical areas should be illuminated to what measurement?

☐ A. 10 feet in height, with 2-foot candle power

☐ B. 12 feet in height, with 4-foot candle power

☐ C. 8 feet in height, with 2-foot candle power

☐ D. 8 feet in height, with 4-foot candle power

8. What type of biometric error is used to signify that an authorized user has been denied legitimate access?

☐ A. Type I

☐ B. Type II

☐ C. Type III

☐ D. Type IV

9. In biometrics, the point at which the FAR equals the FRR is known as which of the following?

- ❑ A. Crossover error rate
- ❑ B. Error acceptance rate
- ❑ C. Crossover acceptance rate
- ❑ D. Failure acceptance rate

10. RSA's SecurID is an example of which of the following?

- ❑ A. SSO system
- ❑ B. Synchronous authentication
- ❑ C. Token authentication
- ❑ D. Asynchronous authentication

11. Which of the following is an example of an SSO technology?

- ❑ A. NetSP
- ❑ B. RADIUS
- ❑ C. TACACS
- ❑ D. WIDZ

12. When discussing the security of SSO systems, which of the following is considered a disadvantage?

- ❑ A. Single sign-on requires much more maintenance and overhead because all systems are tied together.
- ❑ B. The biggest disadvantage to single sign-on is that system time on all systems must be held to very tight standards; if deviated from, this can cause serious access problems.
- ❑ C. There are no real disadvantages to single sign-on.
- ❑ D. If single sign-on is breached, it offers the intruder access to all systems.

13. SNORT is an example of a what?

- ❑ A. Behavior-based IPS system
- ❑ B. Signature-based IDS system
- ❑ C. Behavior-based IDS system
- ❑ D. Signature-based IPS system

14. What type of attack is also known as a race condition?

- ❑ A. Synchronous attack
- ❑ B. Buffer overflow
- ❑ C. Asynchronous attack
- ❑ D. Scanlog attack

15. I/O drivers and utilities are typically found at what protected ring level?

- ❑ A. Ring 1
- ❑ B. Ring 2
- ❑ C. Ring 3
- ❑ D. Ring 0

16. What type of CPU can interleave two or more programs for execution at any one time?
   - ❑ A. Multiprogramming
   - ❑ B. Multitasking
   - ❑ C. Multiapp
   - ❑ D. Multiprocessor

17. This portion of the CPU performs arithmetic and logical operations on the binary data.
   - ❑ A. I/O buffer
   - ❑ B. Registers
   - ❑ C. Control circuit
   - ❑ D. ALU

18. What security model is also known as the Chinese Wall?
   - ❑ A. Biba
   - ❑ B. Clark-Wilson
   - ❑ C. Brewer and Nash
   - ❑ D. Harrison-Ruzzo-Ullman

19. What piece of documentation was developed to evaluate standalone systems and is a basis of measurement for confidentiality?
   - ❑ A. The Red Book
   - ❑ B. The Orange Book
   - ❑ C. Common Criteria
   - ❑ D. CTCPEC

20. Which level of Orange Book protection is considered mandatory protection?
   - ❑ A. D
   - ❑ B. C
   - ❑ C. B
   - ❑ D. A

21. Which of the following is considered the totality of protection mechanisms within a computer system and is responsible for enforcing security?
   - ❑ A. Rings of protection
   - ❑ B. The security kernel
   - ❑ C. TCB
   - ❑ D. Resource isolation

22. Johnny is worried that someone might be able to intercept and decrypt his VoIP phone calls. Which of the following protocols is most closely associated with VoIP?
    - ❑ A. SKYP
    - ❑ B. SLIP
    - ❑ C. S/MIME
    - ❑ D. SIP

23. Which of the following wireless standards uses direct sequence spread spectrum (DSSS) by default?
    - ❑ A. Bluetooth
    - ❑ B. 802.11a
    - ❑ C. 802.11b
    - ❑ D. 802.11g

24. What is a rogue AP?
    - ❑ A. An individual who has connected to an unauthorized modem
    - ❑ B. An unauthorized AP that has been attached to the corporate network
    - ❑ C. An unauthorized modem that has been attached to the network
    - ❑ D. An individual who is intercepting wireless traffic from inside or outside the organization

25. Pulse code modulation (PCM) is used to digitize a voice with 8 bits of sampling for transmission on a DS0 line. What is the max rate of encoding for one of these voice channels?
    - ❑ A. 28.8 Kpbs
    - ❑ B. 56 Kbps
    - ❑ C. 64 Kbps
    - ❑ D. 128 Kbps

26. A T1 uses which of the following to multiplex DS0s into a composite T1?
    - ❑ A. Channel division
    - ❑ B. Frequency-hopping spread spectrum
    - ❑ C. Frequency division
    - ❑ D. Time division

27. Which of the following focuses on how to repair and restore the data center and information at an original or new primary site?
    - ❑ A. BCP
    - ❑ B. BCM
    - ❑ C. DRP
    - ❑ D. BIA

28. This type of service is used to provide protection for source code in case the manufacturer declares bankruptcy or goes broke.
    - ❏ A. Government access to keys
    - ❏ B. MAD
    - ❏ C. Electronic vaulting
    - ❏ D. Software escrow

29. Which of the following describes the cooperative effort between the United States and Europe to exchange information about European citizens between European firms and North American parent corporations?
    - ❏ A. SB 168
    - ❏ B. Demar Act
    - ❏ C. Safe Harbor
    - ❏ D. Safety Shield

30. Which of the following best describes an approved type of forensic duplication?
    - ❏ A. Logical copy
    - ❏ B. Bit copy
    - ❏ C. Microsoft backup
    - ❏ D. Xcopy

31. Which of the following best describes the SET protocol?
    - ❏ A. Originated by Victor Miller and Neal Koblitz for use as a digital signature cryptosystem. It is useful in applications for which memory, bandwidth, or computational power is limited.
    - ❏ B. Originated by MasterCard and Visa to be used on the Internet for credit card transactions. It uses digital signatures.
    - ❏ C. Originated by Victor Miller and Neal Koblitz for use as a key exchange cryptosystem. It is useful in applications for which memory, bandwidth, or computational power is limited.
    - ❏ D. Originated by MasterCard and Visa to be used on the Internet for credit card transactions. It uses the SSL protocol.

32. Which of the following information-management systems uses artificial intelligence?
    - ❏ A. Polyinstantiation
    - ❏ B. Known signature scanning
    - ❏ C. Application programming interface
    - ❏ D. Knowledge discovery database

33. DNS lookups are typically performed on which of the following protocols and ports?
    - ❏ A. UDP 53
    - ❏ B. UDP 69
    - ❏ C. TCP 53
    - ❏ D. UDP 161

34. Bob is worried that the program someone gave him at DEFCON has been altered from the original. Which of the following is a valid technique that Bob can use to verify its authenticity?

- ❑ A. Run AES against the program
- ❑ B. Compare the size and date with the version found on the developer's website
- ❑ C. Run an MD5sum
- ❑ D. Calculate a digital signature

35. Which of the following is not an email-encryption standard?

- ❑ A. VSP
- ❑ B. MOSS
- ❑ C. PGP
- ❑ D. PEM

36. Which of the following best describes link encryption?

- ❑ A. Data is encrypted at the point of origin and is decrypted at the point of destination.
- ❑ B. The message is decrypted and re-encrypted as it passes through each successive node using a key common to the two nodes.
- ❑ C. The KDC shares a user-unique key with each user.
- ❑ D. It requires a session key that the KDC shares between the originator and the final destination.

37. Diameter uses which of the following as a base?

- ❑ A. TACACS
- ❑ B. TACACS+
- ❑ C. RADIUS
- ❑ D. Kerberos

38. The ACID test is used to describe what?

- ❑ A. Behavior-based intrusion detection
- ❑ B. Database transactions
- ❑ C. Signature-based intrusion detection
- ❑ D. The strength of a cryptographic function

39. Which of the following best describes a Fault Resistant Disk Systems (FRDS) system?

- ❑ A. Uninterrupted power supply
- ❑ B. RAID
- ❑ C. Backup power supply
- ❑ D. Hot sites

40. Which of the following is a stream cipher?
    - ❑ A. DES
    - ❑ B. Skipjack
    - ❑ C. RC4
    - ❑ D. Twofish

41. Which of the following is considered the weakest mode of DES?
    - ❑ A. Electronic Code Book
    - ❑ B. Cipher Block Chaining
    - ❑ C. Cipher Feedback
    - ❑ D. Output Feedback

42. Which ethical standard states that "access and use of the Internet is a privilege and should be treated as such by all users"?
    - ❑ A. RFC 1087
    - ❑ B. ISC² Code of Ethics
    - ❑ C. The Ten Commandments of Computer Ethics
    - ❑ D. RFC 1109

43. Which of the following would be considered the oldest and most well-known software-development method?
    - ❑ A. Spiral
    - ❑ B. Clean room
    - ❑ C. Waterfall
    - ❑ D. Prototyping

44. Which of the following types of viruses can infect both boot sectors and program files?
    - ❑ A. File infector
    - ❑ B. Multipartite
    - ❑ C. Polymorphic
    - ❑ D. System infector

45. HTTPS uses which of the following ports?
    - ❑ A. 80
    - ❑ B. 110
    - ❑ C. 111
    - ❑ D. 443

46. Which of the following is considered the oldest type of database system?
    - ❑ A. Hierarchical
    - ❑ B. Network
    - ❑ C. Relational
    - ❑ D. Object-orientated

47. The IEEE separates the OSI data link layer into two sublayers. What are they?
    - ❑ A. Media MAC Control and Media Access Control
    - ❑ B. Logical Link Control and Media Access Control
    - ❑ C. High-Level Data Link Control and Media MAC Control
    - ❑ D. Data Link Control and Media MAC Control

48. What is considered the most current version of wireless cellular technology?
    - ❑ A. Gen4
    - ❑ B. 2G
    - ❑ C. 3G
    - ❑ D. Gen5

49. This protocol started as a simplified version of X.25 and is used in packet-switched networks.
    - ❑ A. Asynchronous DSL (ADSL)
    - ❑ B. Digital Data Service (DDS)
    - ❑ C. T1
    - ❑ D. Frame Relay

50. 802.11 networks are identified by which of the following?
    - ❑ A. Security identifier (SID)
    - ❑ B. Broadcast name
    - ❑ C. Kismet
    - ❑ D. Service set identifier (SSID)

51. ISO 17799 evolved from what regional standard?
    - ❑ A. British standard 7799
    - ❑ B. Canadian Trusted Computer Product Evaluation Criteria (CTCPEC)
    - ❑ C. Information Technology Security Evaluation Criteria (ITSEC)
    - ❑ D. Trusted Computer System Evaluation Criteria (TCSEC)

52. A Common Criteria rating of "Functionally Tested" means the design meets what level of verification?
    - ❑ A. EAL 1
    - ❑ B. EAL 2
    - ❑ C. EAL 4
    - ❑ D. EAL 5

53. Which of the following is *not* addressed by the Clark-Wilson security model?
    - ❑ A. Blocks unauthorized individuals from making changes to data
    - ❑ B. Maintains internal and external consistency
    - ❑ C. Protects the confidentiality of the information
    - ❑ D. Blocks authorized individuals from making unauthorized changes to data

54. Which of the following individuals' roles and responsibilities would include the responsibility for maintaining and protecting the company's assets and data?

  ❑ A. User

  ❑ B. Data owner

  ❑ C. Data custodian

  ❑ D. Security auditor

55. Which of the following is the proper formula used to calculate ALE?

  ❑ A. Single loss expectancy (SLE) · Annualized rate of occurrence (ARO)

  ❑ B. Asset value × Annualized rate of occurrence (ARO)

  ❑ C. Single loss expectancy (SLE) × Annualized rate of occurrence (ARO)

  ❑ D. Asset value · Annualized rate of occurrence (ARO)

56. Which of the following best describes a qualitative assessment?

  ❑ A. A qualitative assessment deals with real numbers and seeks to place dollar values on losses. These dollar amounts are then used to determine where to apply risk controls.

  ❑ B. A qualitative assessment assigns ratings to each risk.

  ❑ C. A qualitative assessment is performed by experts or external consultants who seek to place dollar values on losses.

  ❑ D. A qualitative assessment is performed by experts or external consultants, is based on risk scenarios, and assigns nondollar values to risks.

57. The facilitated risk assessment process is an example of what?

  ❑ A. A BCP analysis technique

  ❑ B. A quantitative-assessment technique

  ❑ C. A DRP analysis technique

  ❑ D. A qualitative-assessment technique

58. Classification levels such as confidential and secret are tied to which data classification scheme?

  ❑ A. ISO 17799

  ❑ B. U.S. Department of Defense (DoD)

  ❑ C. RFC 2196 Site Security Guidelines

  ❑ D. Commercial Data Classification Standard (CDCS)

59. This method of dealing with risk is considered the least prudent course of action.

  ❑ A. Risk reduction

  ❑ B. Risk rejection

  ❑ C. Risk transference

  ❑ D. Risk acceptance

60. Your employer is pleased that you have become CISSP certified and would now like you to evaluate your company's security policy. Your boss believes that encryption should be used for all network traffic and that a $50,000 encrypted database should replace the current customer database. Based on what you know about risk management, what should your decision to use encryption and purchase the new database be based on? Choose the most correct answer.

    ❑ A. If an analysis shows that there is potential risk, the cost of protecting the network and database should be weighed against the cost of the deterrent.

    ❑ B. If an analysis shows that the company's network is truly vulnerable, systems should be implemented to protect the network data and the customer database.

    ❑ C. If the network is vulnerable, systems should be implemented to protect the network and the database, regardless of the price.

    ❑ D. Because it is only a customer database and the company is not well known, the probability of attack is not as great; therefore, the risk should be accepted or transferred through the use of insurance.

Answers to Practice Exam 2

Answer Key

1. D	16. A	31. B	46. A
2. D	17. D	32. D	47. B
3. A	18. C	33. A	48. C
4. A	19. B	34. C	49. D
5. D	20. C	35. A	50. D
6. B	21. C	36. B	51. A
7. C	22. D	37. C	52. A
8. A	23. C	38. B	53. C
9. A	24. B	39. B	54. C
10. B	25. C	40. C	55. C
11. A	26. D	41. A	56. D
12. D	27. C	42. A	57. D
13. B	28. D	43. C	58. B
14. C	29. C	44. B	59. B
15. B	30. B	45. D	60. A

Answers to Practice Exam Questions

1. The correct answer is D. Smoke-activated fire detectors use a photo-electric sensor to detect a fire. Answer A is incorrect because flame-activated sensors respond to the infrared energy that emanates from a fire. Answer B is incorrect because heat-activated sensors respond to the infrared energy. Answer C is incorrect because there is no category of fire detector known as pressure activated.

2. The correct answer is D. Class D fires result from combustible metals. All other answers are incorrect: Class A fires consist of wood and paper products, Class B fires consist of liquids such as petroleum, and Class C fires are electrical fires.

3. The correct answer is A. A deluge water sprinkler system works by leaving the sprinkler head open and filling the pipe only when a fire has been detected. Answers B, C, and D are incorrect: Dry-pipe systems hold back the water by means of a value, preaction systems release water into the pipe only when a specified temperature triggers its release, and wet-pipe systems always contain water that is released by a sensor.

4. The correct answer is A. Magnetic strip card keys contain rows of copper strips. Answers B, C, and D are incorrect: Electronic circuit card keys have embedded electronic circuits, magnetic stripe card keys have a stripe of magnetic material, and active electronic cards can transmit data.

5. The correct answer is D. Hard-drive encryption offers the best defense against the loss of confidentiality. Answer A is incorrect because integrity programs validate the integrity of installed software but do not validate its confidentiality. Answer B is incorrect; reward labels might or might not encourage someone to return equipment and, again, will not protect its confidentiality. Answer C is incorrect because locking cables might prevent someone from removing a laptop but won't prevent someone from accessing data on the device.

6. The correct answer is B. If halon is deployed in concentrations of greater than 10% and in temperatures of 900°F or more, it degrades into hydrogen fluoride, hydrogen bromide, and bromine. This toxic brew can be deadly. Answers A, C, and D are incorrect because concentrations must be 10% or greater and temperatures must reach 900°F.

7. The correct answer is C. The NIST standard for perimeter protection using lighting is that critical areas should be illuminated with 2 candle feet of power at a height of 8 feet. Answers A, B, and D do not match the NIST standards.

8. The correct answer is A. A Type I error occurs when a biometric system denies an authorized individual access. Answer B is incorrect

because a Type II error occurs when an unauthorized individual is granted access. Answers C and D are incorrect because Type III and IV errors do not exist.

9. The correct answer is A. When comparing biometric systems, the most important item to consider is the crossover error rate (CER). The CER is the point at which the false acceptance rate meets the false rejection rate. The CER relates to the accuracy of the biometric system. Answers B, C, and D are not correct because there are no measurements known as error acceptance rate, crossover acceptance rate, or failure acceptance rate.

10. The correct answer is B. RSA's SecurID is an example of synchronous authentication. Devices used in the synchronous authentication process are synchronized to the authentication server. Each individual passcode is valid for only a very short period of time. Answer A is incorrect because RSA's SecurID might be part of an SSO system, but this is not an accurate answer. Answer C is incorrect because although RSA's SecurID might be considered a token, it is not the most accurate answer available. Answer D is incorrect because asynchronous authentication devices are not synchronized to the authentication server. These devices use a challenge-response mechanism.

11. The correct answer is A. NetSP is an example of SSO technology. NetSP is a KryptoKnight derivative that functions at Layer 3 and does not require clock synchronization. Answers B and C, RADIUS and TACACS, are incorrect because they are both examples of centralized authentication systems. Answer D, WIDZ, is a wireless intrusion system that can be easily integrated with SNORT or RealSecure.

12. The correct answer is D. Single sign-on (SSO) offers the attacker potential access to many systems when authenticated only once. Answer A is incorrect because it is can be breached and offers the intruder access to all systems. SSO does not require much more maintenance and overhead. Answer B is incorrect because although SSO systems such as Kerberos do require clock synchronization, this is not the overriding security issue. Answer C is incorrect because all systems have some type of flaw or drawback.

13. The correct answer is B. SNORT is a signature-based IDS system. A signature-based system examines data to check for malicious content. When data is found that matches one of these known signatures, it can be flagged to initiate further action. Answer A is incorrect because SNORT is not a behavior-based IPS system. Answer C is incorrect because SNORT is not a behavior-based IDS system. Answer D is incorrect because although SNORT is signature based, it is considered an IDS system, not an IPS system. IPS systems are unlike IDS systems, in that IPS systems have much greater response capabilities and allow administrators to initiate action upon being alerted.

14. The correct answer is C. Asynchronous attacks are sometimes called race conditions because the attacker is racing to make a change to the object after it has been changed but before it has been used by the system. Asynchronous attacks typically target timing. The objective is to exploit the delay between the time of check (TOC) and the time of use (TOU). Answers A, B, and D are incorrect because they do not adequately describe a race condition.

15. The correct answer is B. Rings of protection run from Ring 0 to Ring 3. Ring 2 is the location of I/O drivers and utilities. Answers A, C, and D are incorrect because Ring 1 contains parts of the OS that do not reside in the kernel, Ring 3 contains applications and programs, and Ring 0 is the location of the security kernel.

16. The correct answer is A. Multiprogramming CPUs can interleave two or more programs for execution at any one time. Answer B is incorrect because multitasking CPUs have the capability to perform one or more tasks or subtasks at a time. Answer C is incorrect because there is no type of processor known as multiapp. Answer D is incorrect because the term *multiprocessor* refers to systems that have the capability to support more than one CPU.

17. The correct answer is D. The ALU portion of the CPU performs arithmetic and logical operations on the binary data. Answers A, B, and C are incorrect because I/O buffers, registers, and the control circuits do not perform arithmetic and logical operations.

18. The correct answer is C. The Brewer and Nash model is also known as the Chinese Wall model, is integrity based, and places all information in a hierarchical structure. Answer A is incorrect because the Biba model is not known as the Chinese Wall model. Answer B is incorrect because although Clark-Wilson is an integrity model, it is not known as the Chinese Wall model. Answer D is incorrect because the Harrison-Ruzzo-Ullman Model is not known as the Chinese Wall model.

19. The correct answer is B. The Orange Book's official name is the Trusted Computer System Evaluation Criteria (TCSEC). It was developed to evaluate standalone systems for confidentiality. Answer A is incorrect because the Red Book was developed to evaluate integrity and availability. It is also known as Trusted Network Interpretation (TNI). Answer C is incorrect because Common Criteria is a combined version of TCSEC, ITSEC, and the CTCPEC. Answer D is incorrect because the Canadian Trusted Computer Product Evaluation Criteria (CTCPEC) is the Canadian version of the Orange Book.

20. The correct answer is C. The Orange Book rates systems as one of four categories. Category A is verified protection, B is mandatory protection, C is discretionary protection, and D is minimal protection. Therefore, answers A, B, and D are incorrect.

21. The correct answer is C. The Trusted Computer Base (TCB) is the totality of protection mechanisms within a computer system. This includes hardware, firmware, software, processes, and some interprocess communications. These items are responsible for enforcing security. Answer A is incorrect because rings of protection are designed to protect the operating system. Answer B is incorrect because the security kernel is the most trusted portion of the operating system. Answer D is incorrect because although resource isolation is an important part of implementing security, it is not the totality of protection mechanisms.

22. The correct answer is D. Session Initiation Protocol (SIP) is an application-layer request-response protocol used for VoIP. SIP is transported by UDP and is vulnerable to sniffing attacks. More details can be found in RFC 2543. Answer A is incorrect because there is no protocol SKYP; the proprietary protocol named SKYPE offers encryption and is used for a peer-to-peer Internet phone service. Answer B is incorrect because SLIP is used by ISPs for dialup connections. Answer C is incorrect because S/MIME is used to secure email.

23. The correct answer is C. 802.11b uses direct sequence spread spectrum (DSSS) technology. DSSS is a transmission method that transmits the data along with a chipping bit to increase the signal's resistance to interference. Answer A is incorrect because Bluetooth uses frequency-hopping spread spectrum. Answer B is incorrect because 802.11a uses orthogonal frequency-division multiplexing. Answer D is incorrect because 802.11g also uses orthogonal frequency-division multiplexing.

24. The correct answer is B. A rogue AP is an unauthorized AP that has been attached to the corporate network. These unauthorized APs represent one of the biggest threats to any secure network. Answer A is incorrect because a connection to an unauthorized modem is not a valid answer. Answer C is incorrect because attaching a modem is not the definition of a rogue AP. Answer D is incorrect because connecting to an unsecured network is not a rogue AP but might be considered an act of war driving.

25. The correct answer is C. Pulse code modulation (PCM) is used to digitize voice with 8 bits of sampling 8,000 times per second, which yields 64Kbps for one DS0 channel. Answers A, B, and D are incorrect because 28.8Kbps, 56Kbps, and 128Kbps are not the rates of transmission for one DS0 channel.

26. The correct answer is D. T1s use time division to break the individual DS0s into 24 separate channels. Time division is the allotment of available bandwidth based on time. It allows the T1 to carry both voice and data at the same time. Answer A is incorrect because there is no system known as channel division. Answer B is incorrect because FHSS is used by mobile devices. Answer C is incorrect because T1s do not use frequency division.

27. The correct answer is C. The disaster-recovery plan (DRP) focuses on how to repair and restore the data center and information at an original or new primary site. Answer A is incorrect because the business continuity plan (BCP) is focused on the continuation of critical services. Answer B is incorrect because business continuity management (BCM) is about building a framework for a capable response. Answer D is incorrect because a business impact analysis (BIA) is the functional analysis that is used to identify the potential impact if an outage occurred.

28. The correct answer is D. Software escrow agreements are used to provide protection for source code in case the manufacturer declares bankruptcy or goes broke. The three items that are most critical in this agreement are where the code will be deposited, under what conditions the code will be released, and the terms of use of the source code upon its release to the user. Answer A is incorrect because government access to keys deals with the government's wishes to maintain cryptographic keys used by industry. Answer B is incorrect because mutual assured destruction (MAD) is a term not associated with software protection. Answer C is incorrect because electronic vaulting is a term that describes the bulk transfer of data.

29. The correct answer is C. The Safe Harbor Act describes the cooperative effort between the United States and Europe to exchange information about European citizens between European firms and North American parent corporations. It was enacted because of the large numbers of individuals who have been victims of identity theft and because of the increase of misuses of personal information laws and agreements. Answer A is incorrect because although SB 168 deals with privacy, it is a state law that took effect in 2002, preventing businesses from using California residents' social security numbers as unique identifiers. Answer B is incorrect because there is no law known as the Demar Act. Answer D is incorrect because the name of the act is not Safety Shield.

30. The correct answer is B. A bit copy, or physical copy, captures all the data on the copied medium and reproduces an exact copy that includes hidden and residual data, slack space, swap contents, deleted files, and other data remnants. This allows the examiner to perform an analysis of the copy and store the original. Answer A is incorrect because a logical copy will not completely duplicate the structure of the original media. Answer C is incorrect because Microsoft backup is not an approved product for forensic analysis. Answer D is incorrect because although Xcopy can duplicate files, it does not provide a bit-level copy of the original medium.

31. The correct answer is B. Secure Electronic Transaction (SET) was developed by MasterCard and Visa to be used on the Internet for credit card transactions. It uses digital signatures. Answer A is incorrect because SET is not used for digital signatures. Answer C is incorrect because SET is not used for key exchange, and Victor Miller and Neal

Koblitz are the creators of ECC. Answer D is incorrect because SET does not use SSL.

32. The correct answer is D. Knowledge Discovery in Databases (KDD) is an artificial intelligence method used to identify useful patterns in data; as such, it provides a type of automatic analysis. Answer A is incorrect because polyinstantiation is a technique used to prevent inference violations. Answer B is incorrect because known signature scanning is a method used to detect computer viruses. Answer C is incorrect because the application programming interface (API) is in no way associated with artificial intelligence.

33. The correct answer is A. DNS lookups occur on UDP 53. Answers B, C, and D are incorrect because UDP 69 is used for TFTP, TCP 53 is used for zone transfers, and UDP 161 is used for SNMP.

34. The correct answer is C. Running an MD5sum would be the best way for Bob to verify the program. MD5sum is a hashing algorithm. Answer A is incorrect because AES is a symmetric algorithm and will not help Bob verify the program. Answer B is incorrect because the size and date might match the information found on the developer's website, but the program might have still been altered. Answer D is incorrect because a digital signature will not verify the integrity of the program.

35. The correct answer is A. There is no email security standard known as VSP. Although answers B, C, and D are all incorrect, they do specify valid email security standards: MIME Object Security Services (MOSS), Pretty Good Privacy (PGP), and Privacy Enhanced Email (PEM).

36. The correct answer is B. With link encryption, the message is decrypted and re-encrypted as it passes through each successive node using a key common to the two nodes. Answers A, C, and D are incorrect because they all describe end-to-end encryption.

37. The correct answer is C. Diameter uses RADIUS as a base and is considered the next generation of authentication, authorization, and accounting services for the Internet. Answer A is incorrect because TACACS is not considered a base for Diameter. Answer B is incorrect because TACACS+ is a Cisco protocol but is widely used. Answer D is incorrect because Kerberos is not associated with Diameter but is considered a single sign-on technology.

38. The correct answer is B. Programmers involved in database management talk about the ACID test when discussing whether a database-management system has been properly designed to handle transactions. The ACID test addresses atomicity, consistency, isolation, and durability. Answer A is incorrect because the ACID test does not deal with behavior-based IDS systems. Answer C is incorrect because ACID is not related to signature-based IDS systems. Answer D is incorrect because the ACID test is not related to the strength or a cryptographic function.

39. The correct answer is B. Fault Resistant Disk Systems (FRDS) are used to maintain services. A technological example of FRDS is RAID. Answer A is incorrect because an uninterrupted power supply is not an example of a FRDS. Answer C is incorrect because a backup power supply is not an example of FRDS. Answer D is incorrect because a hot site might provide backup disk services but is not the best answer.

40. The correct answer is C. RC4 is a stream cipher. It has been implemented in products such as SSL and WEP. Answer A is incorrect because DES is a block cipher with a 56-bit key size. Answer B is incorrect because Skipjack is a block cipher with a default 80-bit key size. Answer D is incorrect because Twofish is a 256-bit key size block cipher.

41. The correct answer is A. Electronic Code Book (ECB) is fast and simple but is also the weakest mode of DES. Answer B is incorrect because Cipher Block Chaining (CBC) is not the weakest mode of DES. Answer C is incorrect because Cipher Feedback (CFB) is more secure than ECB and OFB. Answer D is incorrect because Output Feedback (OFB) is not the weakest, but it can't detect integrity errors as well as CFB.

42. The correct answer is A. The statement "Access and use of the Internet is a privilege and should be treated as such by all users" is part of RFC 1087, which is titled Ethics and the Internet. Answer B is incorrect because the statement is not part of the ISC² Code of Ethics. Answer C is incorrect because the statement is not part of the Ten Commandments of Computer Ethics. Answer D is incorrect because RFC 1109 addresses network management, not ethics.

43. The correct answer is C. The waterfall method is the oldest and one of the most well-known methods for developing software systems. It was developed in the 1970s and is divided into phases. Each phase contains a list of activities that must be performed before the next phase can begin. Answer A is incorrect because the spiral model is a combination of the waterfall and prototyping methods. Answer B is incorrect because the clean room software-development method focuses on ways to prevention defects rather then ways to remove them. Answer D is incorrect because prototyping was developed in the 1980s to overcome weaknesses in the waterfall method. It is a four-step process: develop an initial concept, design and implement an initial prototype, refine the prototype until it is acceptable, and then complete and release the final version of the software.

44. The correct answer is B. A multipartite virus can infect both boot sectors and program files. Answer A is incorrect because file-infector viruses infect files. Answer C is incorrect because a polymorphic virus is one that has the capability to change. Answer D is incorrect because system infector viruses infect system files.

45. The correct answer is D. HTTPS uses port 443. Answer A is incorrect because port 80 is used for HTTP, answer B is incorrect because port 110 is used for POP3, and answer C is incorrect because port 111 is RPC.

46. The correct answer is A. Hierarchical databases link records in a tree structure so that each record type has only one owner. Hierarchical databases date from the information-management systems of the 1950s and 1960s. Answer B is incorrect because network databases were not the first. Answer C is incorrect because although relational databases are the most widely used, they were not the first. Answer D is incorrect because they were not the first but were designed to overcome some of the limitations of relational databases.

47. The correct answer is B. IEEE divides the OSI data link layer into sublayers. The upper half is the Logical Link Control (LLC) layer, and the lower half is the Media Access Control (MAC) layer. The LLC is based on HDLC; the MAC is where 802.3 addressing is performed. Answers A, C, and D are incorrect because none of these terms matches the proper definition of the sublayers of the data link layer.

48. The correct answer is C. Third-generation mobile telephone systems (3G) are being designed and developed by most major manufacturers. 3G is considered the most current version of wireless cellular technology. Analog cellular phones are considered first generation (1G) and digital PCS are second generation (2G); third generation (3G) combines high-speed mobile access with Internet Protocol–based services. If your phone does not support streaming music and video downloads, expect that your next one will. Answer A is incorrect because there is not a Gen4, answer B is incorrect because 2G is not the latest standard, and answer D is incorrect because Gen5 is not a valid answer.

49. The correct answer is D. Frame Relay started as a simplified version of X.25. Frame Relay is a packet-switching technology. One critical concept is the Committed Information Rate (CIR), which is the amount of bandwidth the provider commits to carry. Answer A is incorrect because ADSL is a circuit technology. Answer B is incorrect because Digital Data Service (DDS) is also a circuit-switched technology. Answer C is incorrect because a T1 is another example of a circuit-switched technology.

50. The correct answer is D. A service set ID (SSID) is used to identify 802.11 networks. The SSID is a 32-bit character that acts as a shared password that differentiates one WLAN from another. Answer A is incorrect because a security ID (SID) is an identifier used in conjunction with Microsoft domains. Answer B is incorrect because a broadcast name is not the means of identifying a WLAN. Answer C is incorrect because Kismet is a Linux software program used to sniff wireless traffic.

51. The correct answer is A. British standard 7799 formed the underpinnings of the later-developed ISO 17799. This document is considered the code of practice for information security management. Answers B, C, and D are incorrect because the Canadian Trusted Computer Product Evaluation Criteria, Information Technology Security Evaluation Criteria, and Trusted Computer System Evaluation Criteria did not form the underpinnings of the later-developed ISO 17799.

52. The correct answer is A. An evaluation that is carried out and that meets an evaluation assurance level (EAL) 1 specifies that the design has been functionally tested. Answers B, C, and D are incorrect because EAL 2 = structurally tested; EAL 4 = methodically designed, tested, and reviewed; and EAL 5 = semiformally designed and tested.

53. The correct answer is C. Clark-Wilson does not protect the confidentiality of the information; Clark-Wilson deals with integrity. Answers A, B, and D are all incorrect because the question asks which of the following Clark-Wilson does not address.

54. The correct answer is C. The data custodian is responsible for maintaining and protecting the company's assets and data. Answer A is incorrect because the user is the individual who uses the documentation. Answer B is incorrect because the data owner is responsible for protecting the data. Answer D is incorrect because the auditor makes periodic reviews of the documentation and verifies that it is complete and that users are following its guidelines.

55. The correct answer is C. Single loss expectancy (SLE) × Annualized rate of occurrence (ARO) is the formula used to determine ALE. Answers A, B, and D are incorrect because they are not the formulas used to calculate ALE.

56. The correct answer is D. A qualitative assessment ranks the seriousness of threats and sensitivity of assets into grades or classes, such as low, medium, and high. It is performed by experts or external consultants and is based on risk scenarios. Although purely quantitative risk assessment is not possible, purely qualitative risk analysis is. Answers A, B, and C are incorrect because they do not adequately describe qualitative risk assessment.

57. The correct answer is D. The facilitated risk-assessment process (FRAP) is an example of a qualitative-assessment technique. It is not used for BCP, quantitative assessment, or DRP; therefore, answers A, B, and C are incorrect.

58. The correct answer is B. The U.S. Department of Defense data-classification standard classifies data as unclassified, sensitive, confidential, secret, and top secret. Answer A is incorrect because ISO 17799 is an international security standard policy. Answer C is incorrect because RFC 2196 is the site security handbook and does not address data-classification standards. Answer D is incorrect because there is no CDCS standard.

59. The correct answer is B. Risk rejection is the least acceptable course of action because individuals have decided that it does not exist and are ignoring the risk. Answer A is incorrect because risk reduction occurs when a countermeasure is implemented to alter or reduce the risk. Answer C is incorrect because risk transference transfers the risk to a third party. Answer D is incorrect because risk acceptance means that the risk is analyzed, but the individuals responsible have decided that they will accept such risk.

60. The correct answer is A. Risk management requires that vulnerabilities be examined, that loss expectancy be calculated, that a probability of occurrence be determined, and that the costs of countermeasures be estimated. Only then can it be determined whether the value of the asset outweighs the cost of protection. It is possible that the cost of protection outweighs the value of the asset. Whereas some risk assessments use dollar amounts (quantitative) to value the assets, others use ratings (qualitative) based on breaches of confidentiality, integrity, and availability to measure value.

What's on the CD

The CD features an innovative practice test engine powered by MeasureUp, giving you yet another effective tool to assess your readiness for the exam.

Multiple Test Modes

MeasureUp practice tests are available in Study, Certification, Custom, Adaptive, Missed Question, and Non-Duplicate question modes.

Study Mode

Tests administered in Study Mode enable you to request the correct answer(s) and explanation to each question during the test. These tests are not timed. You can modify the testing environment *during* the test by selecting the Options button.

Certification Mode

Tests administered in Certification Mode closely simulate the actual testing environment you will encounter when taking a certification exam. These tests do not allow you to request the answer(s) or explanation to each question until after the exam.

Custom Mode

Custom Mode enables you to specify your preferred testing environment. Use this mode to specify the objectives you want to include in your test, the timer length, and other test properties. You can also modify the testing environment *during* the test by selecting the Options button.

Adaptive Mode

Tests administered in Adaptive Mode closely simulate the actual testing environment you will encounter when taking an Adaptive exam. After answering a question, you are not allowed to go back; you are allowed only to move forward during the exam.

Missed Question Mode

Missed Question Mode enables you to take a test containing only the questions you missed previously.

Non-Duplicate Mode

Non-Duplicate Mode enables you to take a test containing only questions that were not displayed previously.

Question Types

The practice question types simulate the real exam experience.

Random Questions and Order of Answers

This feature helps you learn the material without memorizing questions and answers. Each time you take a practice test, the questions and answers appear in a different randomized order.

Detailed Explanations of Correct and Incorrect Answers

You receive automatic feedback on all correct and incorrect answers. The detailed answer explanations are a superb learning tool in their own right.

Attention to Exam Objectives

MeasureUp practice tests are designed to appropriately balance the questions over each technical area covered by a specific exam.

Installing the CD

These are the minimum system requirements for the CD-ROM:

➤ Windows 95, 98, ME, NT4, 2000, or XP

➤ 7Mb disk space for testing engine

➤ An average of 1Mb disk space for each test

To install the CD-ROM, follow these instructions:

NOTE

If you need technical support, contact MeasureUp at 678-356-5050 or support@ measureup.com. Additionally, you'll find Frequently Asked Questions (FAQ) at www.measureup.com.

1. Close all applications before beginning this installation.

2. Insert the CD into your CD-ROM drive. If the setup starts automatically, go to step 6. If the setup does not start automatically, continue with step 3.

3. From the Start menu, select Run.

4. Click Browse to locate the MeasureUp CD. In the Browse dialog box, from the Look In drop-down list, select the CD-ROM drive.

5. In the Browse dialog box, double-click on Setup.exe. In the Run dialog box, click OK to begin the installation.

6. On the Welcome Screen, click MeasureUp Practice Questions to begin installation.

7. Follow the Certification Prep Wizard by clicking Next.

8. To agree to the Software License Agreement, click Yes.

9. On the Choose Destination Location screen, click Next to install the software to C:\Program Files\Certification Preparation.

10. On the Setup Type screen, select Typical Setup. Click Next to continue.

If you cannot locate MeasureUp Practice Tests through the Start menu, see the section later in this appendix titled, "Creating a Shortcut to the MeasureUp Practice Tests."

11. On the Select Program Folder screen, you can name the program folder your tests will be in. To select the default, simply click Next and installation continues.

12. When the installation is complete, verify that Yes, I Want to Restart My Computer Now is selected. If you select No, I Will Restart My Computer Later, you will not be able to use the program until you restart your computer.

13. Click Finish.

14. After restarting your computer, choose Start, Programs, MeasureUp, MeasureUp Practice Tests.

15. On the MeasureUp welcome screen, click Create User Profile.

16. In the User Profile dialog box, complete the mandatory fields and click Create Profile.

17. Select the practice test you want to access, and click Start Test.

Creating a Shortcut to the MeasureUp Practice Tests

To create a shortcut to the MeasureUp Practice Tests, follow these steps:

1. Right-click on your Desktop.

2. From the shortcut menu select New, Shortcut.

3. Browse to C:\Program Files\MeasureUp Practice Tests and select the MeasureUpCertification.exe or Localware.exe files.

4. Click OK.

5. Click Next.

6. Rename the shortcut as MeasureUp.

7. Click Finish.

After you have completed step 7, use the MeasureUp shortcut on your Desktop to access the MeasureUp products you ordered.

Technical Support

If you encounter problems with the MeasureUp test engine on the CD-ROM, contact MeasureUp at 678-356-5050 or support@measureup.com. Technical support hours are from 8 a.m. to 5 p.m. EST Monday through Friday. Additionally, you'll find Frequently Asked Questions (FAQ) at www.measureup.com.

If you'd like to purchase additional MeasureUp products, telephone 678-356-5050 or 1-800-649-1MUP (1687), or visit www.measureup.com.

Glossary

access control
Controls that monitor the flow of information between the subject and object. They ensure that only the operations permitted are performed.

accountability
The traceability of actions performed on a system to a specific system entity or user.

Address Resolution Protocol (ARP)
Protocol used to map a known IP address to an unknown physical address.

administrative law
A body of regulations, rules, orders, and decisions to carry out regulatory powers, created by administrative agencies.

ALE
Annualized Loss Expectancy, a formula used to calculate a quantifiable measurement of the impact that a threat will have on an organization if it occurs. ALE is used to calculate the possible loss that could occur over a 1-year period. The formula is SLE × ARO = ALE.

asset
Anything of value owned or possessed by an individual or business.

asymmetric algorithm
An asymmetric key algorithm that uses a pair of different but related cryptographic keys to encrypt and decrypt data.

authentication
A method that enables you to identify someone. Authentication verifies the identity and legitimacy of the individual to access the system and its resources. Common authentication methods include passwords, tokens, and biometric systems.

authorization
The process of granting or denying access to a network resource based on the user's credentials.

availability

Ensures that the systems responsible for delivering, storing, and processing data are available and accessible as needed by individuals who are authorized to use the resources.

baseline

A consistent or established base that is used to establish a minimum acceptable level of security.

Bell-LaPadula

A formal model that is based upon confidentiality. It is defined by two basic properties:

➤ Simple Security Property (ss Property)—This property states that a subject at one level of confidentiality is not allowed to read information at a higher level of confidentiality. It is sometimes referred to as "no read up."

➤ Star * Security Property—This property states that a subject at one level of confidentiality is not allowed to write information to a lower level of confidentiality. Also known as "no write down."

brute-force attack

A method of breaking a cipher or encrypted value by trying a large number of possibilities. Brute-force attacks function by working through all possible values. The feasibility of brute-force attacks depends on the key length and strength of the cipher and the processing power available to the attacker.

CA

Certificate Authority. Used in the PKI infrastructure to issue certificates and report status information and certificate-revocation lists.

catastrophe

A calamity or misfortune that causes the destruction of facility and data.

Challenge Handshake Authentication Protocol (CHAP)

A secure method for connecting to a system. CHAP functions as follows: 1. After the authentication request is made, the server sends a challenge message to the requestor. The requestor responds with a value obtained by using a one-way hash. 2. The server then checks the response by comparing the received hash to one calculated locally by the server. 3. If the values match, the authentication is acknowledged; otherwise, the connection is terminated.

civil law

A law that usually pertains to the settlement of disputes between individuals, organizations, or groups, and having to do with the establishment, recovery, or redress of private and civil rights. Civil law is not criminal law. It is also called tort law and is mainly for the redress or recovery related to wrongdoing.

closed-circuit television (CCTV)

Television cameras used for video surveillance, in which all components are directly linked via cables or other direct means.

A system comprised of video transmitters that can feed one or more receivers the captured video. Typically used in banks, casinos, shopping centers, airports, or anywhere that physical security can be enhanced by monitoring events. Placement in these facilities is typically at locations where people enter or leave the facility, or at locations where critical transactions occur.

closed system
A system that is not "open" and, therefore, is a proprietary system. Open systems are those that employ modular designs, are widely supported, and facilitate mulitvendor, multitechnology integration.

cold site
Site that contains no computing-related equipment except for environmental support such as air conditioners and power outlets, and a security system made ready for installing computer equipment.

confidentiality
Data or information is not made available or disclosed to unauthorized persons.

copyright
The legal protection given to authors or creators that protects their expressions on a specific subject against unauthorized copying. It is applied to books, paintings, movies, literary works, and any other medium of use.

corrective controls
Internal controls designed to resolve problems soon after they arise.

covert channel
An unintended communication path that allows a process to transfer information in such a way that violates a system's security policy.

cracker
A term derived from "criminal hacker," someone who acts in an illegal manner.

criminal law
Laws pertaining to crimes against the state or conduct detrimental to society. These violations of criminal statues are punishable by law and can include monitory penalties and jail time.

DAC
Discretionary Access Control. An access policy that allows the resource owner to determine access.

denial of service (DoS)
The process of having network resources, services, and bandwidth reduced or eliminated because of unwanted or malicious traffic.

detective controls
Controls that identify and correct undesirable events that have occurred.

digital signature
An electronic signature that can be used to authenticate the identity of the sender of a message. A digital signature is usually created by

encrypting the user's private key and is decrypted with the corresponding public key.

disaster

A natural or man-made event that can include fire, flood, storm, and equipment failure that negatively affects an industry or facility.

due care

The standard of conduct taken by a reasonable and prudent person. When you see the term *due care*, think of the first letter of each word and remember "do correct" because due care is about the actions that you take to reduce risk and keep it at that level.

due diligence

The execution of due care over time. When you see the term *due diligence*, think of the first letter of each word and remember "do detect" because due diligence is about finding the threats an organization faces. This is accomplished by using standards, best practices, and checklists.

dumpster diving

The practice of rummaging through the trash of a potential target or victim to gain useful information.

ECB

Electronic Code Book. A symmetric block cipher that is a form of DES. ECB is considered the weakest from of DES. When used, the same plain-text input results in the same encrypted text output.

encryption

The science of turning plain text into cipher text.

fail safe

In the logical sense, fail safe means the process of discovering a system error, terminating the process, and preventing the system from being compromised. The system enters a state in which no access is allowed. In physical systems, a fail safe refers to items such as controlled-access doors. When there is a power failure, the door "fails safe," which means that the door unlocks and people can leave the facility; they are not locked in.

FAR

False Acceptance Rate. This is a Type II biometric device error. It is a biometric system measurement that indicates the percentage of individuals who are incorrectly granted access. This is the worst type of error that can occur because it means that unauthorized individuals have been allowed access.

firewall

Security system in hardware or software form that is used to manage and control both network connectivity and network services. Firewalls act as chokepoints for traffic entering and leaving the network, and prevent unrestricted access. Firewalls can be stateful or stateless.

FRR

False Rejection Rate. This is a biometric device error that is considered a Type I error. It is a biometric system measurement that indicates the percentage of authorized individuals who are incorrectly denied access.

guidelines

Much like standards, these are recommendations; they are not hard-and-fast rules.

hash

A cryptographic sum that is considered a one-way value. A hash is considerably shorter than the original text and can be used to uniquely identify it. You might have seen a hash value next to applications available for download on the Internet. By comparing the hash of the application with the one on the application vendor's website, you can make sure that the file has not been changed or altered. MD5 and SHA-1 are examples of hashing algorithms.

hearsay

Evidence based on what a witness heard someone else say, not what the witness has personally observed.

hot site

A fully prepared and configured site that is ready for use.

inference

The ability to deduce information about data or activities to which the subject does not have access.

Information Technology Security Evaluation Criteria (ITSEC)

A European standard that was developed in the 1980s to evaluate confidentiality, integrity, and availability of an entire system.

integrity

One of the three items considered to be part of the security triad; the others are confidentiality and availability. It is used to verify the accuracy and completeness of an item.

intrusion detection

A key component of security that includes prevention, detection, and response. It is used to detect anomalies or known patterns of attack.

IPSec

An IETF standard used to secure TCP/IP traffic. It can be implemented to provide integrity and confidentiality.

lattice-based access control

A lattice-based access-control model was developed to deal with confidentiality and integrity. It places upper and lower boundary on subjects and objects.

man-in-the-middle attack

A type of attack in which the attacker can read, insert, and change information that is being passed between two parties, without either party knowing that the information has been compromised.

mandatory access control (MAC)

A means of restricting access to objects based on the sensitivity (as represented by a label) of the information contained in the objects and the formal authorization (such as clearance) of subjects to access information of such sensitivity.

mantrap

A turnstile or other gated apparatus that is used to detain an individual between a trusted state and an untrusted state for authentication.

Network Address Translation (NAT)

A method of connecting multiple computers to the Internet using one IP address so that many private addresses are being converted to a single public address.

nonrepudiation

A system or method put in place to ensure that an individual cannot deny his own actions.

one-time pad

An encryption mechanism that can be used only once and this is, theoretically, unbreakable. One-time pads function by combining plain text with a random pad that is the same length as the plain text.

Password Authentication Protocol (PAP)

A form of authentication in which clear-text usernames and passwords are passed.

patent

Exclusive rights granted by the federal government to an inventor to exclude others from making, using, or selling his or her invention.

policy

A high-level document that dictates management intentions toward security.

polyinstantiation

Prevents inference violations by allowing different versions of information items to exist at different classification levels. For example, an unclassified Navy officer might want information about a ship and might discover that it has left port and is bound for Europe. A Navy officer with classified access then might access the same database and discover that the ship has left port but is really bound for Iraq.

preventative controls

Controls that reduce risk and are used to prevent undesirable events from happening.

public key infrastructure (PKI)

Infrastructure used to facilitate e-commerce and build trust. PKI consists of hardware, software, people, policies, and procedures; it is used to create, manage, store, distribute, and revoke public key certificates. PKI is based on public-key cryptography.

RIP

Routing Information Protocol. A widely used distance-vector protocol that determines the best route by hop count.

risk

The subjective measure of the potential for harm that can result from the action of a person or thing.

role-based access control

A type of discretionary access control in which users are placed into groups to facilitate management.

This type of access control is widely used by banks and casinos.

rule-based access control
A type of mandatory access control that matches objects to subjects. It dynamically assigns roles to subjects based on their attributes and a set of rules defined by a security policy.

security kernel
A combination of software, hardware, and firmware that makes up the Trusted Computer Base (TCB). The TCB mediates all access, must be verifiable as correct, and is protected from modification.

sniffer
A hardware or software device that can be used to intercept and decode network traffic.

social engineering
The practice of tricking employees into revealing sensitive data about their computer system or infrastructure. This type of attack targets people and is the art of human manipulation. Even when systems are physically well protected, social-engineering attacks are possible.

spamming
The use of any electronic communications medium to send unsolicited messages in bulk. Spamming is a major irritation of the Internet era.

spoofing
The act of masking your identity and pretending to be someone else or another device. Common spoofing methods include ARP, DNS, and IP. Is also implemented by email in what is described as phishing schemes.

steganography
A cryptographic method of hiding the existence of a message. A commonly used form places information in pictures.

symmetric algorithm
Both parties use the same cryptographic key.

TACACS
A UDP-based access-control protocol that provides authentication, authorization, and accountability.

TCB
Trusted Computer Base. All of the protection mechanisms within a computer system. This includes hardware, firmware, and software that are responsible for enforcing a security policy.

TNI
Trusted Network Interpretation, also know as the Red Book. A document that is part of the Rainbow Series.

trademark
Legal protection for a logo, name, or characteristic that can be identified as exclusive.

Transient Electromagnetic Pulse Emanation Standard (TEMPEST)
A method of shielding equipment to prevent the capability of capturing and using stray electronic signals and reconstructing them into useful intelligence.

Trusted Computer System Evaluation Criteria (TCSEC)

U.S. DoD Trusted Computer System Evaluation Criteria, also called the Orange Book. TCSEC is a system designed to evaluate standalone systems that places systems into one of four levels: A, B, C, or D. Its basis of measurement is confidentiality.

virtual private network (VPN)

A private network that uses a public network to connect remote sites and users.

vulnerability

The absence or weakness of a safeguard in an asset.

war dialing

The process of using a software program to automatically call thousands of telephone numbers to look for any that have a modem attached.

war driving

The process of driving around a neighborhood or area to identify wireless access points.

warm site

An alternative computer facility that is partially configured and can be made ready in a few days.

Index

How can we make this index more useful? Email us at indexes@quepublishing.com

F

J – K – L

M

Mafiaboy, 179

maintenance hooks, 91

maintenance phase of BCP, 206

major service interruptions, 201

malformed input, 159

man-in-the-middle attacks, 262

man-made threats to physical security, 11-12

mandatory vacations, 183

manipulation attacks, 223

mantraps as perimeter security measure, 18

master boot record infection, 156

MD series algorithms, 252

    HAVAL, 253

    HMAC, 253

    SHA-1, 252

measuring impact of service interruptions on businesses, 204

Melissa virus, role of forensics in capturing creator, 232

memory, virtual memory, 94

Merkle-Hellman Knapsack algorithm, 251

message digests, 252

metadata, 171

methods of fire suppression, 26-27

    halon, 27

    water sprinklers, 28

military data classification, 49

MIN (mobile identification number), 119

minor service interruptions, 201

mobile security locks, 21

monitoring, 184

Montreal Protocol of 1987, 27

Morris, Robert, 157

motion detectors, 23

moving encrypted data, 261

MTBF (mean time between failure), 25

MTD (maximum tolerable downtimes), estimating, 203

MTTR (mean time to repair), 25

multifactor authentication, strong authentication, 70

multimode fiber, 124

multiple data centers, maintaining, 210

multiprocessors, 93

multiprogramming CPUs, 93

multistate systems, 96

multitasking, 93

Muslim law, 234

N

Napoleonic law, 234

NAT, 147

negligence, 235

network access controls

    firewalls, 147

        stateful firewalls, 148

    NAT, 147

    packet filters, 147

    proxy servers, 148

    SOCKS, 149

O

Q – R

U – V

W

walkthroughs, 206

WANs (wide area networks)

    ATM, 128

    circuit-switched, 128

    T-carriers, 129

war dialing, 81, 118

war driving, 118, 126

warm sites, 209

warning banners, 185

waterfall model of software development, 164

weaknesses of Kerberos, 72

websites

    Computer Ethics Institute, 226

    ISC².org, 3

WEP (Wired Equivalent Privacy), 125

white noise, 64

wireless networks, 125

    security, WEP, 125

    spread-spectrum technology, 125

    testing, 81

    war driving, 118

wiretapping, 222

working images, 232

worms, 118

    methods of propagation, 156

    Nimda, 157

WPA (WiFi Protected Access), 126

X – Y – Z

X.25, 127

X.509 certificates, 256

X.509 v3 digital certificates, 144

Zimmerman, Phil, 146